OUR STATE OF MIND
racial planning and the stolen generations

The experience of removal never leaves you. No matter how hard you try or how many times you talk about it, you always remember something different, something triggers up your memory — Trish Hill-Keddie.

Since the Second World War, two generations of Aboriginal children have been raised into adulthood as the offspring of the stolen generations. Children of a third generation are still in their teenage years. In a great many cases these young people have experienced a range of emotional, behavioural and adjustment problems. Together they represent the ongoing legacy of assimilation. Its effects are felt in the difficulties parents face in raising their children and in the manner in which contemporary institutions replicate the experience of institutionalisation for Aboriginal children.

Our State of Mind examines the reasons why the policy of assimilation and the removal of Aboriginal children was introduced and maintained for so long. It reveals some of the long term effects of the policy and shows why the stolen generations are as much a part of our present as they are of our past.

Cover: Sandra Hill, *Heartlands*, 1995 (detail), mixed media, transfer with synthetic polymer on paper, 91 x 104 cm, Collection of the Central Metropolitan College of TAFF, Perth. The full as an inset on the back cover.

Dr Quentin Beresford has had a diverse career in teaching, the public service and journalism. He has lectured in politics and public policy at Edith Cowan University since 1993. Before taking up his current position, Dr Beresford was a senior policy officer in the Western Australian office of the Department of Premier and Cabinet. A former editor of *Youth Studies*, he has had long-standing interests in youth policy and juvenile crime.

Dr Beresford is the author of several books and a number of journal articles dealing with diverse aspects of social policy and electoral politics. He lives in Perth with his wife Marilyn and their son, William.

Dr Paul Omaji hails from Nigeria. He is a criminologist and legal sociologist and has lectured in Australian and Nigerian universities. He joined Edith Cowan University in 1993 and served as the coordinator of the Legal Studies program. Since then, Dr Omaji has developed, taught and researched various social and legal issues, some of which directly relate to Aboriginal youth and their interaction with the justice system.

In particular, Dr Omaji has focussed on Aboriginal people and the law, discrimination and human rights, and reconciliation with indigenous populations in the context of international public policy. He is currently Senior Lecturer in the Department of Justice Studies, and lives in Perth with his wife, Alice, and their children Ruth, Reuben, Timothy and Tabitha.

Quentin Beresford and Paul Omaji are also co-authors of *Rites of Passage: Aboriginal Youth, Crime and Justice* published in 1996 by Fremantle Arts Centre Press.

OUR STATE OF MIND

racial planning and the
stolen generations

QUENTIN BERESFORD
PAUL OMAJI

FREMANTLE ARTS CENTRE PRESS

First published 1998 by
FREMANTLE ARTS CENTRE PRESS
193 South Terrace (PO Box 320), South Fremantle
Western Australia 6162.
http://www.facp.iinet.net.au

Consultant Editor B R Coffey.
Designer John Douglass.
Production Coordinator Cate Sutherland.

Typeset by Fremantle Arts Centre Press
and printed by PK Print, Hamilton Hill, Western Australia.

National Library of Australia
Cataloguing-in-publication data

Beresford, Quentin.
        Our state of mind: racial planning and the stolen
        generations

        ISBN 1 86368 235 X.

        1. Aborigines, Australian - Child welfare. 2. Aborigines,
        Australian - Government policy. 3. Aborigines, Australian -
        Social conditions. I. Omaji, Paul. II. Title

362.849915

The State of Western Australia has made an investment
in this project through ArtsWA.

To our parents

Rex William Beresford (1920-64)
and Audrey and Bruce Piggott

Omaji Akwu (who passed away in 1997)
and Ataidu Omaji

CONTENTS

Preface   8

Introduction: Experiencing the Policies of Child Removal   11

1.   Fear of the 'Half-caste'   29

2.   Creating the Poverty of Aboriginal Children   61

3.   Life on the Inside   101

4.   Official Negligence   122

5.   Assimilation in Practice   158

6.   Living with the Aftermath   189

7.   The Inter-Generational Effects   212

8.   The Politics of Removal and Reconciliation   234

Conclusion: The Stolen Generations and Racism   255

Endnotes   269
Bibliography   281
Index   287

PREFACE

The genesis of this book lay in the work we began in 1993 on Aboriginal juvenile crime which was published in 1996 as *Rites of Passage: Aboriginal Youth Crime and Justice.* In the lives of Aboriginal youth who were in trouble with the law, we were confronted with the intergenerational effects of assimilation. Many of the serious and repeat offenders came from a family background where the parents and/or grandparents had been removed by government, leaving a trail of family dysfunction. In the early 1990s there was no comprehensive study which traced either the history of this policy or its effects on Aboriginal family life. This became our objective.

Since beginning research in this area in 1993, several important materials have become available. In 1995 the Aboriginal Legal Service of Western Australia produced *Telling Our Story* which documented the histories of several hundred survivors of removal. The Service also made an extensive submission to the Human Rights and Equal Opportunity Commission Inquiry into the stolen generations, titled *After the Removal.* The Commission's own report was published in 1997 as *Bringing Them Home.* We have been able to draw on the valuable information in each of these publications, and refer those people wishing to gain greater insights into the personal stories of Aborigines removed from their families to these documents.

This book, while complementing the work of the abovementioned organisations, differs substantially in scope and purpose. It is not our intention to speak for the stolen generations. Only those who have lived through such harrowing experiences can adequately explain what it feels like to lose a family, a culture and a sense of identity. Rather, our purpose is to bring into one accessible volume an understanding of the reasons why this policy was introduced and maintained and to show some of its longstanding effects. Our principal purpose is to inform the broader community and other researchers about this tragic episode so that people can be better equipped to understand the past, its effect on the present, and the need for reconciliation.

Our account of the policy of removal is grounded in extensive archival research around which we have built an interpretative framework to examine why Australia held such unshakeable faith in it. In addition, we have conducted a number of interviews with Aboriginal people subjected to forced removal. These stories are used to bring the human face to our account; to link the operation of the policy with the people upon whom it impacted. This book provides a crucial reminder that the policy of removing children forms part of the life experience of many Aboriginal people living today. As well, we interviewed some key officials who had a close working involvement with assimilation, who provided many valuable insights into its operation.

It remains for us to thank the people without whose

assistance this book could not have been completed. Trish Hill-Keddie, Sandra Hill, Phillip Prosser and Rosalie Fraser gave generously of their time for extended interviews about their experiences as Aboriginal children removed from their families. We also appreciate the comments Trish Hill-Keddie, Sandra Hill and Phillip Prosser made on the draft manuscript.

Invaluable material was also obtained from a range of Aboriginal and non-Aboriginal people who were prepared to share their knowledge with us. In particular we would like to thank: Gary Bowler, Gwen Byrne, Frank Gare, Marcia Greer, Bob Hewie, Elsie Hume, Roma Loo, Lena McGrath, Lorry Sims, Heather Vincetti and Maisie Weston.

For assistance in research we would like to express our appreciation to the library staff of the Aboriginal Affairs Department and the State Library.

This book also benefited from discussions with a number of people including Mary Dalyell, staff at the Aboriginal Legal Service, colleagues at Edith Cowan University, and many of our friends. We thank them for their interest.

Our families provided invaluable assistance and encouragement throughout the two years it has taken to complete this project. Our thanks go to Marilyn, Michelle and William Beresford; and Alice, Ruth, Reuben, Timothy and Tabitha Omaji.

Finally, we are immensely grateful for the commitment shown in this project by Fremantle Arts Centre Press and to the helpful advice and editorial skills provided by Ray Coffey.

Introduction

Experiencing the Policies of Child Removal

'We took the children from their mothers,' acknowledged the then Prime Minister of Australia, Paul Keating, in December 1992 during a landmark speech about reconciliation.[1] Visiting the inner-city Sydney suburb of Redfern, only a few kilometres from the site of the first landing of European settlers, Keating expressed the most heartfelt and extensive recognition of the historical injustices against Aborigines ever made by an Australian prime minister. Never before had the nation's leader asked so pointedly for its people to confront the past and its legacy. Of its terrible treatment of Aboriginal people, he said, 'We failed to ask — how would I feel if this were done to me?' There could be few more appropriate comments by which to acknowledge the removal of Aboriginal children from their families. The policy that gave rise to the removal was undoubtedly, as we shall show, one of the most cruel expressions of the prevailing belief in white superiority. By drawing such public attention to this policy, Keating reflected the struggle of other non-Aboriginal Australians who were beginning to ask profound questions about its origin and impact.

Since Keating's Redfern speech many Australians have been challenged to recognise the injustice done. Most Australians who lived through the assimilation era had absorbed the thinking that the policy was for the long-term good of Aboriginal children. Many of this generation still think that the loss of these children's families was a small price to pay for the benefit of gaining access into white society, as if this justified the policy. More recent generations have faced a different problem coming to terms with the sudden attention given to the 'stolen generations'. They know little or nothing about the origins and impact of the policy; it was not part of the school curriculum and rarely, if ever, did it feature in the media, whose coverage of Aboriginal issues in the 1970s and 80s focused predominantly on the struggle for land rights and Aboriginal ill-health, poverty and crime. Archie Roach's poignant 1990 song — 'Took the Children Away' — brought this issue to the attention of a new generation.

In recent times the stories of these stolen generations have been slowly coming to light and with them are details that Australians have not previously had to confront. Foremost among these is the racial underpinnings of the policy of removal. We have set out to challenge the widely held justification that this policy was a well-intentioned attempt to provide a better life for Aboriginal children. To challenge this notion we have placed this policy within the racial thinking of the times. By doing so we are able to construct an understanding of the motives of contemporaries who saw, in the policy of removal, a way to solve the 'Aboriginal problem' as they defined it.

These racial underpinnings are well illustrated in the story of Trish Hill-Keddie and Sandra Hill, sisters who directly experienced Western Australia's policy of assimilation. Now in their forties, both are professionals in their chosen fields; people who have outwardly 'benefited' from having been removed from their family. However, as their story illustrates, the personal costs have been great and attempts to calculate 'benefits' have a decidedly hollow ring. Both have spent years trying to piece together the fragments of their childhood memories and to better understand the system that tore away their childhoods. Even in bare outlines, their childhood experiences are chilling testimony to the scale of the degrading social experiment to which they were subjected. They also serve to amplify the major themes which constitute the focus of this book.

Noongar by birth, the girls were destined to be caught up in the racial policies drawn around Aboriginal families. The history of their family has been shaped by these policies. In 1933, their mother, Doreen, a nine year old, was stolen, along with her seven year old sister, from their family who were living at the Caversham camp, north of Perth. It was a traumatic moment. Police and Native Welfare officers arrived unexpectedly at the camp in a black car. Fearing danger, the children ran to hide in the tall bamboo grass. Pursued and caught by the officers, they were bundled into the car, screaming for their mother. As the car drove off their mother gave chase, shrieking 'give me back my children'. The girls were taken briefly to Moore River Settlement where they were colour-graded and sent off to Sister Kate's Children's Home, in Perth where Doreen lived until she was fifteen. The girls' parents were devastated but refused to bow down to white authority. Despite their lack of income, they hired the services of a solicitor from the firm, Walker and Brockman. A letter from this firm to A O Neville,

Chief Protector of Aborigines, has survived in the records. Here, an attempt was made to show the manner of the children's removal amounted to stealing. The solicitor informed Neville:

> We have been consulted by Mrs Mary Calgaret of Caversham in regard to her two daughters who were taken from their Mother's home at Caversham without their Mother's consent, and placed in Moore River Settlement for aborigines. Mrs Calgaret informs us as follows:
> (a) That she has never been under your department;
> (b) That her mother was half chinese and half English;
> (c) That she has a home, and that Calgaret has employment, and that she can provide for the children.

It was to no avail. State legislation gave Neville the legal guardianship over all Aboriginal children. At fifteen, Doreen was sent out to work as a domestic servant and spent much of her early life working on an isolated country property. She washed, cooked, ironed and scrubbed the floors for her employer. She ate her meals alone on the back verandah. She had learnt nothing about loving family relationships, or of parenting, but she soon found her role as wife and mother. However, she was unable to escape the notice of the Native Welfare Department which continued to show obsessive interest in her racial background. In 1948, after fifteen years under the Native Welfare, Doreen was the subject to a 'genogram' to establish the degree of Aboriginal blood in order to determine whether on not the Department could maintain control over her until she attained the age of twenty-one, a cruel irony given that she was stolen supposedly because she was Aboriginal. The Assistant Commissioner for Native Affairs made his assessment:

> The face sheet of this file indicates that Doreen possesses 13/32 native blood. From appearance I doubt this and have for a long time doubted that Mrs Calgaret (her mother) is a half caste. She is very light in colour and the Bayswater Road Board not very long ago referred to her as a white woman. Whilst I do not class Mrs Calgaret as a white woman I would be prepared to say that she could be an octoroon or no more than a quadroon.

The experience of Trish and Sandra's mother raise crucial questions about the legality and justice of the proceedings. We identify two distinct phases in the use of the law to remove children. One begins with the passage of the 1905 Aborigines Act, extends through to the late 1940s encompassing the 1936 Native Administration Act. Under this phase, Aboriginal families were treated as legal nonentities. The second phase, beginning in the late 1940s, witnessed the application of the Child Welfare Act to 'neglected' Aboriginal children. It was under this regime that Sandra, Trish and their two other siblings were removed from their family. However, we argue that this process of removal frequently occurred in ways which were highly European-centred and, therefore, discriminatory. It certainly took no account of the ways in which many Aboriginal families had already been devastated by the policy of splitting up families. However, it should be noted that this division into two periods related only to the implementation of official policy. Some children continued to be removed after the 1940s without the involvement of the Children's Court, because of pressure from both missionaries and welfare authorities.

On 17 August 1949, Doreen married Herbert Clem Hill, a Noongar who was widely respected in the Busselton and Manjimup area. Herbert had not been removed as a child and, prior to his marriage, had served for fourteen years in the Australian Navy, including enlistment in the Second World War. He was a happy and well-adjusted man yet, like other Aboriginal adults of the post-war era, he was a non-citizen in his own country. As a war serviceman, he was automatically granted honorary Australian citizenship, which simply exempted him from the restrictions of the Native Welfare Act. He refused to apply for full citizenship — granted to a small number of Aborigines from the 1940s — because to achieve equal legal status with whites he had to renounce his connections to his Aboriginal culture. He was unwilling to do so.

The circumstances leading to Sandra and Trish's removal are closely connected to the experiences that their parents suffered under a legislative regime designed to marginalise and consign Aboriginal people to the lowest position in the white social structure. The policy which subsequently removed their children was a planned extension of this body of legislation. But how could such a policy be justified and openly promoted? We attempt to answer this by locating the policy to remove Aboriginal children in the broader scheme of racial theory and, by extension, in its aim to disempower Aboriginal people so that they would not pose any future social and economic threat to white society.

The Hill family moved from Perth to Collie where their father worked as a miner in the local colliery. Though it was always difficult to make ends meet the family enjoyed a comfortable lifestyle and the living conditions were more than adequate. However, by 1955 the parents' marriage had run into problems; their mother was unable to cope with parenting and relationships, problems which stemmed from her own background as a stolen child. Herbert was left to look after his children which he struggled to do whilst still maintaining his long hours at the mine. During these times there were no pre-schools, and assistance with child care was usually provided by family, friends or neighbours. It was an impossible task for Herbert and he was forced to send the three children to Sister Kate's for temporary respite while he arranged suitable care for them during his working hours. The Child Welfare Department thought differently; the children's file was stamped 'Notice of Removal'. A short time later Herbert and Doreen reunited and the children were returned to their care. However, from the moment of welfare intervention the family file would remain open until all the Hill children were eighteen years of age. Government policy favoured taking young Aboriginal children for the purposes of assimilation. In a 1949 memo, the Commissioner for Native Affairs stated: 'Children under six years of age are definitely preferable. From two to six years is the ideal age. Babies in arms are acceptable and often preferred.'[2] The logic was, the younger the children, the easier the assimilation process.

At the prospect of earning higher wages Herbert moved the family north to the Pilbara. They lived in the town of Wittenoom Gorge where Herbert was employed as a miner in the asbestos industry. During this period Herbert was called up to do two years service in the Armed Forces. According to Sandra, 'the level of isolation, alienation, responsibility and loneliness that Doreen experienced when Herbert was away was overwhelming.' She now had five children under the age of eight. Tragedy struck the family when David, the youngest child died suddenly and as a consequence of all these issues and events the marriage deteriorated and finally broke down. Doreen left the family, entered another relationship and eventually settled at Point Sampson. At first Herbert struggled to care for the children but this proved to be an impossible task and, as a last resort, contacted Doreen to try to work out a solution. Doreen agreed to care for the children temporarily and they were transported to Point Sampson to live with their mother.

The house in which the children lived was a basic State Housing Commission dwelling, situated close to the beach and tucked up against a sand dune. Sandra and her elder sister, Barbara, recall having to sweep the floor every day because the sand blew in through the windows. The family had very little and the children slept on mattresses laid out on the floor. Doreen had no income other than that which Herbert sent her, no material possessions and was left alone with the children. She also had another child and was pregnant again. Even though their living conditions were poor, both Trish and Sandra remember playing down the beach every day and they do not remember being unhappy, although all the children missed their father terribly.

The difficult living conditions for Doreen and her children reflected the racial divisions not just in northern mining communities but throughout the State. Whites received higher wages and were afforded greater opportunities relating to housing and jobs. Even though Trish and Sandra's father was a hard-working man, he struggled to maintain a standard of living for his family that was 'acceptable' to the Welfare Department. This book challenges the mythology prevailing at the time, and subsequently, about 'neglected' Aboriginal children. It does so by placing the poor living conditions of most Aboriginal families — about which negative judgements concerning the condition of their children could be so readily made — within a social justice perspective. We argue that these families were poor because government, and the wider community, had intended this fate for them.

The Child Welfare Department and the Roebourne police periodically called at the house and eventually expressed concern about the family's living conditions. In 1958, a decision was taken to remove the four Hill children to Sister Kate's Orphanage For Half Caste Children. For Sandra, the memories remain vivid:

> We were told to get in the car and we did. We trusted the policeman. I thought he was taking us for a ride. We were four small children, how could we know that this would be the last time we would see our mother? We were looking out of the back window and could see our mum as we drove off. She got smaller and smaller and I thought this is far enough away and told the policeman to take us back home. The little ones started to cry for Mum and we screamed at the policeman to stop the car. He didn't until we reached Roebourne. I didn't see my mother for another twenty-nine years. I will never forget the pain and the fear I experienced in that car on that day, it was absolutely devastating.

The children were taken to the nearest police station, fed and later flown south to Perth where they were admitted to Sister Kate's. The Department billed all these expenses to Herbert who had written to the Department assuring them that 'he will not wilfully neglect his children' and that he 'does not want committal'. Worse was to follow. He was issued with an order to pay maintenance for his children — taken at a difficult moment in his life. The order for maintenance dragged him into a decade long battle with the Child Welfare Department which served to compound the injustice meted out to him by white society.

At a pound per week per child, maintenance consumed one-third of his weekly salary of thirteen pounds. From the late 1950s he steadily fell into arrears and ran up a large debt with the Child Welfare Department. He wrote a number of letters to the Department seeking their understanding and requesting reductions in payments. The letters fell on deaf ears. In 1963 he was apprehended and imprisoned with debts to the Child Welfare Department of over one thousand pounds. He served twelve months in prison.

Sent three thousand miles south to Sister Kate's, the four Hill children saw their father briefly on three occasions over the next three years, but not their mother for nearly three decades. Such a draconian act demands the most thorough explanation of the motives behind the removal of thousands of children like Trish and Sandra. An essential part of the racial theory behind this policy was to culturally transform these children into whites — albeit, marginalised ones. Thus we have to examine the racial thinking about Aborigines and their culture. What did contemporaries find so disturbing in the Aboriginal make-up to cause this compulsion to wipe out Aboriginality in the children?

Sandra and Trish's experience in Sister Kate's provides

some early insights into this thinking. These were the 'light coloured' children destined to be assimilated into white society.

In the Home Sandra and Trish were allocated different cottages. Each of the cottages had a 'Mother' and a 'Father' who were also raising their own children. Yet, the appearances of normal family life were contrived. To many of the Home's children, the purpose of Sister Kate's was to sever them from their backgrounds and crush their spirits as individuals. The daily routine, even for children as young as four or five, was run along Dickensian lines. The day began at 6 am and beds had to be made with 'hospital corners'. Children were then allocated different jobs: 'Most of the cottages had wooden floors so we had to polish wooden floors with rags on our knees and do every board in a long dormitory doing one board at a time. You had to wash your own sheets and underclothes, sweep and garden.' Children then walked over to the dining room for breakfast at 7 am. As Trish recalls:

> If you hadn't finished your jobs you missed out on breakfast. So a lot of kids went without a meal. I remember I did because I'm very stubborn. Each cottage had its own table and there was limited interaction with children from other cottages. I didn't even think my siblings went to Sister Kate's at one stage because I hadn' t seen them for so long.

Sandra remembers the unceasing regimentation of the Home:

> Every function was systematically organised. It was like rounding up the cows. Every detail of our daily lives was done to a plan. It was a way of controlling

kids. It disempowered us. It took away all our thought processes. You didn't think of doing anything different because you would get the stick. We were put to bed every afternoon at 4.30; tucked up looking out at the daylight wishing we could be playing.

Much of what happened to both Sandra and Trish constitutes child abuse by any standards. On one occasion, Trish was belted so severely her sisters found welt marks down the length of her back. Sandra was force fed because she wouldn't eat the food which she found to be horrible. Numerous times her head was held back by her cottage 'mother' and food was shoved down her throat until it spilled out over her face and clothes. Clothing for the children was basic and limited; secondhand items given to the Home as charity. Children were allocated their clothes from stacks of boxes marked according to age. Children only wore shoes when white families took them out for weekend visits. Around the Home they went in bare feet, in winter as well. The cottage 'Father' sexually abused the girls. He liked to spank them over his knee while they were naked.

School brought little relief. Children from Sister Kate's attended the Queens Park primary, a State school conveniently located at the back of the Home. But for many it was a horrible experience. There was a stigma attached to being at Sister Kate's in the minds of the non-Aboriginal children. Trish recalls: 'I can remember being teased, picked on and belted because they knew where you came from.'

Parents and relatives were discouraged from visiting. In 1941 Sister Kate had complained to the Commissioner for Native Affairs about the visits from relatives. She claimed not to mind visits from the mothers, but felt that the presence of other relatives was 'unnecessary' and that they 'disturbed the children.'[3] By the 1950s this attitude was extended to many of the parents themselves, although Sandra remembers a few visits from their father. Trish recalls feeling very confused throughout her time at the Home: 'I didn't the hell know what was going on and why I was there in the first place and what my parents had done that was so bad. You started to think that your parents did it because they didn't want you.' Sandra confirms that the staff went to great lengths to get across, almost on a daily basis, 'that we were abandoned. We began to hate our parents because we thought they didn't want us.'

The opportunity the Home provided for weekend visits with white families paved the way for their eventual release. Families wishing to sponsor weekend visits came into the cottages and looked the children over. Neither they nor the cottage 'parents' explained anything to the children about this process. The children were just told where they would be spending the weekend. Trish was sponsored by a wealthy family who, after several visits, became concerned about the ill-treatment she was receiving at the Home and arranged to foster her. A similar experience later happened to Sandra. The family which sponsored her on weekend visits became alarmed about the distress Sandra expressed when being driven back to Sister Kate's. Both she and her older sister, Barbara, were fostered by a family of market gardeners. Fostering of children was encouraged; it was 'a very white way' to raise the children for eventual assimilation into society. It also helped relieve the government of the subsidies needed to run Sister Kate's. Native Welfare contributed to the family for the upkeep of fostered children. In Trish's case, in particular, her foster parents were thought to be ideal. The family was wealthy, and 'this was seen as a positive because I would be given great opportunities.'

However, the attitudes that underpinned the foster care of Aboriginal children in the 1950s and 60s meant that the so-called great opportunities often exposed children to a crippling experience. These attitudes were a refinement of racial theory which held that, under favourable circumstances, Aboriginal background would naturally give way to the superiority of European civilisation. Trish's foster-parents were the very embodiment of this belief. Professional by background and by social habits, her foster-mother in particular, 'honestly believed that she was doing me a great service in that she was going to train me to become a very well-adjusted young woman full of etiquette, full of very English behaviour.'

Nothing was spared to effect the transition into someone able to succeed in a white world. She became a young lady attending the best of schools, supplemented by ballet and linguistics classes. Socialisation even extended to how to behave in the presence of Aboriginal people: 'I can remember being told that if an Aboriginal person comes towards you when you are walking down the street you must cross the road. And I actually did it. I can't believe that I did it, because I was so conditioned towards Aboriginal people as being very dirty and fearsome.'

During the years that she was in foster care Herbert and Doreen continued to search for their children, although they had little way of knowing where they were. Herbert Hill continued to struggle to pay his maintenance debt and to seek the return of his children. His letters show how Aborigines were forced to account to the Child Welfare Department for every penny spent. By 1966 he had not seen his children for over nine years; the eldest two were approaching sixteen years of age, but he did not know where they were living. His son was still at Sister Kate's. In May of that year Herbert wrote a letter to the Department, the tone of which gives some small insights into his feelings of being ground down by the years of financial impost and emotional loss. However, he never reneged on his commitment to his children. He began his letter:

A note to say I am posting you part of the money, as I have been off work sick, and they [his firm] had a week's holiday which I was not paid for as I was not here long enough. Could you tell me how I go about getting the money reduced, because I cannot afford it. [After expenses of rent, smokes and food] I am left with 12 pounds and I need 18 pound for under-clothes and outer clothes and a little pocket money, so how can I get it reduced, to about 6 – 7 pounds a pay. I would like to know how to get my son home.

This failure to take account of the human dimension of separating children from parents has left many with ongoing painful emotional struggles, the severity of which has its toll on their well-being. If the non-Aboriginal community is to develop a deeper understanding about the suffering endured by the stolen generations it must come to grips with the long-term impact inflicted by racial policies which removed children from their families, isolated them in institutions which used authoritarian methods to make them learn to be white, and fostered them to families where many suffered problems of identity and abuse. Sandra remembers that, while she came to love and respect her foster mother, she grew up feeling that she and her sister 'were just the foster kids'. Her foster parents actively discouraged her from reading about Aborigines and at school she had to counter racially derogatory remarks by saying, 'I'm not black, I'm white. As she explains: 'It really hurt me when the other kids called me names. I kept telling them I was white because I wanted to be like them, accepted. I really started to believe that I was white. I resented my Aboriginality and spent much of my childhood trying to pretend it didn't exist.'

Those who administered this policy of removing children from their families gave little thought to subsequent reunions with families. For Sandra and Trish this has been a painful experience and has involved different levels of acceptance and understanding. By the time the first meeting was arranged, where both their parents were present, neither had seen each other for over twenty years. It was an occasion full of apprehension. As Sandra explains:

Although I wanted to see my parents we had built up a lifetime of resentment for my mother. I questioned who this person was and even thought she might be an imposter. When I walked into this room and this lady looked exactly like my sister I knew she was our mum. We all talked for several hours about our lives and our families and, though I wanted to, I never asked Mum and Dad what happened to us and why. It was a bittersweet reunion. It was awkward and there was a level of detachment in me that was disconcerting but, it was and will always be, the most significant and the most cherished event in my entire adult life.

For Trish reuniting with her parents has been harder.

Even several years later, reunions with her mother were painful. On one occasion:

> I stayed inside almost like a child that was being terrorised, hiding behind the door. She got out of the car and I saw a very short, chunky little lady. I'm still hiding inside and Sandy says, 'Come on out, and say hello to Mum,' and I thought, 'well I'm not going to call her Mum, she's not my mother, what has she done for me.' So I eventually went to the front porch and she walked up to me with open arms and as she embraced me it felt as if I had just fallen off a rock; no emotion, nothing, and my hands were flopping down by my thighs. I thought 'why do you want to find me now, when I was stuck in that wretched place for so long as a little kid and you left me there.' Mum kept her arm around me and walked inside with me. I was busting to ask her why she didn't fight to keep us, why she didn't run after the car, and why she didn't come down and see us more regularly. But I couldn't, and I never have asked her. She has just gone through so much herself and it wouldn't be right.

Meeting her father was also traumatic. On one occasion, he arrived from Bunbury with a suitcase wanting to stay but he left soon afterwards. The reconnection never took place and Trish did not see him again. He died in Collie a short time later of asbestosis. She now deeply regrets those hours that she did not spend with him. 'He was just wonderful. He walked up the steps and said, "Oh, how are you love?"' But Trish was overcome with panic. Succumbing to all the hurtful memories of the things Sister Kate's told her about him she froze at the thought of what to say. The words would not come for all those questions she wanted to ask him. The sadness of such a moment is almost unimaginable. 'I really believe that he was very hurt by it and I left very quickly because I did not want to face up to those things. I did not want to have feelings and be hurt again.' The sense of loss is permanent. 'I wanted so much to tell my father I loved him — but now it' s too late.'

Stories such as this are still new to most Australians. They have a power that shocks and deeply unsettles those that hear them. This became clear to us when we first heard Trish Hill-Keddie give an outline of her childhood experiences at a seminar for social workers. The audience was stunned into respectful silence. It seemed possible to hear everyone in the room ask themselves the same question: how did this happen in Australia and within the lifetime of everyone present? This became our question too, and the motivation for this work. While it is difficult to speak of any individual being 'representative' of such a large group of adults removed as children, Trish Hill-Keddie and Sandra Hill's story is certainly disturbingly common.

1

FEAR OF THE 'HALF-CASTE'

In 1937 delegates representing State and Commonwealth Aboriginal administrations met in Canberra to chart the future direction of Aboriginal affairs in Australia. It was the first national meeting of its kind, and described by delegates as 'an epoch-making event.' Significant political pressures had been behind its establishment. It was intended as a compromise to the calls for the Commonwealth to assume control of Aboriginal affairs from the States. Neither the States nor the Commonwealth supported such a transfer of power but agreement was reached on the desirability of holding periodic conferences.

History has not recorded the full importance of this, the first such conference. Its principal resolution paved the way for the full-scale implementation of the policy of removing Aboriginal children from their families, schemes for which had been advocated since the turn of the century. This resolution set in train an Australia-wide government policy which lead to the removal of thousands of children like Trish Hill-Keddie, well into the 1960s.

In a motion which, much later, would trouble the conscience of many Australians, delegates unanimously resolved that:

> the destiny of the natives of Aboriginal origin, but not of the full blood, lies in their ultimate absorption by the people of the Commonwealth, and it therefore recommends that all efforts be directed to this end.[1]

Delegates knew this resolution was a watershed in the treatment of Aboriginal people. It represented official government policy, sanctioned by the Commonwealth of Australia, to embark on practices aimed at controlling the destiny of the Aboriginal race. For observers of today, the resolution raises several critical questions: What led them to adopt it? Why did they draw a distinction between 'full-blood' Aborigines and those of 'Aboriginal origin'? Why was it thought this latter group could not exist in its own right? What did delegates mean by their concept of 'absorption'? We have addressed these questions in this book.

The motion was framed and submitted by Western Australian delegate to the Conference, A O Neville. He was to emerge as the foremost thinker on race in government circles at the time. Neville was able to speak about his observations of the 'Aboriginal problem' from his long experience as Commissioner for Native Affairs in Western Australia, in the course of which he had developed a long-range 'solution'. Neville brought to the Conference an unusual combination of qualities and experience. He was a capable administrator who had spent a decade overseeing the Department for Native Affairs in Western Australia bringing unusual commitment and a sense of duty to an area nearly everybody else in government regarded as a backwater.

There is little doubt Neville was one of the prime architects of the formal policy of separating Aboriginal children from their families, not only in Western Australia but, through the force of his contribution at the 1937 Conference, throughout the other Australian states. He was keen to explain to delegates the policy of removal already underway in the West. At one point he laid bare the operation of the policy: 'The child is taken away from the mother and never sees her again. Thus the children grow up as white, knowing nothing of their environment.'[2] It is hard to imagine the values which drove Neville to implement and so proudly champion such a policy. This man's talents and energies were directed at solving what he perceived as an emerging racial problem in Australia.

Neville's own background is the starting point for understanding his ideas on race. An immigrant to Western Australia in the closing years of the nineteenth century, he had a near idyllic early life as the son of an Anglican minister on a wealthy but isolated estate in Northumberland. Raised in an environment dominated by Christianity, order and tradition, his values were well suited to romanticising the expansiveness of the British Empire. Stories of heroic missionaries were among the few outside influences to penetrate the quiet valley of his childhood. Empire and Christianity fused in his mind. It was the duty of the British, he came to believe early in his life, to bring Christianity and peace to 'the remote and barbarous parts' of the Empire.[3]

Of course, Neville shared this ideal with many of his contemporaries. It was one driven by racial ideology. Indigenous races were widely thought of as irredeemably inferior beings; their very blackness signifying their membership of a separate branch of humankind.⁴ When Neville became part of the wave of young civil servants to migrate to the far flung parts of the Empire he most likely carried with him a clear imprint about the organisation of humanity. The second half of the nineteenth century, when Neville's views were being formed, was an age dominated more than any before it by the idea of race being the single most important factor governing human behaviour and, hence, the worth — or otherwise — of the world's different peoples.

It is important to locate Neville within this intellectual climate because men like him applied their reasoning about race to policies and practices which culminated in the solution he eventually put forward to the 1937 Conference. Neville's resolution on absorption is an example of race as an instrument of policy; such policies grew out of two centuries of thinking about race.

The link between race and behaviour was first articulated by the great Swedish botanist, Carl Linnaeus who, having worked on classifying plants, went on to develop in the 1750s a three-fold classification of humans — Europeans, Asiatics and Africans. The European was 'of gentle manners, acute in judgement', the Asiatic 'of grave, haughty and covetous manners', and the African 'of crafty, indolent and careless dispositions'. Of course, there was no factual evidence to verify any element of this theory.⁵

In the wake of Linnaeus came several generations of scientists who completely abandoned any pretence to scientific method in order to propagate their theories about race, behaviour and culture. Robert Knox, a Scottish lecturer in anatomy, echoed Linnaeus in his 1850 book, the *Races of Men*, adding that 'the dark races' were psychologically as well as physically inferior. In the late 1850s,

Charles Darwin had recently returned from his voyage on the *Beagle*, with his revolutionary view of all humans originating from the same stock. His work had the potential to completely undermine the flimsy foundations propping up racial thinking, but some of his utterances showed the extent to which it had become woven into the fabric of Western thought. He predicted that 'the civilised races of man will almost certainly exterminate, and replace, the savage races throughout the world.'[6]

Darwin's principal contribution to science — the concept of evolution through natural selection — profoundly impacted on racial ideas. Herbert Spencer, a social philosopher, adapted Darwin's model of natural science to create a 'grand theory of the social world' incorporating 'the survival of the fittest.'[7] Known as Social Darwinism, this view was elevated into a theory which purported to explain the existence of 'superior' and 'inferior' races, the former being able to overrun the latter with greater energy and mental ability. No more powerful idea had entered the debate on race. Black, inferior races would die out because they were biologically inferior to Europeans. When called upon for proof of his assertion, Spencer was merely to reply: 'what is evident does not need proof.'[8]

Social Darwinism spawned its own solutions to the problem of 'inferior' social groups. Francis Galton, a cousin of Darwin's, introduced the idea of eugenics, which spread widely throughout the Western world in the nineteenth and early twentieth centuries. Advocates promoted measures to improve the quality of the racial stock by influencing the breeding rates of different sections of the population. It was a deliberate program to not only let the 'inferior' races die out but also focus attention on a problem perceived to be particularly menacing: the 'half-caste'.

The children of mixed parentage were widely thought 'to present the worst characteristics of both races'. The overt prejudice they suffered sprang from a deeply unsettling fear in the white population that this 'half-caste' race would breed up to become a social menace. Just how it was perceived this menace would manifest itself varied; however, common threads run right through white statements on this issue throughout the nineteenth and the first half of the twentieth centuries. It was feared 'half-castes' would be more black in their outlook than white; they would constitute a potentially numerically strong population to threaten white interests, especially in the north of the country; they would represent a source of racial conflict along American lines; and they would threaten established white social and moral standards. Moreover, their very presence signified the ease with which some whites could break the ultimate racial taboo and enter sexual relationships with blacks. Laws were passed in many colonial societies, including the United States and Australia, outlawing 'miscegenation' — the interbreeding of races. [9]

By the time Neville set foot in Western Australia in 1897 as a young man of promise and good connections, he had internalised one of the most influential ideas of the nineteenth century: that humankind was a hierarchy of races and it was the business of government to protect and advance those thought to be 'superior'. Soon after arriving Neville started his rapid rise through the ranks of the public service in Perth, then little more than a conservative colonial outpost. He reached a pinnacle of his career in 1902 when he became Registrar of the newly created Colonial Secretary's Department.

Coinciding with Neville's ascendancy in the public

service were growing concerns about the 'Aboriginal problem'. In 1904 these culminated in the appointment of a Royal Commission on the Condition of the Natives. The outcome of the inquiry was a landmark report, the first official document which canvassed the need to remove Aboriginal children from their families as a deliberate policy of government. Headed by Queenslander Dr E W Roth, the Commission was given broad terms of reference focused around the treatment and conditions of Aborigines. Roth's Commission was notable for drawing attention to the emergence of a 'half-caste' population. Nearly all the witnesses Roth interviewed expressed concern about the growing number of 'half-caste' children. Summing up the evidence given to him, Roth made the following comments:

> Of the many hundred half-caste children — over 500 were enumerated in last year's census — if these are left to their own devices under the present state of the law, their future will be one of vagabondism and harlotry. In speaking of the numerous aboriginal and half-caste children around Carnarvon, the Resident Magistrate says they will spend their lives in gaol or as prostitutes if nothing is done with them. He would suggest their being sent to some reformatory or mission *whether their parents wish it or not*; [italics added] but at present he has no power to deal with such cases. With regard to the 20-30 half-caste children around Broome, the officer in charge of police considers they should be taken right away ... At Roebourne the Sub-Inspector of Police is of the opinion that such children should be removed from the blacks' camps altogether: a shame that they should be

allowed to run wild ... At Derby, the Resident Magistrate considers that these are people that should be got at. There is a large number of absolutely worthless blacks and half-castes; if they are taken away young from their surroundings of temptation much good might be done with them.[10]

As these comments clearly show, significant community support existed for a policy of forced removal from the earliest years of the new century. To the people in the north, especially, the call for these children to be removed merely extended and formalised existing practice. As Roth discovered, Aboriginal children, often younger than ten years old, were regularly stolen to work in the pastoral and pearling industries where they were indentured as unpaid and uneducated apprentices. In the North-Western districts, Roth reported, 'the pastoralists have taken most of the boys from the tribes'. Probing this issue further with the District Medical Officer in Broome, Roth discovered a virtual slave system involving Aboriginal children who were taken without authorisation of the Aboriginal Affairs Department and almost certainly without the consent of their parents.

Do you know whether any of these children under indenture are ever visited by a Justice? — I have not heard of it being done. What is the usual trade to which these children are indentured? — I should think that quite half of them are indentured to the pearling industry. The remainder are mostly girls indentured as domestic servants. Are these children indentured to the pearling industry taken out on to the pearling boats? — Yes. Do the boys ... receive any wages? — It is almost certain that they do not.

At what age are these boys signed up? — I think the age ranges from ten years upwards ... As far as you know, are such apprenticed children signed on with the consent of their parents? — I do not know.[11]

Roth did not approve of this treatment of Aboriginal children and, when he came to weigh up the evidence submitted to him about their conditions and treatment, he recommended the Chief Protector of Aborigines be made the legal guardian of every Aboriginal and 'half-caste' child until such child attains the age of eighteen. In effect, he set out the foundations for the later wholesale removal of children from their families. In addition to justifying this measure, he went on to highlight the main implications of his major recommendations:

There can be no doubt that of the 500 half-caste children many will, when the necessary protective legislation is provided, become a charge upon the Executive, and the question will then arise as to whether a special Government institution or one of the other mission stations will receive them.[12]

Roth's recommendation about legal guardianship was eventually embodied in the 1905 Aborigines Act which subjected Aborigines to tyrannical control. In addition to the power of legal guardianship over Aboriginal children, the 1905 Act empowered government to force the fathers of 'half-caste' children sent to missions to pay for their children's upkeep. Moreover, it brought existing church missions dealing with Aboriginal children under the Act by classifying them as 'Aboriginal institutions' in order to formally separate the care of Aboriginal and white children.[13] The mobilisation of the law in such a draconian way against Aboriginal people was a reflection of the legal treatment of Aborigines since the earliest days of settlement. Events from the early nineteenth century showed that white men who murdered Aborigines were rarely tried; if tried rarely convicted; and if convicted, rarely punished. In other words, Aborigines were regarded as legal nonentities, denied the legal rights which white society otherwise thought belonged to all humans. It was the evolution of this attitude which culminated in the use of the law to uphold the right of white society to remove Aboriginal children and to care for them separately.

Although by 1905 the Western Australian Government possessed sweeping powers over all Aboriginal children, the provisions of the Act to remove children were not extensively used in the years immediately after its passage through Parliament. Insufficient funds to cover the costs of transporting the children from their homes to the various missions was cited as the principal reason behind the fall in the number of children in institutions between 1906 and 1911.[14] However, the administrative drive to make full use of the provisions was also lacking. Neville's appointment in 1915 to head the Aborigines Department brought a new sense of urgency and purpose to the task. Although he had no prior knowledge or experience in Aboriginal affairs he 'began a career that would consume the rest of his life.'[15]

Neville took up his post at a time of growing animosity among whites towards Aborigines, particularly in the south of the State where the ever encroaching pastoral and agricultural industries ensured a process of forcing Aborigines off their land and marginalising them as seasonal workers or dependents on government rations.

Farmers and townspeople alike began clamouring for the exclusion of Aborigines from contact with white society. With characteristic enthusiasm and drive Neville set out in September 1915 on his first tour of inspection of the southern regions of the State and encountered, for the first time, large numbers of 'half-caste' children. Their living conditions shocked him but the trip marked the 'beginning of the persistent search for solutions.'[16]

The first plan Neville implemented was the establishment of isolated 'native settlements', run by the government, where children could be physically separated from their parents, then educated and trained for unskilled occupations. Two key objectives were met by the plan for reserves: the anger of townspeople over the presence of Aborigines on the edges of towns would be appeased and children would be given the opportunity to shed their Aboriginal background and be accepted into white society. Two settlements were established — Carrolup, outside Katanning and Moore River, north of Perth.[17]

The fate of families and children on these settlements showed how Neville's ideas on absorption were beginning to be implemented. At the Moore River Settlement, for example, children were removed from their parents, names and birth dates were arbitrarily assigned to them on arrival and they were told their parents had lost interest in them. Those who absconded were severely flogged.[18] The high costs of operating the settlements were soon found to be crippling and Carrolup, which Neville had envisioned as 'a thriving, self-supporting community'[19] was forced to close. The inmates were taken to Moore River which then became the only place in the southern part of the State where Aborigines could be sent for 'training'.

A subsequent Royal Commission into Aboriginal Affairs, set up in 1935, and headed by H D Moseley, condemned the conditions of this institution as over-crowded, dilapidated and vermin-ridden.[20] Although the settlement at Moore River limped on, a telling reflection of Western Australian's concern for its Aboriginal population, Neville's hope that the settlement idea would offer a solution faded.

The 1930s were a time of unrestrained growth in racist attitudes towards Aborigines among the broader community and of continuing developments in 'scientific' theories about race. Racist attitudes permeated thinking about Aborigines. Racial prejudice, especially towards 'half-castes', was paraded as the 'aboriginal problem'. Commissioner, H D Moseley travelled 14,000 miles around the State collecting information from which he warned government 'that the great problem confronting the community today is that of the half-caste.'[21] Other investigators of the time agreed: 'half-castes' were a blight on the community. For instance Paul Hasluck, a young journalist on the *West Australian* in the mid 1930s, undertook a detailed, and largely sympathetic, investigation into the 'half-castes'. However, beginning his account, he acknowledged:'The problem of the half-castes in this State is best shown by the numbers. In 1901 there was a total of 951 half-castes in Western Australia; in 1935 there were 4,245. In 1901 only one out of every 200 persons was a half-caste; today one out of every hundred is a half-caste.'[22] Moseley's first concern was also the rapidly multiplying number of 'half-castes'. For both men, however, numbers alone hid deeper fears. For Hasluck, the conditions in which they lived, especially the children, were a grave concern:

The children are at once the section of the half-caste population that causes most alarm and gives ground for strongest hope. They might be able to profit from a chance to do better for themselves, but no chance is given. Today they are swarming about the native camps without proper care. Many of them — laughing, ragged urchins, keen in intelligence — are almost white and some of them are so fair that, after a good wash, they could probably pass unnoticed in any band of whites.[23]

Hasluck saw the rise of a 'separate caste'; a race of outsiders, of 'coloured people' with no place in the community. They married among their own 'colour' and, he observed, 'to an increasing extent with full-bloods', so that 'colour is not being bred out. More is coming in. We are pushing the half-castes back to the Aborigines.'[24]

The idea that 'half-castes' were a threatening, separate race attracted Moseley's attention. In a classic display of contemporary racial theory he linked their 'race' to their collective mode of behaviour. 'Half-castes', he wrote, were 'disinclined to work'; they were 'loafers' and naturally possessed of 'begging habits'. If nothing was done, he warned, 'the time is not far distant when these half-castes, or a great majority of them, will become a positive menace to the community: the men useless and vicious and the women a tribe of harlots.'[25]

When Hasluck and Moseley discussed solutions to this 'problem', both agreed the best chance lay with the children. Whereas Hasluck was content to canvass the various proposals circulating among the interested community to provide education and training for the children, Moseley had settled on a solution: 'a gradual weaning from the aboriginal influence and an encouragement to fit themselves for life in a white community, so that when they reach adult age, they may, if inclined to forsake their bush life, be acceptable in other places.'[26] In other words, Moseley favoured absorption, the idea that these children could be stripped of their cultural background and be made over as whites. However, he saw this as a gradual process which could be put into effect through the establishment of settlements where families could be housed and employed on local farms. Children could be given their own quarters 'where, although not debarred altogether from seeing their parents, they may be gradually weaned from the aboriginal influence.' Moseley also flirted with the contribution that eugenics could play in this cultural transformation. He gave considerable space to the evidence of a local medical practioner, Dr H C Bryan, who spoke

> strongly against the mating of half-castes with half-castes, on the ground that it will perpetuate the black and coloured elements. And still, without advocating the marriage of whites and half-castes, he does support the mating of a half-caste with a coloured person higher in the white scale. To further this scheme, he says, we should do all in our power to prevent a half-caste marrying another half-caste, and to encourage him to look higher.[27]

Neville's thinking had been moving in the same direction for several years. The earliest indication of his emerging theories on race were outlined in an article he wrote for the *West Australian* in 1930. Here he revealed his ideas on genetic inheritance. He reassured readers that throwbacks to Aboriginality would not occur in unions between 'half-castes' and whites. He also raised a more far-reaching goal offered by genetics: 'Eliminate the full-blood and permit the white admixture [to 'half-castes'] and eventually the race will become white.'[28] This was no idle interest; it was being fashioned into a policy. In the early 1930s, Neville began to openly worry about the emergence of 'an outcast race'.

Acting on his concerns, Neville took a critical step in his quest for a new direction towards Aboriginal affairs. In 1933 he had overseen the establishment of a government-funded 'home' for 'quadroon' (quarter-caste) children, the first of its kind in Australia. Its founder, Katherine Clutterbuck (Sister Kate), was of a similar cast of mind to Neville. A devout, English-born Christian with a sense of moral duty about doing good works in the colonies, she, too, embodied prevailing racial theory and applied it in her attitudes towards Aborigines.

Sister Kate wrote to Neville in 1932 seeking his support to help establish the home. This was achieved and Sister Kate built the home amid spacious grounds in Perth's southern suburbs, which she than ran until her retirement in 1946. Constructed along the pioneering 'cottage model' she had developed at the Parkerville Children's Home orphanage before her retirement, each cottage at Sister Kate's operated as a separate 'family' staffed by a 'mother' and a 'father'. This model became the centre-piece of the homely image which she managed to project to the outside world, ensuring Sister Kate's became one of the most fashionable charities among Perth's social set. Sister Kate was a woman of certainties. She had no doubts the neat cottages and artificial family structure bubbled with a 'happy atmosphere'. Material issued by the Home described it as offering a natural environment 'where Dad goes to work and Mum prepares and cooks the meals'.

She was convinced Aboriginal children found a 'sense of belonging' and 'felt part of a family' for the first time in their lives. By the early 1940s, Sister Kate claimed the dozens of cases with whom she had maintained a personal contact proved the work of her Home 'a success.'[29]

Behind these folksy claims lay the real purpose of the institution — Social Darwinist, racial engineering. Sister Kate explained: 'We desire to have the quarter caste children treated like white boys and girls under similar circumstances.'[30] Moreover, she had hopes to 'breed out the colour' from this group. As she explained once to Neville, she objected to the marriage of two 'quadroons', preferring instead these girls married white males.[31]

Children were brought to the Home from all over the State; nearly two-thirds were from the pastoral areas where, in the late 1930s, 'the mothers [had] been leading useful lives on the stations.'[32] Officials from the Department of Natives Affairs gave her whole-hearted support in her enterprise. District officers were reminded that 'colour is to be the deciding factor' in the selection of children to be sent to the Home, because 'it is desired to maintain trueness of colour as far as possible.'[33]

The role performed by Sister Kate's had legislative backing. Neville succeeded in having Parliament pass the 1936 Native Administration Act which brought the 'half-castes' under the same provisions as those of the 1905 Act and extended guardianship of children from sixteen (in the 1905 Act) to the age of twenty-one. Henceforth, government, through the Department of Native Affairs, had the power to remove any Aboriginal children from their parents, to institutionalise such children and, later, to control whom they married.

Thus, when Neville, at the peak of his drive and

purpose, travelled to Canberra in 1937 to attend the Commonwealth Conference on Aboriginal Welfare, his plan for absorption was the most developed of any of the States. Delegates showed a keen interest in Western Australian developments, outlined by Neville, and ultimately supported his motion that absorption became national policy. How did they justify coming to this agreement?

Concerns about race, and about the threat from 'inferior half-castes' in particular, dominated procedures. A backdrop to these discussions were the latest developments in racial 'science' which saw the application of intelligence testing, developed by Frenchman Alfred Binet in 1905, and by researchers committed to eugenic principles. In many parts of the Western world debate over the causes of black under-performance attracted interest.[35] This was the peak era of the eugenics movement, which had gained supporters among conservatives and progressives alike, and which spread with astonishing speed through Western society. Advocates of this pseudo-science were united in a common commitment to controlling reproduction to prevent the 'degeneration' of the European races. 'Inferior' social groups were variously defined as people of mixed races, the feeble minded and the insane, and they became the target of programs of forced sterilisation.[36] While there is no direct evidence that this particular plan was ever contemplated by government officials as a solution to Australia's 'half-caste' population, the ideas central to the eugenics movement certainly did: government intervention, racial planning and the pursuit of human perfectibility.

Australia became a testing ground for another pioneering development in racial 'science' — the 'culture free' intelligence test. An American professor, Stanley D Porteus, claimed to show that Aborigines always performed worse than whites, but that their scores improved the greater their contact with whites.[37] While Porteus remained convinced his tests proved the inferiority of Aborigines, broader scientific opinion questioned the reliability of 'culture free' intelligence testing. The ensuing debate in academic journals about this matter during the 1930s stimulated new understandings about race and human potential. In the forefront of this debate was Australian anthropologist, E P Elkin. In 1937 Elkin wrote an article published in a reputable journal, *Oceania*, in which he warned: 'We must beware lest we undervalue their intelligence because of certain aboriginal cultural traits which seem to us superstitious or primitive.'[38] Elkin advanced a radically different view about Aboriginal potential. He believed they were capable of being educated and that differences in the scholastic achievements between them and whites could be explained by cultural factors and by the lack of a home environment which encouraged scholastic learning.

However, such informed views failed to shape the thinking of delegates to the 1937 Conference. Social Darwinism prevailed. It was generally agreed that 'full-blooded' Aborigines would soon die out. Dr Cecil Cook, Chief Protector of Aborigines in the Northern Territory, explained: 'If we leave them alone, they will die out, and we will have no problem, apart from dealing with those pangs of conscience which must attend the passing of a race.'[39] This was similar to Neville's view:

> In my opinion, however, the problem is one which will eventually solve itself. There are a great many full-blooded aborigines in Western Australia living

their own natural lives. They are not, for the most part, getting enough food, and they are, in fact, being decimated by their own tribal practices. In my opinion, no matter what we do, they will die out.

Neville had no evidence for this view. Nevertheless, the practices of infanticide and abortion raised a deep moral issue for him; 'should [we] allow any race living amongst us to practice the abominations which are prevalent among these people.'[40]

In his major address to the Conference, Neville urged delegates to adopt the long-range plan being developed in his own State. He saw the Aboriginal situation in three phases: the 'pure-blooded' Aborigines in the far north who, he predicted, would eventually die out; a growing number of detribalised and 'half-caste' Aborigines in the middle-north; and a growing number of 'coloured people' or 'half-castes' in the south. It was this third group which was at the centre of Neville's racial planning. If they were not absorbed into the general population, he rhetorically asked delegates, what is to be the limit to their number? His answer provoked the ultimate fear about Aborigines: 'are we going to have a population of one million blacks in the Commonwealth?' There was plenty of support for a play on these sort of fears from other delegates.

Professor J B Cleland, Chairman of the South Australian Advisory Council on Aborigines who, in drawing attention to the increasing population of 'half-castes', concluded that a 'very unfortunate situation would arise if a large half-caste population breeding within themselves eventually rose in any of the Australian States.'[41] Cecil Cook expressed a similiar concern when he said that 'the preponderance of coloured races, the preponderance of coloured alien blood and the scarcity of white females to mate with the white male population' would create 'a position of incalculable future menace to the purity of race in tropical Australia.' Worse could happen. Cook believed a large population of blacks 'may drive out the whites.'[42]

Delegates from Queensland, Northern Territory and Western Australia were unanimous on one point: white interests must be protected. As Cook argued, continuing with an elaborate system of protection would end up producing 'an aboriginal population that is likely to swamp the white.' Neville believed he could meet this emerging 'menace' head-on. He spoke to delegates about his twenty-five year plan 'to merge the two races.' This involved 'breeding out' Aboriginality through intermarriage in the white community, although the full explanation of his vision requires study of his book, *Australia's Coloured Minority* which he wrote in 1947 after his retirement. Neville envisaged a three-part, interlocking plan set against the Social Darwinist belief that 'full-blood' Aborigines would eventually die out. For the remaining 'half-castes', the plan was to take the children away from their mothers; to control marriage among 'half-castes'; and to encourage intermarriage with the white community. In this way, it would be possible to 'eventually forget that there were ever any Aborigines in Australia'.

Of the crucial first part of his plan, Neville explained:

> we must take charge of the children at the age of six years; it is useless to wait till they are twelve or thirteen years of age. In Western Australia we have the power under the act to take any child from its mother at any stage of its life, no matter whether the mother is legally married or not. It is, however, our intention to establish sufficient settlements to

undertake the training and education of these children so that they may become absorbed into the general community.

Neville described to the Conference details about the work of Sister Kate's in implementing his policy. By way of background, he explained the key principle upon which the Home operated: 'you cannot change a native after he has reached the age of puberty, but before that it is possible to mould him.' In other words, the objective of the Home was cultural transformation. At this time Sister Kate's was home to over a hundred children and, as Neville described:

> when they enter the institution, the children are removed from their parents, who are allowed to see them occasionally in order to satisfy themselves that they are being properly looked after. At first the mothers tried to entice the children back to the camps, but that difficulty is now being overcome.[43]

Neville made one startling admission about this aspect of his long-range plan. He admitted it was 'well known that coloured races all over the world detest institutionalisation.' Neville knew why: Aborigines 'have tremendous affection for their children.'

The operation of Sister Kate's excited considerable interest among delegates from other States. It is clear no one had so far established anything quite like it.

The second part of Neville's racial plan — controlling marriage among 'half-castes' — was a matter on which he had already acted, as he explained to the delegates:

> in order to prevent the return of those half-castes who are nearly white to the black, the State

Parliament has enacted legislation including the giving of control over the marriages of the half-castes. Under this law no half-caste need be allowed to marry a full-blooded aboriginal if it is possible to avoid it.

Neville was at the forefront of racial thinking in advocating marriage between lighter coloured Aborigines and the white population as a desired outcome. Most of the community was appalled at the idea, including Neville's own field officers. In *Australia's Coloured Minority* he recalled the attitude of white superiority among his officers:

> I remember one of my senior officers, when discussing the future of a coloured girl, declaiming in florid language that 'we of the blood of a Gladstone, a Shakespeare, or a Kitchener should not plant our seed in the womb of a native', and that 'for the half-blood child the slogan should be, back to the aborigine ever — marry a white man never.'

However, Neville regarded intermarriage as a practical solution to Australia's race problem. He possessed highly refined racial arguments in support of his view. His own observations told him that 'incorrect mating' among the 'half-castes' had steadily produced an inferior 'breed'. In Neville's mind, a better type of 'half-caste' had existed thirty or forty years previously. These were robust, vigorous people, who travelled the country as 'good, hard workers'. However, they intermarried and 'became lethargic'. Only with the admixture of further white blood did they, according to Neville, recover some of the original traits, eventually 'acquiring part of the good qualities of both races; the physical improvement being notable.'[44] Herein lay the crux of Neville's plan. It was critical, he wrote, to encourage 'the white rather than the black through marriage.'

In his 1947 book, Neville writes in lyrical terms about the potential for his scheme. Conceding momentarily that it 'is not always wise for people of widely diverse races to intermarry', it is nevertheless possible:

> The young half-blood maiden is a pleasant, placid, complacent person as a rule, while the quadroon girl is often strikingly attractive, with her oftimes auburn hair, rosy freckled colouring, and good figure ... As I see it, what we have to do is to elevate these people to our own plane, and if inter-marriage between them and ourselves becomes more popular, then we shall be none the worse for it. That will solve our problem of itself.[45]

Existing law was designed to prevent miscegenation. Neville was only too aware of the legal difficulties involved, not least because the Act 'said that cohabitation was an offence, but did not mention sexual intercourse.'[46] Faced, on the one hand with these legal difficulties, and on the other with the need to solve the 'half-caste' problem, Neville pinned his hopes on intermarriage. 'I know of some 80 white men who are married to native women, with whom they are living happy, contented lives, so I see no objection to the ultimate absorption into our own race of the whole of the existing Australian native race.'[47] The key aspect of this plan needs re-emphasis. In Neville's mind absorption did not mean merely co-existence on equal social terms. His was a larger vision. He believed that, through intermarriage, children of such unions would become steadily lighter in colour until, ultimately, the race of Aborigines ceased to exist.

Neville gave considerable space in his 1947 book to detailing the genetics behind his plan for 'correct mating'. In fact, one key section has the appearance of a 'how to' manual for breeding out the Aboriginal race. It contains a range of photographs of Aboriginal people captioned as various racial 'crosses'.

> It seems apparent with these people of European-Aboriginal origin that like breeds like — two half-bloods will produce children of similar blood and not of quarter blood as many people think — and therefore it requires the admixture of further white blood to alter the ratio and produce the quadroon ... the more they mix with us the more like us they become, and the less likelihood of reversion to the aboriginal type.[48]

For Neville, 'the question of marriage' was 'of paramount importance.' As Commissioner for Native Affairs he had the power to dictate his vision for genetic extermination. Time and again, he explained to readers of *Australia's Coloured Minority*, he was asked by white men, wishing to marry a 'coloured' girl, whether their children would be black. As the law imposed upon him the responsibility 'of approving or objecting to the proposed marriage', his answer was vital. Marriages between women of European-Aboriginal descent were clearly approved because: 'the children would be lighter than the mother, and if they later married whites and had children these would be lighter still, and that in the third or fourth generation no sign of native origin whatever would be apparent.'

These ideas had the status of official policy in Western Australia by the mid 1930s. Moseley, in his 1935 report to government, provides telling confirmation: 'If this scheme of breeding out the colour is really effective, and if these people [Aborigines] assist in the policy by choosing the appropriate partners, well and good.'[49] Neville advocated the key parts of this long-range plan to the 1937 Conference, but not in all their lurid details. It is not clear from the minutes of the Conference the extent to which other delegates shared his belief in breeding out Aboriginality through intermarriage. The Queensland delegate, for example, reiterated the determination with which his State 'rigidly restricted' marriage between whites and blacks, giving every encouragement 'to marriage of cross breed aborigines amongst their own race.'[50] Therefore, delegates could read into absorption one of two meanings: that Aboriginal children should be taken from their parents and raised as whites to mix as non-Aborigines in the general community; or, the term could be used as Neville intended it: children should be removed from their parents and brought up as whites for release into the general community where they would be encouraged to marry whites and, through procreation, further weaken the genetic strain of Aboriginality. Neville's was by far the more controversial of the two interpretations but both were outcomes of widely held racial beliefs and both involved draconian intervention to break up Aboriginal families. Professor Cleland seemed apprised of the full implications of Neville's motion for absorption:

> there can only be one satisfactory solution to the half-caste problem, and that is the ultimate absorption of these persons into the white population. I think that this will not necessarily lead in any way to

deterioration of type, inasmuch as racial intermixtures seem, in most cases to lead to increased virility.

Neville never found cause to retreat from his views about race. He continued to head the Department of Native Affairs until his retirement in 1940. Throughout this time he stuck rigidly to his plan. A telling correspondence in 1939 between Neville and the Director of Gnowangerup Mission, H W Wright, shows the extent of his commitment. Wright wrote to Neville questioning his policy:

> In reference to the light coloured children which you saw here, these are all offsprings of fair and legally married parents and if these folk are keen on sending their children to school and are trying to live as independent, law abiding citizens, I felt it would be unwise to break up their families.[51]

Wright was one of very few whites — missionaries, departmental officials, or ordinary members of the public — to uphold the rights of Aboriginal families. Not surprisingly, it failed to move Neville who replied:

> their parents may be married, but my impression was that some of the children were the offspring of white fathers. Even if the children belong to legally married parents, I feel that it would be wrong to allow light-coloured children to grow up as white natives. They must be given an opportunity in life … I have no wish to break up families, but other aspects must be considered besides sentiment. We must go on weeding out the light-coloured children.[52]

Neville took great satisfaction in his powers under the

1936 Native Administration Act to personally remove children from their parents and in watching them fulfil his expectations for them. He was a virtual dictator over Aborigines. He told readers in his 1947 book that many 'half-caste' young women with children fathered by white men came to see him 'to discuss the disposal of their children.' Neville wasted no time in telling these mothers the fate of their children: 'I explained to them that separation was inevitable for their children's sake.' He convinced himself that memories of their mothers 'faded quickly from their minds.' He kept a watchful eye on these children. They attended school and mixed as white children. However they would never be able to meet their real parents later in life because, by this time, 'both would realise the position sufficiently well to avoid any adverse consequences from it.' This was as close as Neville could bring himself to acknowledging that forced removal carried long-term emotional damage. In his mind, the national need was more pressing. As he reminded readers in *Australia's Coloured Minority*, 'Should there pass another fifty years of social ostracism for these people, our descendants will see a new race evolve and one they may well blame us for bequeathing them.'[53]

Neville left his legacy of racial practices firmly embedded within the Department of Native Affairs. In 1943 his successor, F I Bray, wrote to the Victorian Aboriginal Group outlining the Department's racial guidelines for removing children from their families:

> Although some half-castes are tribal in character, we usually endeavour to treat them as non-tribal, and when we discover a half-caste who is the off-spring of a full-blood mother, or a quarter caste child who is the off-spring of a half-caste mother,

we usually segregate them into native institutions or missions.[54]

Issues of race and colour continued to dominate departmental policy as the following letter from Commissioner Bray to a government officer stationed in the North-West clearly indicates. He began by expressing his refusal to the request from one Aboriginal man for the release of his son from Sister Kate's:

> James is a near white boy. He is being reared as a white boy at Sister Kate's Home, and in due course he will be placed out in employment, and will live as a white person. It would be detrimental to his future welfare to permit him to return to his mother who lives in association with natives. If this were agreed to it would undo all the good work in rearing James to white standard.[55]

The passage of the 1936 Native Administration Act in a country without a Bill of Rights which might have offered some protection to the minority Aboriginal population, conferred the aura of legality around the policy of removing Aboriginal children from their families. The use of the law in this way lasted until the early 1950s when a system of removing Aboriginal children under the Child Welfare Act was instituted. Thus, the period between 1936 and 1950 represented unchecked power to dismantle Aboriginal family life. The law was clearly discriminatory because it did not apply equally to everyone. It was specific to one race only. The extent of this discrimination is revealed when the practice of removing Aboriginal children is contrasted with practices relating to white children who were the responsibility of the Child Welfare

Department. The Child Welfare Department's 1946 Annual Report loudly proclaimed the sensitivity of its policy towards children who came under its notice. 'The Departmental officers', it explained, 'have been able to effect improvements in the best interests of the children, without removal. Every effort is made to prevent broken homes and to preserve the parental tie.' Yet, the breaking up of Aboriginal homes was instituted by law.

Further, the 1936 Act contravened the legally accepted notion of due process in public administration. Victims of State policies have the right to be heard, to be represented and to appeal decisions. Aborigines were conferred with no such rights under the 1936 Act. This opened the way to the practice of the indiscriminate rounding up of children which forms the tragic central theme of many Aborigines' personal testimonies. A 1946 journal entry from the work diary of a Department of Native Affairs Inspector shows this process of indiscriminate removal at work:

Proceeded to Mount Wellard and picked up a quadroon girl Amy, daughter of half-caste ... and unknown white man and her brother or half brother, Fred. Amy is aged about 15 or 16 years and Fred about 11 years. The former definitely quadroon and the latter doubtful, might be half caste. Great difficulty was experienced in removing these children and it was only through the firmness of Sergt. McGeay that it was possible and even then the mother had to be taken also to accompany them to Roeburne.[56]

This was not an isolated incident. Indiscriminate removal of children is recalled by Frank Gare who began his career in the Department of Native Affairs in 1946. He explained in an interview:

> Police would go around on their patrols and go to a bush camp and find two or three lighter looking children ... they just used to go and pick them up. When I went up to Carnarvon in 1949 I read a police manual which told police officers what to do. In a section under natives it said that if a police officer finds light caste children in a native camp they are to pick them up and send them to the nearest mission or, failing that, down to Sister Kate's in Perth. They just picked them up and took them away. It was all done at the request of Neville to the Police Department.

These acts contravene international law, including the 1946 United Nations declaration against genocide and the 1948 Declaration on Human Rights. The specifics of these acts, as they applied to the practice of removing Aboriginal children from their families, is discussed in chapter eight.

However, issues of international illegality did not appear to concern those who devised and implemented the policy of removal. The 1930s were the high point of the racial thinking which had seeped into mainstream attitudes. Similar racially inspired schemes were being implemented in other parts of the colonial world. In Canada, the 1930s witnessed a high point in the expansion of the residential school system, whereby native children from across the country were forcibly removed from their communities and placed in schools to be educated in white civilisation. They were to be exposed to a 'curriculum aimed at radical cultural change

... the 'savage' child would surely be remade into the 'civilised adult.' This scheme, too, was motivated by the ultimate ideal to 'kill the Indian in the child' so that 'all the Indian there is in the race should be dead.'[57]

The 1930s also witnessed the first awful stirrings of Nazi racial policies against the Jews and the Gypsies. The parallels between these groups and Aborigines cannot be ignored even though the ghastly death camps of the Holocaust have tended to mask them. Both schemes were the product of racial ideas which justified the division of humanity into 'superior' and 'inferior' racial groups; a division which was used to justify schemes to inflict suffering on these so-called 'inferior' groups.

While few public objections were raised against proposals to remove Aboriginal children and institutionalise them, agreement was not unanimous. When the 1936 Native Administration Bill was discussed in the House of Assembly, A A Coverley, Member for Kimberly and a long-time critic of Neville in Parliament, seized on the expanded powers it gave the Commissioner to criticise the injustices the measure would inflict on Aboriginal parents. These people, he said,

> should be allowed to see [their children] and talk with them and go back [to their communities] and say how well they are cared for. That would do something good and ease the minds of the aboriginal people who have to lose their half-caste children. These people do not understand. They have not any idea where their children are taken and whether they are dead or alive.[58]

Over the next three decades, isolated voices were raised against this scheme by some influential people, including several parliamentarians. However, this alternative voice was never sufficiently strong to dent the prevailing view.

Planners behind the policy — such as Neville and Sister Kate — have left to contemporary society the problem of interpreting their work. Were they, as many people seem to think, merely well-meaning individuals who should not be judged by today's standards? From their own perspective they had perceived a pressing social problem, defined it by the values of their own day, and resolved to find a solution. In adopting absorption, they were applying the thinking about race that had seeped into the Western conscience. By this reasoning, the early architects of Australia's racial policies have received the lesser judgement of misguided philanthropists. However, it should never be forgotten that, in its initial form, Neville's was a plan to annihilate a race by planned, genetic extinction. This was racial thinking at its most gruesome. When can this ever be excused?

2

CREATING THE POVERTY OF ABORIGINAL CHILDREN

Following the end of the Second World War, important changes occurred to the policy of removing Aboriginal children from their families. International forces compelled government officials to re-shape the reasoning behind its continuation. The defeat of the Nazis and the world-wide denunciation of their horrific crimes against humanity forced politicians and scientists to publicly distance themselves from a belief in racial policies. As one recent historian of racism has commented, 'after the death camps and the Holocaust it became nigh on impossible openly to espouse belief in racial superiority'.[1] The Western Australian Commissioner of Native Affairs in his Annual Report for 1945 conceded that 'today it is considered that any human being is entitled to consideration irrespective of the colour of his skin'.[2]

Thus, white Australians' vision for 'breeding out' Aborigines had to be rethought. The official policy now became known as assimilation. To white elites this meant 'educating and training the natives in order to fit them into our own economic and social life.'[3] The situation for

Aboriginal children hardly changed. A central plank of assimilation remained the removal of children from their families and their placement in missions and foster homes. Here it was expected they would be fitted into the lower end of the white social structure 'under conditions similar to our own'. In other words, they were no longer to live as Aborigines.[4] The planning behind this cultural transformation continued to be motivated more by fear of Aborigines than by any genuine humanitarian concern for the children.

The adoption of assimilation also brought changes to the means by which children were removed. The old practice of indiscriminate rounding up had become unacceptable. The broader changes in racial thinking made it necessary to find 'non-racial' justifications and 'legal' mechanisms for the practice to continue. Thus, the unacceptable living standards of Aboriginal families was emphasised. Henceforth, Aboriginal parents would be punished with the forced removal of their children for failing to rear them according to white standards. The Commissioner, in his 1945 Annual Report, added an important qualifier to the new standard of racial tolerance: acceptance of an Aborigine depended upon their preparedness 'to live under civilised conditions'.[5] The Department of Native Affairs together with the Child Welfare Department became the arbiters of the new standards within the judicial framework of the Children's Court. However, the attitudes behind assimilation and the use of the courts to decide the fate of Aboriginal children opened up a number of troubling issues.

In the post-war era when these changes were being planned, Aborigines were still widely regarded as racially inferior and a potential threat to social stability. Removing them, for whatever reasons, carried the benefit of stripping away their culture. In the immediate post-war period, few questioned whether Aborigines desired to be offered this opportunity to become like whites. In 1957 social activist and progressive, Jessie Street, raised one of the few voices of dissent against this racial planning. After an exhaustive tour of Aboriginal settlements around Australia she wrote a report in which she questioned the appropriateness of assimilation on cultural grounds. 'Is there any evidence at the present time', she asked, 'that Aborigines, with very few exceptions, wish to live as whites?' She worried about the loss of Aboriginal culture and especially their communal way of life which, she argued, was incompatible with the competitive individualism of white society. Moreover, the Aboriginal concept of 'success' was, she felt, too different and unlikely to be valued: 'Among the aborigines the material success of the individual means more of everything for the tribal community ... but it is regarded by many uninformed whites as further evidence of the lack of a sense of responsibility on the part of blacks instead of evidence of their innate generosity.'[6]

Jessie Street's comments exposed the extent of the cultural change which assimilation sought to impose on the Aboriginal population. Children were to bear the brunt of this cultural transformation, the need for which continued to be justified in racial terms. Those living in the southern part of the State, the 'half-castes' as contemporaries categorised them, remained the key target group. Contemporaries continued to worry that the children would pick up the cultural values of their black parents if they remained with them. As Neville had recognised, 'Seldom were the lighter coloured children treated other than as natives.'[7]

Assimilation, as it came to be understood in the post-war years, was first detailed in the 1948 parliamentary *Report on Survey of Native Affairs*, conducted by Western Australian magistrate, F E A Bateman. His report showed how the new policy was driven by long-standing racial attitudes and fears. Most of Bateman's views, and those of others who supported them, were a reworking of pre-war attitudes and prejudices towards Aborigines. However, it is important to see them in their new context to emphasise the point that the foundations of assimilation were laid in racial theory.

Bateman certainly echoed the stereotypes about 'half-castes' which had been circulating for half a century. 'The average half-caste in the towns', he reported

> is an undesirable type, idle, unreliable, fond of drinking and gambling and generally useless. In liquor they are noisy, obscene, disorderly and often violent. In the majority of instances they move from town to town, never remaining settled in one spot for very long and living on the various native reserves adjacent to the towns.[8]

There were 1500 'half-castes' in the south of the State at this time and when Bateman, like others before him, projected his understanding of their current problems into the near future, he found a 'definite menace', requiring an urgent resolution. The appalling conditions endured by most Aborigines in the southern part of the State, where most lived on ramshackle reserves on the outskirts of towns, compelled Bateman to consider the fate of the children. He firmly believed an unbridgeable gulf separated Aboriginal family life from whites. Any attempt to raise the status of the children in such circumstances was 'absolutely hopeless' and would only 'prolong the native problem for generations.' The key difficulty, as Bateman saw it, was that any good done during the day at school was immediately reversed the moment the child returned home to its parents:

> How possibly can children progress when after the day's schooling is over they are forced to return to the disgraceful verminous conditions of native camps, where six or seven children together with their parents and perhaps an adult relation or two and more often than not a dog, occupy on a communal basis a shack, inadequate in size and constructed of old kerosene tins and bags.[9]

Not only were the physical conditions of Aborigines threatening their children's future, but Aboriginal culture was widely seen by white officials as frustrating children's 'sense of responsibility' and stimulating 'that urge to ignore moral standards as laid down by us', leading them 'to yield to those pleasurable impulses the flesh is heir to.'[10] The belief in white superiority which lay behind such views underpinned a disdainful attitude towards Aboriginal culture generally and in particular to the perceived lack of any culture whatsoever among the 'half-castes'. Some of the most florid examples of this outlook can be found among the letters and diaries of Department of Native Affairs inspectors and patrol officers who wrote regular memos to the various commissioners. One such memo written in 1952 glorifies 'we whites' who are 'controlled by hundreds of years of Christian background.' It mattered not to the author that 'we do not believe or accept a word' of this background; it 'still acts as a guide or control of our living.' 'Half-castes', brought up 'by their mothers with the Aboriginal background' have lost these restraints 'in their contact with civilisation'.[11]

A O Neville, in his book published in 1947, provides some additional insights into the way in which the concept of race was used to construct the 'problem' of Aboriginal children in this post-war period. The children growing up on the reserves, he argued, acquired 'a warped outlook difficult to eradicate'. This, he believed, was the fault of their 'coloured' parents: 'The bad habits of the grandparents and parents are bequeathed to the children ... The elders are indifferent to the lack of improvement in the children. What was good enough for them is good enough for the children.'[12] Thus, 'the children are still the main problem.' Neville's solution was unchanged, but it is important to highlight his reasoning. On the reserves, he wrote, 'you will find a bright spot due to the fact that some mother has worked at one time in a white employer's house and has there learnt the rudiments of cleanliness of person, care of children, and the protection of foodstuffs.'[13]

In canvassing solutions to these perceived problems of 'half-castes', Bateman rejected an obvious answer: to improve the living conditions on the reserves. 'Even if the present economic condition was such to make this possible', he reasoned, 'there is considerable doubt as to whether this would bring about a satisfactory solution.' In these, and later comments, Bateman reflected the prevailing community views on race. Describing all the adults as 'beyond redemption', he believed that 'these types if provided with a new home would have it as filthy as a native camp in a matter of weeks.' Such thinking made drastic solutions appear reasonable. Henceforth, Aborigines should be subject to our own law regarding neglected children. If white parents neglected their children the children are removed from their control. The same action should be adopted in respect to the native children. The welfare of the children is the only thing which should be considered and the fact that the parents are likely to be heart-broken for a few weeks should not influence the administration any more than the fact that white parents in similar circumstances suffer grief. Those native parents who will not make any effort to improve their conditions and help their children are not fit to retain them. I feel sure that the fear of losing their children would be a tremendous spur for those borderline cases ... and compel them to do something for themselves and their children.[14]

The filth and lethargy which they allegedly tolerated were, in his mind, all of their own making. Moreover, they were disinterested in their children's schooling and wandered carelessly from town to town, 'exposing them to all kinds of harm.' Such children were 'neglected a thousand fold more than any white child deemed to be neglected under the Child Welfare Act.' Their perceived absence of worth as people is revealed in his assessment of parents; any grief at losing their children would only last 'for a few weeks.' Bateman's proposed solution had a familiar ring: segregate the children in institutions and fit them to take their place in white civilisation. So pleased was he with his conceptualisation of the problem and his diagnosis of the remedy, he relished its potential to do good: 'I feel that it would be advantageous for all native children to spend some time at these children's institutions'. In outlining his scheme, Bateman was reflecting current practice within the Department of Native Affairs. Neville's successor as Commissioner of Native Affairs, F I Bray, was convinced that 'no substantial progress is possible unless children are separated from their parents and cared for in dormitories.'[15] Here was the long-standing and entrenched view of whites — reformulated for a new era.

However, there is an extraordinary shallowness about Bateman's approach to defining the problem of Aboriginal child poverty. He, and countless others like him, were unwilling to properly confront the reality of Aboriginal life, and to acknowledge the role governments and ordinary people had played over the years in creating and sustaining the very poverty about which they now moralised. Most Aboriginal people — and especially those in the south of Western Australia — did live in abject poverty and this poverty did, very frequently, restrict the life chances of their children. However, Bateman not only failed to acknowledge the causes of Aboriginal poverty, he overlooked the abiding strength of the family in Aboriginal culture, despite the impact of severe material deprivation. Moreover, he chose to ignore the real desire — against impossible odds — of many Aboriginal people to improve their life circumstances and the chances for their children. These were rarely listened to, and certainly not by Bateman. His legacy was to further extend the use of race as a political means to control and oppress Aboriginal people, but this time under the guise of humanitarian concern.

Neville and Bateman reflected the views of the wider community. Erected around them was a framework of logic which justified drastic action. They neutralised the inhumanity of removing these children by claiming a higher moral concern: 'half-castes' were inferior parents; their children were being damaged; only by taking them into the 'superior' care of white society would their future be guaranteed. Solid as this framework of logic appeared to them it was held together by a fabricated theory on race. The justification for removal — that these children were wilfully neglected — was a facade. When the circumstances of Aboriginal poverty are carefully examined, it is clear that this was a deliberate imposition by government, widely supported by the community. Contrary to the moralizing, Aboriginal children in the post-war era were taken from their families for reasons over which they had no direct control.

Indigenous people everywhere who are dispossessed of land are prone to social and economic marginalisation. Such a process occurs from the beginnings of colonisation. In the twentieth century, the descent of Western Australian Aborigines into poverty was entrenched by the passage of the 1905 Aborigines Act, the impact of which has been well documented elsewhere.[16] Briefly, and in respect of the Act's effect on the future living conditions of Aborigines, any Aborigine who was not in lawful employment could be removed to a reserve or expelled from any town or municipality which had been declared a prohibited area. Reserves expanded in number from the 1930s, and well into the 1960s, existing on the outskirts of many country towns.

Usually, the outcry from locals protesting the 'nuisance' from natives compelled local authorities to establish a reserve, which only ever offered temporary control of land to Aborigines. In these reserves, also known as camps, Aborigines congregated in family groups as dispossessed and displaced people, effectively denied any opportunity to enter the mainstream economic life. Governments spent virtually nothing on establishing or maintaining these reserves, a fact that was reflected in the low levels of spending on Aboriginal affairs. Western Australia had the lowest spending of all the States: in 1935, the government spent little more than one pound per head on Aborigines; New South Wales spent £5.5.3; Victoria — £13.4.4; Queensland and South Australia — £5.10.10.[17]

Few white people had bothered to become acquainted with these poorly serviced reserves and to understand the lifestyle and the problems of the people who lived on them. *West Australian* journalist, Paul Hasluck, was one of the few who had and his detailed portrait, while not free of the racial biases of the time, offers a most comprehensive portrait of these communities. His work, originally published as a series of newspaper articles was subsequently bound as a small book, *Our Southern Half-caste Native and their Conditions.*[18] Hasluck's richly informed observations help to expose Bateman's later report as the product of cultural blindness and racial stereotyping.

Hasluck did not mince words in describing the appalling living conditions on the reserves. 'Most half-castes,' he wrote, 'live in habitations rather worse than the poorer class of suburban fowlhouse.' He identified three types of living quarters. The most basic were the mia-mias, traditional dwellings which, in the camps Hasluck visited, were built with five or six poles erected to make a pyramid. Around the windward side of the structure were strewn old bags, blankets or bushes. Inside, a whole family slept on the ground. A step higher were 'rude tent-shaped huts' made of bags and kerosene tins which had been flattened and opened out. In wet weather a cooking fire was made inside. Thirdly, the 'superior sort of hut' was made more substantial by the addition of old timber and galvanised iron. These had a chimney 'of sorts', a door and two or three compartments separated by hanging bags.

Hasluck tried hard to see through the prevailing myths and stereotypes about these people. He observed that families living in the more substantial huts went to considerable lengths to keep their places clean and tidy. He also noted that the status of Aborigines in the white community as a 'bad lot' was far from accurate:

> Farmers who had employed half-castes for many seasons, the police, the local protectors and a few school-masters who had anything to do with their children — that is, people who were in constant touch with them — gave them a much higher character than did the people who 'would not tolerate them anywhere about the place' and who presumably seldom met.

As well, Hasluck encountered communities founded on the strength of the family unit. Although legal marriages scarcely existed, 'most unions so simply made in the camps seem to be lasting' and these couples were 'devoted to their children' for whom they had strong aspirations: 'most of them were very eager for their children to go to school.'

However, Hasluck found that Aborigines faced an impossible task in realising these ambitions. By the late 1930s, Aborigines living on the reserves had been reduced to a marginalised workforce of odd job labourers. A common means to earn money was the picking of 'dead wool' which involved wandering around the paddocks until a dead sheep was found and then, squatting beside the carcass, plucking the wool from it by hand. Snaring foxes and rabbits for their skins occupied some, while a few were hired as a semi-permanent casual labour force on the farms, contracted to perform seasonal work at hay carting and shearing times. However, the money earnt from these varied odd jobs was never sufficient to make Aborigines independent of government rations.

Hasluck reserved his harshest criticisms for the failure of governments to ameliorate the hardship and privation endured by the reserve dwellers. 'It is impossible to find evidence', he wrote,

> that in recent years the Government has taken any positive action to better the conditions of the people living on the reserves ... They have given no education to the children, no encouragement to the families to do better, and have offered no means of improving their living conditions.

Virtually none of the reserves were connected to town water or sewerage systems making it difficult to encourage cleanliness. It was clear that government intended these people to be marginalised and impoverished.

Conditions for some Aborigines brightened considerably during the Second World War, demonstrating a crucial point which contemporaries mostly chose to overlook. With access to regular employment at award wages, Aborigines could avoid the poverty which led officials to justify the removal of their children. Nevertheless, it was never the intention of government to allow Aborigines into the economic mainstream. However, labour shortages, due to the war effort, created unprecedented employment and high rates of wages for many Aborigines. The Annual Report from the Department of Native Affairs for 1945 noted that the 'detribalised native people are now in better economic circumstances'. They had plentiful employment, higher earnings than in previous years and, 'as they are drawing Child Endowment as well, many of them are trying to improve their social conditions.'[19]

The upward trend in favourable circumstances faltered after the war ended. In the southern part of the State, many Aborigines continued to receive award wages but most could only find part-time employment.[20] The operation of the work permit system for employing Aborigines was a further impediment to obtaining regular work. This system required any employer to take out a permit with the Department of Native Affairs to hire any Aborigine of 'more than quarter caste', and for any period of more than one month, except those who held citizenship. It absolved employers from the provisions of the Workers Compensation Act, enabling medical expenses incurred while working to be met by the Department. However, the main purpose was to exert control over the lives of Aborigines. Employers were expected to lodge a proportion of Aboriginal wages with the Department for banking in a Trust Account. The permit system had two detrimental effects on the employment of Aborigines. Firstly, is was a bureaucratic inconvenience to farmers wishing to employ Aborigines on a casual basis. 'It is extremely annoying,' wrote one Beverley farmer to the local Native Affairs District Officer in the early 1950s,

> to have to keep on applying for permits for natives
> casually employed. There are many occasions when
> a native could be employed for a few days but

farmers don't give them the job because they have to go to the trouble of getting a permit.

Secondly, in a labour market being opened up to migrants, permits created an unnecessary additional cost to farmers, making Aboriginal labour unviable. This was acknowledged by a Bunbury Patrol Officer for the Department of Native Affairs in 1951 when he wrote:

Just about every employer of labour has Compensation Insurance covering two or three men. He pays his premium each year ... I don't think that after he has paid that premium he is going to employ a native and pay another twenty five shillings for a permit.[21]

The permit system not only acted to restrict Aboriginal employment, for some it operated as a form of bondage, a fact acknowledged by the Commissioner for Native Affairs who, writing in his 1953 Annual Report, acknowledged: 'Under current legislation a native is under the supervision of a police officer or Protector and may not absent himself from his service or quit his work without reasonable cause. Thus he is not permitted to barter his service or change his place of employment.' Apart from receipt of a small wage, there is not much difference between this system and slavery.

Downward pressure on wages paid to Aborigines followed a 1947 Arbitration Court decision on farmworkers employed in the South West Land Division. Clause 13 of the Award made provision for 'the less efficient class of native worker' and, in consequence, a reduced wage. A memo from the Secretary of Labour to the Commissioner for Native Affairs preceding the decision provided the justification for the new discriminatory measure. 'Natives are generally less efficient', he wrote, and belong to the 'sub-economic group' compared with 'white men'. Therefore, they 'must be dealt with more generally as less efficient workers'.[22] In his 1954 Annual Report, the Commissioner of Native Affairs acknowledged that: 'By and large natives are still a sub-economic unit of our community, living in sub-standard conditions, dressed in the raiments of civilisation, but mere caricatures of the white man'.[23] In other words, all Aborigines were ascribed a characteristic based on their race.

Racial attitudes were, at times, quite explicit in the post-war drive to reduce Aboriginal wages. Nowhere is this better illustrated than in Bateman's report. After castigating the 'half-castes' in one breath for their failure to uphold white standards and care for their children he went on to justify the necessity to lower their wages. The contortions of his reasoning are worth examining. Rejecting the rationale for Aborigines to receive the same wages where they clearly performed equal work, Bateman explained:

> It is obvious that their living conditions cannot be compared with those of the white man who is in an elaborate social structure and who must receive a comparatively high wage to live up to the required standard. The basic wage of the white man ... is based on the need to maintain a home and family. The white man has to make certain provisions regarding old age, sickness, education of his children, etc. None of these matters concerns the average native. Neither his living conditions nor his commitments are comparable to those of the whites.[24]

Other forces at work during the 1950s conspired to deprive most Aborigines a living wage. Catch-up work necessary after the war such as clearing, burning, root-picking and fencing had kept Aboriginal men and their families living on the farms and in seasonal work, but it came to an end in the early 1950s. Many displaced workers shifted onto the reserves near towns.[25]

Additional unfavourable forces appeared as the fifties progressed. Technological changes in farming such as the spread of chainsaws, motor vehicles and tractors largely excluded Aboriginal people as contractors because they lacked capital to purchase such equipment. Newly arrived migrants competed with Aborigines for farm jobs while a rural downturn in the late 1950s robbed what little casual work remained for Aborigines.[26] Estimates by the Department of Native Affairs, and reported in the 1953 Annual Report, claimed fewer than five per cent of Aborigines in the South West were in permanent employment. At best, the rest worked for eight or nine months a year, placing 'a severe strain on the native breadwinner.' Some supplemented their diet with kangaroo meat but 'these are the fortunate few … who happen to live near uncleared bush country.' As a consequence, poverty increased among Aboriginal families, again making them extremely vulnerable to having their children removed for 'welfare' reasons. Even when Aborigines derived limited, but important, additional assistance from the introduction of Child Endowment payments in 1943, the Department of Native Affairs increased its surveillance of Aboriginal families to ensure these monies were being spent 'wisely'. For those unable to satisfy the Department, 'consideration [would] be given to the removal of their children to Missions and Government Institutions.'[27]

In 1955 reserves in the Geraldton area had witnessed, according to the Department of Native Affairs, 'too much sickness, sometimes followed by death among the children'.[28] Bronchial complaints and gastric upsets were the most frequent illnesses, and these were related directly to the standard of living of the parents: 'Generally speaking these people are unable to afford ample nourishment for their families, but too many of them live in tents and humpies, with completely inadequate ablutions and sanitation.'

The neglect of Aboriginal housing by successive State governments in the post-war period greatly exacerbated the impact of poverty on Aboriginal people. With the number of reserves growing from thirty-six in 1949 to seventy by 1964, an escalating crisis resulted. Throughout this period most of the reserves were a sorry spectacle. They continued to be located within a few kilometres of country towns but on sites not wanted for anything else. Often they were in close proximity to rubbish tips, sanitary depots or abandoned dumps. Only half had running water and earth closet latrines. Those reserves without these basic services were a dangerous health risk. An inspector from the Health Department visited the Borden Reserve near Gnowangerup and found atrocious conditions:

> The water supply is from a dam on the reserve. This dam is not fenced and is used for watering stock and dogs as well as for human consumption. The dam was just a mud hole at the time of inspection. There was all types of debris and manure in it. This water must be considered very dangerous ... On these reserves the native camps consist of tent and bush huts. Some of the camps have beds, but the majority of the natives sleep on the ground.[29]

In the worst of these camps, 'half-clothed or naked children, filthy and invariably covered with flies, played among the rubbish which always accumulated in the camp.'[30]

A state of virtual apartheid existed in many country towns during the 1950s. In Roebourne, for example, very few Aborigines lived in the town. However across the river, three-quarters of a mile away, was a reserve where 150 Aborigines lived. The numerous corrugated iron huts were self-built. They were small, unlined, unlit, and poorly ventilated. Each day, about thirty of the sixty children set out on the one kilometre walk to school. A 1956 Department of Native Affairs report into this reserve was couched in the language of blaming the victims. The living conditions of these reserves, the Report noted, 'do much to hinder any opportunities the natives might have in this area of attaining some small measure of social acceptance and assimilation.'[31]

The Commonwealth Government considered the need to upgrade Aboriginal housing as early as 1945, acknowledging that many Aborigines were then striving to improve their living conditions and social circumstances but, 'where an aborigine desires to have good housing he is frequently frustrated by his low level of income.'[32] However, the State Government made little effort to improve these conditions until the late 1950s, and then only modestly. In fact, State Governments in the post-war era were deliberately reluctant to spend adequate amounts of money for the social benefit of Aborigines. The continued removal of Aboriginal children from their families on the grounds of neglect must be seen against this moral failure by the State.

The reserves presented Aboriginal families with

impossible conditions under which to parent effectively, at least in ways which avoided the condemnation of white officials. At one level, the alleged neglect of children was a direct outcome of the impoverished conditions imposed on Aborigines by the reserve system. Worse still, officials knew this was the case. The Commissioner of Native Affairs was well aware that social conditions beyond the control of Aborigines, were leading to children being removed into State care. Documents relating to an investigation carried out by department patrol officers into three malnutrition cases among Aboriginal children in the Beverley-Brookton area in 1958 show government's full knowledge of this link. The patrol officer began his report with a disturbing observation. Malnutrition among native children in his district, he wrote, 'poses a very serious problem'.[33] He noted that lack of knowledge about mothercraft was one of the causes for the poor health of babies. It is possible many of these mothers had themselves been childhood inmates of institutions where there was limited exposure to parenting skills. However, a range of environmental and economic causes were also noted in the report. Firstly, the only source of water for the infants had an unpalatable taste. This led to a dangerous reduction in fluid intake by the infants, especially over the summer months. Secondly, home conditions encouraged fly-borne diseases and infections which left them 'unfit for camp conditions and camp type food.'

These people were in a classic poverty trap. They had no regular employment and, consequently, no income with which to improve conditions for their children. As the Patrol Officer's report noted: 'most of the malnutrition in native children is found in those families whose breadwinners through lack of sufficient employment or because of very irregular employment are not able to adequately provide for their families.' Compounding the problem was that very few Aborigines qualified for Commonwealth Social Service benefits. Commonwealth governments had decreed that Aborigines with 'a preponderance of Aboriginal blood', even though they may have been living alongside white society, were ineligible for benefits with the exception of child endowment.

Most were forced to accept government rations, especially during the idle months of December through to February, when no casual work was available on the district's farms. However, these rations did not make adequate provision for the needs of infant children. Of the three cases of malnutrition which came to light in the Beverley-Brookton area in 1958, one died, one was admitted to the care of the State as neglected and one was admitted to hospital. As officials continued to remove the children, a blind eye was turned to the very conditions — and the very reasons of neglect — which they used to justify their actions.

In a broader sense, the poverty imposed upon Aboriginal people had a crippling effect on the education of children. Among those Aborigines trying to instill ambition in their children, overcrowding severely limited the ability to study. On a 1949 inspection at Pinjarra, a Department of Native Affairs officer visited the Corbett family who lived in a hut two miles from the school. The parents and seven children shared four rooms, ten feet square in all, with numerous cracks in all the walls and only rough-laid planks as flooring. The children slept two to a bed in three beds in one bedroom, the parents and the baby in the other bedroom. The father was in regular employment and the hut was clean. The inspector talked to the eldest daughter — 'a quiet, attractive, well mannered girl' — who, he discovered, wished to become a nurse. However, he acknowledged it would 'be almost impossible for her to study in the limited space available with six younger brothers and sisters.'[34]

The difficulties faced by Aboriginal parents in their struggle to improve their material conditions — and many expressed a desire to do so — were greatly compounded by community racism. In the mid 1930s, Perth had been declared a prohibited area for Aborigines. To gain entry to the city, Aborigines were required to obtain a pass which would only be granted to those in employment.[35] Throughout the 1940s and 50s, racism was explicit at all levels of society. Annual Reports from the Department regularly referred to the 'wall of colour prejudice' that existed in the community.[36] Social ostracism was widespread. Commissioner F I Bray had acknowledged in the early 1940s that it was impossible for Aborigines and whites to cohabitate. Even where 'detribalised natives become educated and desire to live as whites, they are not accepted socially by whites.' With 'few exceptions', whites were hostile to the idea of social equality with Aborigines and Bray believed this prejudice forced Aborigines to live 'as a class unto themselves'.[37]

Aborigines living in Perth were concentrated in the slum area of East Perth and efforts to establish a reserve for them in the metropolitan area were bitterly and successfully resisted by pressure exerted from white residents backed up by local authorities. 'Natives,' commented the Department as late as 1959, 'were not wanted anywhere in the metropolitan area.'[38] It had been compelled to acknowledge some years earlier that majority white opinion 'insists on natives "being kept in their place" which means, in effect, keeping them socially ostracised and under-privileged.'[39]

Socially, Aborigines were kept at a tightly drawn distance from the white population. Throughout the southern part of Western Australia, they were widely debarred from attending trotting and race meetings, the cinema and from playing in organised football competitions. This last restriction in particular exacerbated Aboriginal marginalisation. 'A game at which most native youths excel is denied to them because of what can only be termed blind colour prejudice. Instead, natives spend their Sunday afternoons — the football afternoon in the country — playing two-up at their camps.'[40]

Even the Western Australian police were noted for 'their extremely harsh attitude' towards Aborigines; Bateman argued they were totally unsuited to act in the capacity of protectors, a role they held in country centres.[41] Hospitals in the southern part of the State were reluctant to admit Aboriginal people during the 1940s,[42] but it was schools that became the principal battleground over race and the continuing desire among many West Australians for segregation between themselves and Aborigines. The situation prior to the 1940s was summed up by A O Neville. In a frank admission in his 1938 Annual Report he acknowledged that, throughout his period of service, 'a whole generation of [Aboriginal] children has grown up who have missed being educated through natural prejudice.'[43] The situation improved somewhat in the late 1940s, when it was claimed Aborigines were attending over a hundred state schools, although usually only in very small numbers and with little community acceptance.

Officially, schools in Western Australia followed a

policy of non-segregation. In reality the system was not only highly discriminatory against the attendance of Aboriginal children, but also State Government policy allowed for such discrimination. In the early 1940s, a member of the Legislative Council, Mr Roche, called on the Commissioner for Native Affairs, to pursue the complaints of white parents at the Orchid Valley School who were objecting to the attendance of three Aboriginal students. 'I gather from Mr Roche's remarks,' the Commissioner later wrote, 'that the objection of the parents would rest entirely on the colour question and not on account of the living conditions of the children concerned [as the family] live under reasonably satisfactory conditions.' Mr Roche indicated he favoured 'the complete exclusion of native children from all schools', but the Commissioner was more pragmatic: 'no action will be taken about Orchid Valley at the moment', he wrote. 'We must await events and see whether a protest is made by the white parents.'[44]

In country towns especially, parents were able to use a provision in the Act which allowed children to be excluded if they 'suffer from any contagious, offensive or infectious disease or are habitually of unclean habits.'[45] Even in the late 1940s, the Minister for Education, Mr Watts, was proclaiming the policy of coeducation of white and 'native' children while upholding the need for government to be sensitive to 'the conditions prevailing at the school and in the district concerned'.[46] It is difficult to determine how frequently this provision was used by local communities to exclude Aboriginal children as not all cases necessarily came to light. However there are a number of instances on record in the 1940s.

Bateman's observations about prevailing community

opinion on the racial composition of schools give some telling insights. Fear of moral contamination from camp-dwelling children, he explained, drove white attitudes:

It is unarguable that the environment of the native camp can only result in a low code of morals, bad habits and serious exposure to infection. In these circumstances it is not a strange phenomenon, but only a natural consequence that parents of white children object to their children being compelled to associate with children reared in such an environment.[47]

In 1947 parental opposition to the education of Aboriginal children in state schools in Carnarvon flared 'into bitter antagonism.' Following the establishment in the town of the Church of Christ Mission, parents carried on a campaign for several months to bar the entry of mission children, 'openly threatening to restrain their children from attending school.'[48] It is likely that non-Aboriginal children in such schools would 'tease, pick on and belt' students from missions, as Trish Hill-Keddie recounted in her story.

In 1949, a District Officer from the Department of Native Affairs visited the Pinjarra School where he talked with the headmaster. From this conversation, it emerged that Aboriginal children were barely tolerated at the school:

He [the Headmaster] spoke with obvious repugnance of the condition in which they came to school but he had no knowledge of their living conditions. To illustrate his remarks he took me around to the classrooms and brought different native children to me. They were without exception, reasonably clean, particularly when one takes into consideration the fact that the inspection was made after the lunch break. He admitted that his wife (who teaches in the school) is very prejudiced against natives and said that when square dancing is contemplated, native boys are told to fall out, as 'She couldn't bear the thought of white girls having to hold their hands.'[49]

In the face of these attitudes, it is perhaps not surprising Aboriginal children frequently absconded from school and most did not attend at all beyond the age of eleven or twelve.

The reaction of Aboriginal parents to these difficulties varied. Some Aborigines who still followed a traditional way of life, even though they may have been classified as 'detribalised', were keen to have their children accompany them on their trips around the country. Others following a settled and largely urban existence harboured aspirations for their children and were distressed that prejudice blighted their prospects. In a rare example of cultural empathy, a District Officer from the Department of Native Affairs detailed in a report to Head Office the feelings of the Aborigines living in Northampton. 'Coloured parents,' he said,

show interest in seeing that their children are educated better than they themselves have been. Many have sent or are intending to send their boys and girls through High School to at least Junior Examination Standard. However, by several such native parents it has been said 'What will they do then?' Even those parents with their children now at High School can see no clear future for their offspring. They feel that prejudice in their field of employment and socially will prevent them from ever becoming more than just 'another nigger'.

The only heartening sign, according to the Northampton Patrol Officer, was the refusal of these parents to adopt a defeatist attitude.[50] This is remarkable given the scale of hostility facing Aborigines over education. In September 1949, a meeting was held between the Native Affairs and Education departments about the irregular attendance of Aborigines at school. The Commissioner, S G Middleton, believed the provision of scholarships for Aboriginal children to stay on in high school, together with accommodation in Perth for those coming from the country, would be practical solutions to the problem. However, he was not hopeful of achieving either quickly because of the 'public outcry and prejudice'. He put the problem bluntly: 'In this State a solution to the problem could be seen but the Department was up against a wall of prejudice.'[51] How, then, could these children get an education? Middleton put to the meeting a plan to extend in scope the existing practice of removing children from their families. He explained:

> One of their [Education Department's] inspectors had already accompanied an Inspector of Native Affairs on a tour of some camps, with a view of getting evidence to the effect that parents were nomadic and not sending their children to school, with the idea of having them brought before the Children's Court.

Middleton foreshadowed one of two approaches: either, the introduction of amending legislation to give his

Department power 'to take children away in such circumstances and put them into institutions', or the utilisation of existing legislation to do the same. In fact, Middleton would have been aware that the practice of removing children to missions for reasons of non-school attendance had been occurring in country districts since at least 1945.[52] The Department's determination to pursue this policy was cruelly ironic. Many, if not most, schools did not welcome Aboriginal children, but it was the parents and their children who were to be punished for their failure to attend. It was not until the early 1950s that full responsibility for the education of Aboriginal children was accepted by the Education Department. Even then community hostility remained. Alan Kickett clearly remembers, as a young Aborigine growing up at Roelands Mission, an incident at Bunbury High School in the mid 1950s. He described in interview the attitude of the school's head master at the beginning of one year when the bus carrying the mission children arrived at the school. He tried to prevent the children from attending the school saying 'the school was for whites only'.

Similar discrimination faced Aborigines granted citizenship rights. In 1944, the State Labor Government succeeded in passing a Bill through Parliament allowing Aborigines to apply for citizenship. Previously, the rights extended to Aborigines had been limited to the granting of a certificate of exemption under the Native Administration Act; that is, they were no longer bound by the repressive provisions of the Act. Even this limited freedom carried strict racial guidelines. Aborigines granted exemption were barred from associating with other Aborigines who had not been given this status, including members of their own families.[53]

The State Government was eventually forced to concede legal status to a limited number of Aborigines. To those living settled lives and holding down responsible jobs, as well as to the four hundred who had enlisted for war service, the Government was prepared to grant full citizenship. However, the privilege demanded a harsh concession from Aboriginal people. In granting citizenship, the State's parliamentarians insisted it should contribute to the process of eradicating Aboriginal culture. To be granted citizenship an Aborigine needed to be able to satisfy a magistrate that 'he has adopted the manners and habits of civilised life.' A stringent test applied. An applicant needed to provide evidence that 'he has ceased from observing his tribal habits for at least two years and has lived since in accordance with the standards of the white race.'[54] This tight restriction, it was argued, would 'open up more clearly the transitional path from native circumstances to white standards'.[55] Or, as Hugh Leslie, Member of the House of Assembly explained: 'The intention of the Bill is to cause a definite segregation of the native from from his relatives and friends' so that he will 'be able to lead a life of white citizenship.'[56] Thus, Aborigines in Western Australia were forced to choose their cultural identity: they could be Aborigines or citizens, they could not be both.

This record of racism occurred in the face of Australia's nominal commitment to the principles set out in the United Nations Declaration on Human Rights. In the mid 1950s, this had become 'so often quoted but seldom practiced where natives are concerned.'[57] So immersed were the vast bulk of Western Australians in racist attitudes towards Aborigines that, any attempt by the authorities to advance coexistence between the races was fiercely opposed. In 1949 Middleton worried that most residents 'would never accept our policy of assimilation with any feeling other than hostility'. He was certain that 'this tragic fact' of 'bitter class [sic] feeling is manifest … in even the high level of senior public servants, party members, local authorities etc.'[58] Why, then, did the policy persist? Partly because it had become accepted at the State and Commonwealth level, but also because it was still being driven by the fears of elites. Those who thought through the issues as they perceived them remained convinced that, without assimilating the Aborigines, the State faced threats to its future welfare. In July 1950 Middleton went on ABC Radio and lashed out at community attitudes. He pinpointed the deeply ingrained public fear widespread during and after the war that Aborigines, because of the ill-treatment they had received, would link up with a potential Asian invader to Australia.

> It's time that white people in the south realised the danger of their attitude towards natives. They despise them and refer to them as 'niggers'. This sort of thing made the native very bitter … the attitude of white people … has turned the natives into a fifth column.[59]

In playing upon public fears, Middleton hoped to shift public attitudes. Former Commissioner for Native Affairs in the 1960s, Frank Gare, explained in interview that: 'People did not want to admit that Aborigines had been ill-treated but they knew they had. Anyone who was conscious that Aborigines had lost their country to these British invaders feared that they might welcome some other invader to fight off the colonisers.'
Future social stability, then, depended on assimilating

Aborigines into wider society, but on white terms, according to white values. The continuing removal of children was the key to this policy. According to white officials, they needed to be taken out of their poverty-stricken and culturally inferior Aboriginal environment and trained for their assimilated role in white society. They needed skills and, above all, attitudes to fit them for this role.

Officials had a simple but clear-sighted view on the resocialising process for Aboriginal youth. To take their place in society they needed to be offered a strong dose of Christian religion. The prevailing view about Aborigines well into the twentieth century held that, as the *Cyclopedia of Western Australia* expressed it, they were 'low in the moral scale'; their sense of 'right and wrong is not so strongly developed', with a conscience 'that is little more than rudimentary'.[60] 'Half-castes' presented a different version of the problem. Neville put the case as strongly as anybody. Detribalised Aborigines, he argued, had drifted entirely away from the spiritual beliefs of the 'bush blacks'. Few had learned anything to replace these beliefs so that, collectively, they were 'in great need of spiritual teaching.' Neville lamented the failure of Aborigines to emulate the American negroes who lapped up an adopted religion like mother's milk ... and what spiritual relief they enjoyed.'[61] For Aborigines, Christian ethics had to be grafted on.

Resocialising the youth also necessitated the development of vocational skills. But here again racial thinking predominated. The widely held view was that Aborigines lacked intelligence for any occupation other than unskilled labour. 'The mental characteristics of the native are comparatively of a low order', asserted the *Cyclopedia of*

Western Australia.[62] This view took deep root in the public's mind. The near universal opinion, born of ignorance or sheer duplicity about the impact of Aboriginal living conditions and the differing styles of Aboriginal learning, was that Aboriginal children were not capable of being educated beyond year 3 or 4 of primary school. 'There are some who maintain', Bateman argued 'that the half-caste child has equal ability to the white but this is not borne out by the facts.' What were these 'facts', according to Bateman? Principally that 'every teacher I have discussed this matter with held the same view'. Teachers daily witnessed the sight of Aboriginal children 'of 11 or 12 years of age in the 3rd or 4th standards side by side with white pupils eight or nine years old.'[63]

According to this thinking, Aboriginal youth could only aspire to the lowest rungs of white society. 'The view is widely held', reflected the Under Secretary of the Premier's Department in 1950, 'that native youths in this State should be absorbed into rural industries because their intelligence quotients preclude consideration of any other occupation for them.'[64] Education was therefore deemed relatively unimportant, as was induction into the skilled trades. However, the ultimate testimony to the racism behind the policy was acknowledged by the Commissioner of Native Affairs in his Annual Report for 1945. In a frank admission, clearly designed to placate community concerns about the policy of assimilation, he wrote: 'So far as education is concerned, our aim is to educate the children of detribalised natives who live in or near the white centres of population, and our object, too, is to subsequently bring them into employment which will *not* bring them into economic or social conflict with the white community.'[65] (Italics supplied) In other words, the official architects of removal intended to limit the degree of assimilation of Aboriginal children in order to prevent them competing with whites for skilled jobs.

This explains much about the subsequent development of the policy, and why successive governments ignored key parts of the Bateman Report. In articulating his view for post-war assimilation, Bateman tried to set high standards for government. For assimilation to work, he reasoned, missions would not only have to improve the effectiveness of their operations, but government must also lay down a 'positive policy' to oversee their work. Bateman believed evangelism must go hand in hand with practical training and every effort had to be made to ensure Aboriginal youth were given full opportunity 'to play their full part in the uplifting of the native race.' Racially inspired his vision may have been, but it was not to be had on the cheap.

> Mission workers should be carefully chosen and the Superintendent if possible should have anthropological training. Teachers including educational, technical and agricultural, nurses, etc., should be specialists and not as at present obtains in some instances persons of poor capacity who have heard the call and find something agreeable to them in mission activity.[66]

Bateman's call for a purposeful direction for assimilation was not heeded, with tragic consequences for children in missions and foster homes. This failure to fully implement assimilation, however undesirable it may have been, exposes the motive of the policy-makers. Assimilation was not intended, as is often claimed today, to be 'in the best interests of the children.' Rather, it was pursued largely as a convenient cover to continue with pre-existing policies aimed at the social and economic marginalisation of Aborigines. Removal and institutionalisation of children denied them their culture, as did the efforts to prevent contact with their families. Moreover, the lack of provision of adequate education and training ensured most would pose no future threat to white interests. If the 'best interests' of these children were uppermost in the minds of policy-makers, Bateman's recommendations on the quality of care needed for them would have been followed through in tangible ways. It was not.

Lack of political interest in the provision of care for these children did not stop the presentation of this scheme as a humanitiarian mission; one designed to rescue Aboriginal children. Missionaries, especially, were prone to this justification. R Mitchell, from the United Aborigines' Mission at Kellerberrin, articulated how the act of removal could be justified as a higher moral good. 'Where parents fail to measure up,' he argued, 'then they should be compelled to place their children in the care of Missions, always bearing in mind that the object is not to destroy the parents' affection for the child, but for the necessary welfare of the child itself; a system such as this would be just and fair to everybody, one to which no one could raise any objection.'[67]

The use of the court system to achieve these ends raises some of the most troubling issues about the entire process. There is great uncertainity as to when the practice of indiscriminate rounding up of Aboriginal children actually ended and the practice of charging the children with neglect in a Children's Court began. Ostensibly, S G Middleton was appointed by the State Government to implement the Bateman Report. However, by this time the practice of removing children had become deeply entrenched within the Native Affairs Department and he encountered fierce opposition in his attempt to introduce a package of sweeping reforms to the structure and operations of the Department.[68]

In any event, the new legalism of using the courts for the removal of children amounted to another manifestation of injustice for Aboriginal families. Just as the 1936 Act had done, the mobilisation of child welfare legislation to charge children with being neglected gave legal authority to the practice, an authority which in most cases it did not warrant. The practice of charging children with neglect was a stipulation of the 1947 Child Welfare Act and was applied to all children. As one parliamentarian explained during debate on the measure: 'we are trying to make a charge that a child is neglected by its parents and is destitute and a second charge that being a neglected child it is definitely guilty of an offence.'[69] This was the mechanism chosen to give the State power to overcome the problems associated with abandoned children and to control children's subsequent living arrangements. Although applying equally to Aboriginal and non-Aboriginal children, the former were particularly vulnerable to its application. In fact, there are a number of grounds upon which most of the children taken from their families after 1948 could be regarded in the same category of 'stolen' as those children taken before this time.

Firstly, removing Aboriginal children because they were neglected was a convenient means to ignore the deeper issues of disadvantage among Aborigines, and especially those living in or close to urbanised areas. There is no doubt many Aboriginal children were materially deprived and that some may have been raised in families which were dysfunctional in some way. Frank Gare's recollection of one case in the early 1960s is a reminder of the difficult situation facing authorities.

> I remember a case in Geraldton in which a couple — who were living in town — but who were fond of drinking put a child to bed one night and rolled on top of the baby, smothering it. That was a case where we should have acted and saved that child's life. If we had acted and taken that child she would now be in her late 30s and, in all likelihood, complaining about being one of the stolen children.

The real issue, however, is not how many cases of this type there were but whether it was a just policy to remove Aboriginal children, considering their institutionalised disadvantage and that little or nothing was being done to prevent the underlying circumstances leading to their removal. In 1967 the Commissioner for Native Affairs in his annual report belatedly acknowledged this reality. 'The unfortunate environment', he wrote, 'in which so many have to live, makes nearly all of them more prone to child welfare problems than the other sections of the community.' In Port Hedland, the Commissioner explained how disadvantage led to an upward rise in the number of children brought before the court for neglect. Families had been moving from the southern regions of the State in search of employment but 'they find themselves without homes and the wherewithal to support a family, thus leading to the neglect of their children.' In cases such as this, there is no indication parents were inadequate; they were simply denied the means to meet the needs of their children. Thus, the Child Welfare law was used to legitimise the broader failure of government policy.

In the post-war era, the removal of Aboriginal children continued to occur in a discriminatory fashion. While most governments throughout Australia created a distinct legal framework for the welfare of white children, generally through the Child Welfare Act, welfare provided to Aboriginal children was not only different but was subsumed under Aboriginal-specific legislation. Thus, in Western Australia a law for the welfare of children was enacted in 1907, however it would be another four decades before Aboriginal children became a legitimate concern of the Child Welfare Department. Even then, Aboriginal children continued to be treated first under the 'native' welfare legal regime, in preference to general child welfare provisions. This situation remained until the early 1970s.

At the ground level, assimilation perpetuated a value system of discrimination among officials charged with its implementation. According to a former employee of the Child Welfare Department, the Native Welfare Department had established a mentality towards Aboriginal people based around twin principles; a disregard of the Aboriginal family as an institution, and the need to have Aboriginal children in institutions. This manifested in a practice of threatening some parents with the Child Welfare Act, thereby obtaining their consent under pressure to have their children placed in institutions. Throughout the 1950s and early 1960s most continued to be sent to missions where they were subjected to the practices of stripping them of their cultural background and limiting, or denying, contact with parents.

Child welfare legislation was not applied impartially. The general child welfare law of most Australian states required that a child be found to be 'neglected', 'destitute' or 'uncontrollable' before he or she could be removed from their parents. The expectation that such requirement would apply equally to all children was not borne out in practice. As the Human Rights Inquiry found, these terms 'were applied by courts much more readily to indigenous children than non-indigenous children as the definitions and interpretations of those terms assumed a non-indigenous model of child-rearing and regarded poverty as synonymous with neglect.'[70]

There are additional concerns about the nature of the court process. The reliance on evidence obtained from police and departmental officers to secure convictions is wide open to potential miscarriages of justice and especially in light of the cross-cultural issues involved in such complex legal proceedings. Even Bateman acknowledged the hostility police displayed to Aborigines. He went further, claiming their role as agents of the Department of Native Affairs was an undesirable one. Aboriginal parents were nominally given the right to attend court hearings but they were not supplied with legal counsel.

Significant community pressure throughout the 1950s and 1960s to have children removed was brought to bear directly and indirectly upon the magistracy. According to a former employee of the Child Welfare Department, sections of the business community disliked the presence of Aboriginal children around commercial areas and initiated contact with the Department to have certain children removed. Magistrates did not always scrutinise the reasons behind these removals.

Court proceedings were open to abuse. Aboriginal parents were represented in some instances by welfare officers, usually the female, from the Department of Native Welfare. These officers were apparently employed to act in a more sympathetic manner with Aboriginal people. But, however well meaning individual officers may have been, the conflict of interest involved in the Department both prosecuting and supposedly defending Aboriginal parents creates an obvious denial of natural justice. It is extremely doubtful Aboriginal parents felt they possessed either the power or the knowledge to intervene effectively on behalf of their children. Aboriginal people had been subjected to the tyrannical power of the Native Welfare Department for more than half a century. In this time, a 'departmental culture' had taken firm root. Native Welfare officers typically talked down to Aborigines and treated them as inferior and subservient. None of this is surprising given the power that legislation conferred over the lives of these people, but such an imbalance of power undermined the ability of individual parents to defend their right to retain their children.

There are few records on the operation of the Child Welfare legislation which can throw more light on the operation of this law. Records are in the form of personal files and are inaccessible to the general public. However, the Commissioner of Native Welfare during the 1960s, Frank Gare, explained to us in interview the practices during his time.

> A child could be charged with being neglected if its moral or physical welfare was in jeopardy. Well we forgot about the moral business. This just meant that they were behaving in their Aboriginal culture. And we said if a child's life is in jeopardy we would have to take action — but no less — their life had to be in jeopardy. And this meant that the cases brought before court were very few ... The patrol officers of the Department got feedback all the time

from the police who always knew everything going on in a country town. And if two parents were spending all their time in a pub they know that the kids are neglected. They see kids hanging around pubs for hours on end waiting for their parents to come out. They know that back home there is a baby waiting for Mum — that would be brought to our attention, if we hadn't picked it up ourselves. We would then start watching that family. Judgements were made about children's poor living conditions but not in isolation. There would have to be some other factor, usually associated with alcohol. I can't recall a case that we took to court just because the camp conditions were poor. It wasn't enough and it was too prevalent; they practically all lived in those conditions.

These may be important qualifications as to how the scheme operated in the mid to late 1960s when an evolving awareness about the removal of children began to became apparent. The extent to which Gare's explanations applied during the 1950s is harder to establish. In any event, court processes which rendered children as being neglected in his period were still subject to potentials flaws. The case of Rosalie Fraser outlined in Chapter Three suggests court proceedings left much to be desired. Moreover, there is evidence — discussed in Chapter Six — that some magistrates openly held prejudicial views about Aborigines as late as the 1960s.

Assimilation as practised amounted to legal discrimination against Aboriginal people. The foundations of the policy lay in racial theories and the policy itself was little more than a mask to perpetuate the ongoing desire among most whites for segregation. Officials, like the community at large, had convinced themselves of the inferiority of Aborigines and of the self-inflicted nature of their poverty. They rationalised that children could only benefit from being separated from their families and sent to isolated missions to be brought up as whites. It occurred only to a very few to challenge this set of racial beliefs.

3

LIFE ON THE INSIDE

Acts of extreme violence began and ended for Phillip Prosser in the nine years he spent in Roelands Mission outside Collie in the 1940s and early 1950s. Rosalie Fraser suffered daily emotional and physical abuse throughout the childhood she spent with a foster-mother and her financially struggling family during the 1960s. The mission and the nuclear family were the two institutions given responsibility for caring for Aboriginal children taken away from their families. There are similarities in their aims and operations. Both played a deliberate role in the cultural transformation of these children. They were both conveyors of white values and barriers to reconnection with the past Aboriginal culture. In both settings many Aboriginal children suffered horrific abuse. The sources of this abuse had similar origins. With probably rare exceptions, neither 'respectable' white families nor 'saintly' missionaries valued much about Aboriginal culture. Both regarded the Aboriginal child as a potential convert to christianity and white culture.

Phillip Prosser is easily established as typical of the children who went through the missions: there is a significant volume of documentary material revealing life in these institutions. By contrast, the private arrangements underpinning fostering left little documentary evidence outside of individual files which are inaccessible to the general public. Rosalie's abuse, as we show, may have been extreme, but it was certainly not isolated.

Roelands was one of twenty-seven missions run under the auspices of the Native Welfare Department in the 1950s and 60s. Missions had had an uneasy relationship with government over the years. Under Neville their activities were barely tolerated because of his fears over lack of control of their activities. Under Middleton it became government policy to subsidise an expanding number of missions to house the increasing numbers of children taken from their families. Missions spanned the length and breadth of Western Australia. Most sizeable country towns supported a mission on its outskirts where Aboriginal families, dispossessed of their land, were fed, clothed and evangelised. However, it was in the south-western region of the State where the purpose-run missions for children were mostly located.

Roelands was one of these missions. Three months after Phillip Prosser arrived as a five year old, he received a flogging from the Acting Superintendent of such severity its callousness can now be barely imagined.

> I had my first flogging three months after I arrived in the Home by a man that stood around six feet five inches. I was accused of something I hadn't done along with three or four other lads. It was a cold winter's morning and we were flogged with a sewing machine strap. I was given six across my arms, turned around and flogged from my

shoulders down to my legs. To get rid of the pain we rolled around on the icy ground.[1]

Phillip Prosser left in 1953 following a raging confrontation with another of the Home's hierarchy. It was summer and he and two other boys had been called up to the compound about a missing piece of iron. They knew who had taken it but all three refused to 'lag' on their mates. For punishment, they were told to dig out a sun-dried claypan which was so hard the pick bounced back with every blow. Phillip revolted. He was told to get back to work, but he refused. The supervisor went off to get a cane and Phillip used the opportunity to arm himself with a copper stick which he hid behind his back. When the supervisor returned Phillip pulled out his weapon and an uneasy stand-off between child and adult occurred. To defuse the situation, each agreed to put down their implement. However, as Phillip went to place his copper stick on the ground, he was struck behind the ear with a painful blow of the cane:

> For the first time in my life I retaliated. I latched onto his ear lobe to bite it off. I punched into him. He dug his metal tipped boots into my feet and peeled back my skin. I just went berserk but he laid into me with a split cane.

Phillip subsequently informed an area officer for the Department of Native Affairs about the incident, who managed to have him released from the Home. However, as far as he could tell, there were no repercussions for Roelands or its staff. Phillip claims documentary evidence from Native Affairs shows the incident was covered up.

It was not uncommon for 'closed' institutions such as

Roelands to successfully maintain an 'official' version of their activities which conflicted with the 'private' experience of them. The incident involving Phillip Prosser and, clearly, a number of others like it, could never be gauged from the information received by the public about Roelands' operations. In 1952, for example, the Superintendent, Mr K C Cross, wrote of his young charges:

> Excellent reports continue to be received from employers of the young people who have left the Mission. During the year one boy entered into an apprenticeship agreement with an electrical engineer. One of the older girls has passed her entrance examination set by the Nurses' Association ... For the young people who have completed their training and are away working in various parts of the State, a Convention and a reunion was arranged during January of this year. I am pleased to report that this reunion and also the holiday periods spent by the folk at the Mission, which they call Home, proved an inspiration and a sense of accomplishment to the Mission staff as they again met the young people and noted the manner in which they have, in most cases, maintained the Mission training standard, and to some extent improved their acceptance in the community.[2]

From such a glowing account no one would ever have known such disturbing incidents of the sort experienced by Phillip Prosser ever occurred. However, a closer reading of Cross' account of the preceding year might suggest that all was not as indicated. There is a lack of specific details and a clear message that young Aborigines were being driven to meet some 'standard' imposed by the mission. The reunions about which Cross expressed such enthusiasm appear not quite so overwhelmingly attended as he indicated. In 1950, a decade after its establishment, a press report on Roelands claimed that 'as many as 14 old farm children return to see their friends'.[3] This represents only a small fraction of those who, by that time, had gone through the place. A reunion of ex-Roelands children was organised by Aborigines in 1996. The atmosphere had a highly charged undercurrent to it. 'You could feel the hate, the bitterness that was oozing out of the things that happened to those kids in Roelands.'[4]

It is the clash of these rival perspectives — Aborigines with memories of cruelty and missionaries executing God's work — which makes any assessment of places like Roelands so very difficult. It is more than likely some Aborigines received positive opportunities due to their time in the institution. The standard of primary school teaching is remembered by Phillip Prosser to have been high and he believes children with talent were given some encouragement. But equally, there is a dark side to the work of Roelands which continues to affect many of those who spent time there. It would be surprising if this was not the case in light of the backgrounds and motivations of those who established and operated the place.

Controversy still surrounds the exact origins of Roelands Home. It was founded as an experiment by dairy farmer and prominent Church of Christ member, Albany Bell, in the late 1930s to help Aborigines grow food while living on his property. For reasons unknown, this arrangement did not work out. However, later on the Department of Native Affairs struck up an arrangement with Bell for the farm to be used to look after Aboriginal children removed from their families. The Department had a clear vision of its place in the network of institutions opening up to cater for these children. In 1947 Middleton noted to one of his officers about to inspect a family with children earmarked for removal: 'I would personally require to see all the children involved, and doubtless they could be placed at Roelands Mission Farm if they were considered to be too dark in colour to be successfully absorbed ultimately as whites.'[5]

The limited expectations held for these children because of the colour of their skin probably underscored the harsh discipline used by some of the staff. At the same time, the staff were deeply motivated by their Christian faith and their commitment to the Church of Christ. Roelands Home was administered by a committee composed mainly of active members of the Church of Christ, although the present hierarchy of the Church claims it was organisationally separate from the main body of the Church. There are no documents available which shed further light on the links between the Home and the Church and, indeed, between the Home and the State Government. It appears to have been an unstated and loose arrangement between all three parties.

Controversy also surrounds the qualities of the staff and its long-serving Superintendent, K G Cross. There are indications that Cross believed himself to be motivated by human compassion for the 'half-castes'; he saw them as outcasts in both races and believed no one cared for them. It is also claimed some Aboriginal parents urged him to take their children because they wanted them to receive an education and to be given an opportunity in white society. Other children were brought to the Home from the courts having been charged with offences.

Administering to this diverse group of children required a selfless, even saintly, outlook, according to one view.

> Some of the staff worked for 20–25 years because they could not stand seeing neglected and disadvantaged children, children who were not accepted in their own society. Being Christian they had a responsibility to help the disadvantaged. Who today would work in such an isolated place, look after so many children and be paid virtually nothing? People worked for 20–25 years and walked away with nothing.[6]

However well-intentioned the work, as experienced by the children it was quite different. Part of the problem of assessing Roelands — and other missions like it — is the need to challenge the Christian ideology which drove such people to believe they could do 'good work' with children taken from their families. Cross certainly had lofty, but limited ideals, for the Home. He wrote that the purpose of the mission was 'to provide training in the Christian life as revealed in the Message of the Gospel of Jesus.'[7] In other words, his first priority was conversion. In implementing this evangelical approach, some staff held a dogmatic, intolerant and even hostile attitude towards their charges. To the children this was often expressed as righteousness and cruelty. Competing with Christianity in driving this attitude was disdain for the children's Aboriginality. At times they were treated as less than human. The practice of making examples of senior boys (thirteen to fourteen years) who had not fed or tended the animals to the satisfaction of the staff demonstrates this. These boys were sat in the dining room and humiliated in front of the other children. Each received two rusty tin plates, the smaller containing a slice of dry bread while on the larger was placed dried bracken fern and dried bran. The message was not lost on younger boys forced to watch such humiliation. Phillip Prosser explains: 'if you don't feed the animals properly, you're not fit to eat either. We'll treat you no better than the animals.'

Phillip Prosser vividly remembers that Cross and his staff viewed Aboriginal culture as pagan. He also has a clear recollection of these officers' self-appointed role in life: 'they were sent on a mission by God to train us into Christian society.' This 'training' meant prayers morning and night and church every Sunday. Their attitude was 'tunnel vision; they were right and we were wrong'.

> Every little thing you did in their eyes was a sin and you were punished and that involved corporal punishment. They used any utensil they could get hold of. I've seen boys flogged with a garden hose. Another young boy nearly had his eye knocked out because he was belted with a thick belt with a huge metal buckle on it and the buckle cut him across the eye.

The staff saw physical discipline as the way to resocialise these children's behaviour. In the early 1950s the Home housed over seventy children. The mission was built around a 1,500 acre farm which produced dairy goods, vegetables and fruit. The children's labour was an integral part of the farm economy. It not only sustained the Home, it provided salaries for the staff. In the 1940s and 50s, government subsidies paid to missions such as Roelands were so low that, at Roelands, it is estimated they covered barely one-third of the operating costs.

It is possible to look upon the involvement of the

children in the labour of the farm as part of their training and part of normal childhood chores. After all, these children were being prepared for future occupations on the land. However, the picture is more complex and disturbing. From the recollections of those who spent their childhoods in Roelands work was all-consuming. 'In the Mission we were literally little slaves. Just work and religion', remembers one ex-inmate. The daily routine seems to bear out the comment: up at 6 am; beds made and prayers at 6.30; chores before breakfast; breakfast at 7.30; religious teaching after breakfast; attendance at school on the Mission; chores all over again after school. Saturday morning involved still more work: filling up the wood boxes, cleaning out the pigsties and the chicken pens: 'we were a labour force for the Mission, for nothing', argues Phillip Prosser. He has clear memories of making up to five hundred fruit cases a day at the ages of ten and eleven while, at the same time, girls were spending all day grading fruit. This labour serviced the Mission's export fruit business.

This work routine raises some important questions about the claim that these institutions were training grounds for children's future occupations. In reality, these children were an unpaid labour force; they were, in effect, unwilling servants in their own institutionalisation. Their work provided the funds to enable missionaries to conduct their self-appointed roles of resocialising them. To sanction the removal of these children from their families is one part of the injustice they suffered; forcing them to work for the upkeep of the institution they were sent to, as was the case at Roelands, is little short of an outrage. On leaving the Mission most of the boys from Roelands found little more than low-paid labouring jobs, mostly on farms where it was not uncommon for them to have to sleep in a shed. However, the meticulous regime of early rising and work did perform an essential part of the cultural shift being inculcated in these children. Work, and the discipline which often accompanied it, were to be the means by which these children would abandon the ways of the 'native' and take up an industrious life in white society. They first had to be shown how this was done.

Christian zealotry drove the staff at Roelands to wipe out as much as they could of the children's Aboriginal heritage. This process began the moment a child arrived. Children came to Roelands from many different parts of the State and, therefore, from different language and tribal backgrounds. On arrival, many had their names changed to disconnect them from their parents. Children were forbidden to speak in their native languages, and were severely punished if found doing so. Parents were discouraged from visiting and some children harboured suspicions that mail to their parents was censored.

The missionaries' evangelical drive was so strong it impaired their ability to show affection to the children. Ex-inmates remember a place with 'no love or care'. Staff interactions with children frequently spilled over into frustrated anger. Some remember being repeatedly told: 'you're never going to make it. You're a liar, a thief, you're going to Hell.' At other times interactions resulted in outright cruelty. Girls were thrashed for loosing hair clips or ribbons. One girl was beaten when, after her stubbed toe was placed in a bowl of clean water, she described the now coloured water as 'bloody'.

Bed-wetting incurred severe reprisals. 'A kid who wet the bed had to have his face rubbed in it first before the sheets were taken off and washed.' Sometimes these children would be forced to wear a sign around their necks on which was written: 'I am a bed wetter'. Cruelty was also endured daily in the poor standard of clothing the children were issued. Commonly, they had no shoes to wear around the mission. In winter the ground could be freezing and their feet became painfully numb. During these months, Phillip Prosser remembers children walking with a stooped hunch trying to protect themselves from the biting cold, pulling the few woollen clothes with which they were provided tight over their hands.

Some of the staff engaged in sexual abuse of the children. On one occasion, a prowler was found roaming around the grounds and caught trying to break into the senior girls' room. It was a staff member, who was recognised by his dog lying at the base of a tree he had climbed to try to avoid detection. He had a reputation of being particularly cruel. He used to carry around an old tractor pulley — about two feet long and four inches wide — with which he used 'to flog the boys.' Once it had become common knowledge that he had been trying to sexually abuse the girls he was sent packing from the Home. However, one of the problems that places like Roelands experienced was obtaining suitable staff. The low pay and isolated conditions made it inevitable some unsuitable people would be attracted to the place. Most were untrained and had little but professed Christian faith to recommend them.

There was little attention to the children's emotional needs or the development of essential living skills. Girls, for example, received no education about the onset of menstruation. When it did occur, many were overcome with fear and uncertainty about what was happening to them. Some thought they were dying from internal bleeding and openly wept. Understanding about money and wages was similarly lacking. Children were forced to devise their own simple entertainments; little or nothing was provided by the mission staff. Their moments of lively interaction between themselves provide, for most, the only source of happy memories of Roelands.

The reality of Roelands as it was experienced by many of its inmates completely contradicts its public image. 'The outstanding thing about this mission farm', glowed the *West Australian* in a 1950 article, 'is the atmosphere of happy trust.'[8] Almost nothing could be farther from the truth. There was little resembling 'normal' childhood activities at Roelands, even by the standards of the day. Comments made by the *West Australian* show how easy it was for contemporaries to look at the surface features of a place — 'the tidiness of the well-stocked cupboards' — and assume this reflected the inner, emotional life experienced by the children.

Missions were only one part of the experience of assimilation for many Aboriginal children. Being fosted into white families was equally common. The white family was seen as a valuable institution in the service of assimilation because of the opportunities it presented for the acquisition of white values and behaviours. As most of the records on fostered Aboriginal children are inaccessible to the public, much of what follows was gathered through interviews.

One of the striking aspects of the system of fostering children was the diversity of family types prepared to take in children. Generalisations about motives are therefore very difficult to make, however, we have been able to detect at least four categories of families, each with distinctive attitudes to fostering. Firstly, were the wealthy elite who regarded fostering as a form of social status. In their upper-class and religious world-view, fostering Aboriginal children was a public sign of 'goodness' both as Christian compassion and as commitment to the perceived benefits of active involvement in assimilation. Welfare authorities sought out such families knowing the strength of conditioning Aboriginal children would be exposed to. A second category were families motivated by humanitarianism. These expressed some affinity with Aboriginal people and positively liked Aboriginal children. Such families straddled the socioeconomic divide; some were rural battlers while others were well-off professionals. Thirdly, were parents seeking to care for children, usually because they were unable to have any (or any more) children of their own. Such parents genuinely wanted more children and most did not see colour as an issue. Lastly, were struggling families whose motivation was economic gain. They were attracted to fostering because of the weekly cheque they received from the government to look after these children.

Of all the categories, it seems that many, if not most, children went to the fourth family type where they were at high risk of abuse and exploitation. In the worst cases, they were regarded merely as a commodity to be treated at the whim of the foster-parents, who were mostly outside any official scrutiny. Whatever the motivation, fostering involved a painful cross-cultural experience which has left many damaged and confused.

Rosalie Fraser is among those fostered into a poor white family. Here she suffered in every way as griev-ously as those children abused in missions. Now in her late thirties she can reflect on her experience with the strength which comes from having confronted and

mastered a period of emotional ill-health, brought on by
the lingering and intrusive memories of abuse, the depth
of which is almost unimaginable.⁹ Rosalie's case raises
many disturbing issues about the system which administered assimilation. It underlines the extent to which
Aboriginal families continued to be the subject of judgements based on race. It highlights the arrogance of a State
which exercised those judgements and then failed to act
in its duty of care. Rosalie's mother had all her ten
children taken from her over a period of time.

Rosalie's removal from her family was swift and
clinical. In 1961, when she was two and a half year's old,
a welfare officer visited her parent's home in rural
Beverley. The officer judged her parents unfit to care for
children largely on the basis of the condition of their
house, which was home to three other children. Her
father, a ganger with the railways, had only recently
started work. He had previously experienced difficulty
finding regular employment. The family had no money
saved and their State Housing home had no furniture in
it. The welfare officer thought the house was unclean and
the children neglected. The following day the Health
Department sent an inspector who also said that it was
not up to standard. All four children were removed.
There was a subsequent court hearing; the parents were
present but were unrepresented. The outcome was predictable. Despite acknowledging the bond between
parents and children, the overriding assessment of the
parents was negative: 'they lacked responsibility.' Many
years later Rosalie's mother explained there was nothing
she or her husband could do: 'the welfare and the police
had all the power.' It was a familiar story.

There was a sad irony for Rosalie and her sister in the

events which followed. Requests by other members of her parent's immediate family to foster the children were turned down by the Child Welfare Department because the homes to which they might go — Aboriginal homes — were judged to lack suitable space. Yet the home selected by the Child Welfare Department was anything but suitable. They were sent to a 'lower class white family' in Glendalough — on the 'other side of the lake' — where State Housing owned a number of houses. The three-bedroomed house was already home to six children, and the family was under financial strain.

Rosalie has long pondered why her foster-mother became involved in their lives. Under the Child Welfare Act she was required to be licensed to take children under six years of age. However, Rosalie does not believe her foster-parents underwent any prior screening to determine their suitability because records show it was only a matter of a few days after they were removed from their parents that her foster-mother received a telegram from Child Welfare asking her to take the children.

By the early 1960s, the Department was unable to manage the system of fostering it was overseeing. The Annual Report for 1962 makes this clear: 'In the last year there has again been an increase in the number of children being cared for by foster-parents. Several appeals have been made through the newspapers for homes for children ... the response was not overwhelming.' In other words, it was under pressure to find families, almost any family. It is possible to see how, in these circumstances, screening could rate a low priority. In Rosalie's case the choice of family does seem extraordinary, even at face value: a struggling family in modest circumstances already straining for space is allowed to accept two more children. Rosalie thinks it is possible her foster-mother simply did not know how to turn down the Department once she was approached. However, she cannot overlook one awful possibility, that the family was attracted by the considerable financial benefits they received from the Department to foster herself and her sister. 'When they got the money through the post every Saturday they went and did the food shopping.'

Clearly, the financial state of the family should have precluded them from fostering. The Spartan circumstances of the Glendalough household impacted directly on Rosalie and her sister in ways which made them marginalised members of the family. For years the sisters were forced to sleep in the same bed. They were treated differently from the other children in ways which were simply demeaning. The parents fully equipped their own children for school, but Rosalie and her sister wore thongs in winter and, on wet mornings, arrived wearing only an old plastic table cloth to protect their clothing. They owned no toys.

However, the material deprivation to which they were subjected pales against their experience of neglect and abuse. Before the age of five Rosalie was admitted to hospital suffering from rickets for which she received medication. If this was indicative of lack of basic care, the torrent of emotional abuse which daily poured from her foster-mother confirms the complete unsuitability of this foster family.

> Every day of my life that I stayed in that foster placement I was referred to as a fucker, a boong, a bastard or a slow-learning cunt. My name was never used. I didn't really have a name.

The foster-mother harangued Rosalie for her

Aboriginality. She was told: 'You're nothing but a black boong, just like your mother'. This abuse was not just occasional but repeated throughout each day. 'If we were outside we were told "get in here you black boongs."' On a broader level, her foster-parents openly talked about Aborigines in derogatory terms, calling them 'dirty, no-hopers and drunks'.

The physical abuse was just as persistent and threatening. 'At one time my foster-father insisted that we be sent to the Mount Lawley Receiving Home [for Aboriginal children] because of the abuse we were getting and because he thought she would kill us.'

The welfare system failed the girls when it allowed them to return to the family after a short stay at the Receiving Home. For years on end the house was regularly in uproar because of the abuse the sisters received from the foster-mother. Rosalie's foster siblings were often distressed over their treatment and protested to the mother that they 'should be gotten rid of'. One, however, did try to intervene to offer protection.

The most extraordinary aspect of Rosalie's experience of foster placement in this dysfunctional family is the role of the Department of Child Welfare. Their failure to exercise duty of care continued throughout her placement. The family was visited, briefly, about once a year.

> We were always warned prior to them [the Child Welfare Department] coming and we were drilled not to say anything. When they came everything was different. The house was cleaned up, it was made to look like my sister and I had separate beds to sleep in and we had toys put on our beds. We were told by our foster-mother that if we were asked if we liked living there we were to say yes.

On one visit a welfare officer criticised Rosalie's foster-mother for failing to ensure the girls' hair was brushed after which she contemptuously ranted: 'The fucking welfare have a cheek to criticise — who else is going to look after boongs?' However, the Child Welfare's apparent concern for the well-being of the sisters on this occasion did not extend to careful checks which might have revealed the mistreatment taking place. On the occasional visits from the Department, the children were spoken to separately from the foster-mother, but only very briefly, and in the most superficial manner. Equally disturbing were the racial comments some of these officers recorded in their departmental files. In 1966 an entry read: 'these were two ugly girls who had prominent Aboriginal features including broad noses and protruding lips.' In 1970 another commented that Rosalie 'would no doubt marry an Aboriginal person because she will find it too hard to live up to a white standard.'

From time to time welfare officers suspected that the sisters were not being properly cared for. On their files was noted clear indications all was not well in their home. They were described on one occasion as 'two very skinny and undernourished children, small for their ages.' There are also notes from teachers indicating the sisters were coming to school 'unkempt' and without proper equipment. Department files also reveal that a series of complaints were received from neighbours about the treatment of the children. Nothing was done to follow up any of these concerns.

Rosalie is understandably angry at the treatment she received at the hands of the Child Welfare Department. She wonders about the justice of a system which made harsh judgements about her parents and yet failed to show equal rigour with her foster home. She asks why the money which government paid to clothe and feed her at her foster family could not have been given to her natural family to assist them. As events turned out her own family fractured. Her father, who became so ashamed after losing all his children, disappeared after he fell behind with the compulsory child maintenance payments he had to make for the upkeep of the children taken from him. Her mother succumbed to alcoholism.

Rosalie herself became a mother at a young age and began to come under the notice of the Child Welfare authorities. For a time she suffered repeated flashbacks about the abuse she had suffered in the foster home and this finally led to a nervous breakdown. She recovered by writing out her torment in her own full account of life as an Aboriginal child in a white family.

Rosalie's greatest sense of tragedy is the loss of her Aboriginal heritage.

The two stories at the centre of this chapter — Phillip Prosser in the 1950s and Rosalie Fraser in the 1960s — raise disturbing issues about the involvement of government agencies in the assimilation process. There is, according to some legal authorities,[10] a strong case to be made that, in removing children from their families, government entered a fiduciary relationship; that is, it agreed to act for or on behalf of, or in the best interests of, these children. In the case of Western Australia, this relationship is potentially all the stronger given the legislation which made the Commissioner for Native Affairs the legal guardian of all Aboriginal children until they turned twenty-one years of age. This legal responsibility has already been tested in some recent court hearings.

Sweeney sums up the findings:

> In the recent case of *Williams v The Minister,*
> *Aboriginal Land Rights Act,* the New South Wales
> Court of Appeal held, by a majority, that it was
> arguable that the Aboriginal Welfare Board (a
> statutory body) was under a fiduciary obligation to
> Aboriginal children placed in its care. It also held
> the Board was arguably obliged to have 'truly
> provided, in a manner apt for a fiduciary, for [the
> plaintiff's] 'custody, maintenance and education'.

Similarly, Justice Toohey in *Mabo (No2)* stated:

> executive actions by the government gave rise to a
> policy of protection by which government, together
> with the particular vulnerability of Aboriginal
> people to the exercise of power by the Crown to
> adversely affect their interests, gave rise to a
> fiduciary relationship.[11]

The issue becomes the extent to which government
breached its obligations under law to provide for the best
interests of these children. There are strong grounds for
believing this was the case with both Phillip Prosser and
Rosalie Fraser. Phillip Prosser was sent to an institution
which not only failed to guarantee his physical safety but
which contained (even by the standards of the day) an
institutionalised culture of violence exceeding the known
experiences of children in State Government schools.
Officials knew about the violence at Roelands. In Rosalie's
case, the foster home to which she was sent failed to
guarantee her best interests in a physical and emotional
sense. The persistence of this gross abuse while under the
care of the Child Welfare Department, is the strongest

illustration possible that government did not provide for the best interests of many of these children. Rosalie's was one of a series of test cases brought against the Western Australian Government in the early 1990s for its failure to act in its duty of care to children removed from their families. In 1995 the Minister for Community Services, Mr Nicholls, rejected the claims, 'fearing a flood of claims from thousands of Aborigines displaced by the Government's 'welfare' department.' Rosalie told the press at the time: 'All the abuse we suffered as children, the department failed in its duty of care … to not even allow our parents the right to know where we were, to not let them know we were abused, when we were hospitalised, it's wrong.'[12]

In both cases government agencies were neither trained nor resourced to adequately fulfil their duty of care. This, of course, exposes the sham of the State's concern for Aboriginal children. Many were sent to places where they were infinitely worse off in a material and emotional sense than the homes from which they were taken.

4

OFFICIAL NEGLIGENCE

In February 1969 the Western Australian Minister for Child Welfare, L A Logan, received a letter from Mrs Pamela Morris of Gooseberry Hill outlining a series of startling allegations about the treatment of Aboriginal boys at the New Norcia mission, north of Perth. On three occasions Mrs Morris had sponsored holiday stayovers for boys from the mission, one of whom was with her family for ten weeks. From the things the boys told her, and from what she had observed, she felt compelled to 'express my deep concern for these boys' to someone in authority. Immediate issues such as inadequate food and clothing worried her as did their poor state of general health. However, the lack of supervision exercised by the Child Welfare Department was one of her more pressing concerns. Mrs Morris told the Minister the Department had insisted she gain prior approval for the boys to stay for the holidays. She was visited by an officer from the Department. However this officer had admitted to her that she was one of the few prospective families ever visited for inspection. The consequences of this worried her. As she told the Minister, most of the children from New Norcia 'would be going to homes which would not be approved.' While the boys were in the care of her family 'no contact was made [by the Department] with them. Had the boys been miserably unhappy and ill-treated, none would have known.'

Mrs Morris also expressed her fears about the future prospects for these boys. They had no house-mother or matron — 'as recommended by child psychologists' — and little meaningful contact with the two Brothers who were 'fully occupied with administration and discipline'. Consequently, the boys' socialisation had been stunted: 'when they first came to us [they] were quite unable to converse with adults.' Their educational development was similarly retarded. One of the boys, who was 'reasonably bright' was not able to tell her how well he had done at school because he had not received any formal assessment that year. Although twelve years of age he was still in grade four and he did not think he would be progressing beyond the end of primary school. Otherwise, he received no instruction 'in any of the things which could be useful to him', such as carpentry, car or tractor maintenance, or farming which, Mrs Morris told the Minister, surely 'precludes him from anything but a labouring position.'[1] None of this, she concluded, would be tolerated in an orphanage for white children.

The Minister duly replied to her concerns and allegations. However, instead of assuring Mrs Morris he would investigate and act upon these, he sought to excuse the government from any direct responsibility for the operation of the mission. 'The task of changing people's ideas toward the best forms of child care, is unfortunately, a slow process, and we all from time to time chafe under the irritations of limited finance and the lack of any other quicker alternative.'[2]

This exchange is significant. The problems Mrs Morris identified were far from isolated ones and the Minister's lame excuses were made in full knowledge of a recent departmental investigation into New Norcia and other missions. For several years, officers from both the Child and Native Welfare Departments had been investigating aspects of abuse and neglect of mission children. However, no systematic action was taken and none of this investigative activity reached the public. Even if it had, there is no certainty public clamour would have forced government to take the appropriate action — force the closure of missions by removing government subsidies given to them for looking after Aboriginal children made wards of the State. Consequently, only a few members of the public, such as Mrs Morris, who undertook to look after these children in the holidays, knew the full, and shocking, picture of life inside an isolated and secluded mission.

Long before L A Logan brushed aside the concerns of Mrs Morris, government in Western Australia had shown its indifference to opposition voiced against its policy of assimilating Aboriginal children through their forced separation from parents. Political opposition to the policy sprang up unexpectedly in 1956 when a Select Committee of Parliament was established to inquire into the conditions of Aborigines in the Laverton-Warburton range. Extraordinary circumstances surrounded the establishment of this inquiry. The lifestyle of the still mainly traditional Aborigines in the area, many of whom had little prior contact with white civilisation, was being disrupted in a startling way. British nuclear testing was taking place in the area at the Maralinga site. This meant some contact was necessary to warn Aborigines in the area not to go east of the Warburton Mission, into the danger zone. While some ignored the warning, others were encouraged to 'hang around' the Warburton Mission.[3] These Aborigines had 'no hope of work' and police barred them from coming into the small towns in the area without police permission. Another impact of white civilisation also worried some officials. The Agricultural Department had been baiting dingoes from aircraft. Aboriginal children especially were at risk from poisoning because they hunted the goannas which were known to eat the fatty meat baits dropped from aircraft around the desert waterholes.

Serious as these risks were to Aborigines, the Member for South Perth, Mr Grayden, who moved the motion to establish the Committee, raised a dramatic allegation which, he believed, warranted investigation:

> The Native Welfare Department has in hand plans to remove all the children from the Warburton Range area, without the consent of parents, and to take them 400 miles away across an area most of which is barren, waterless country, to Cosmo Newberry, the parents being left in the ranges.[4]

According to Grayden, the Department believed the move would assist their employment opportunities, and hence 'their integration into the Australian way of life' as the Warburton Mission was unable to find them work. It was the intention of the Department 'to make a clean sweep' and compel children of school age to go to the Cosmo-Newberry Mission, several hundred miles across the desert to the west of Warburton, where a program of part-time employment on the mission was offered. There was no intention to take the parents because no facilities were provided for them there. However, Grayden did not believe 'for one minute' that when these children were educated they would be able to find work in the Laverton area. However, under the Native Welfare Act, the Commissioner still retained powers to effect such a move. These children, in Grayden's words, 'were being sent into exile'. Even before Grayden began his work of chairing the Committee he was convinced the children's rights were being violated.

> What are the reactions of these children going to be when they are taken away from their parents, and sent 400 miles away from them until they reach the age of 21 years of age, when they will be required to work on stations in the vicinity? In other words they will not see their parents again unless they are prepared to walk 400 miles back to the [Laverton] mission. This enforced separation of the children from their parents is contrary to the universal declaration of human rights which has been agreed to by the United Nations Council, and of which Australia is a signatory.[5]

This was a profound speech. It was likely that it was the first time any Western Australian parliamentarian had directly invoked the United Nations Declaration against the practice of removing children from their families. Furthermore, Grayden had indicated that removal would be subject to review by his Committee at least in its application in the Warburton area. However, once the Committee got down to work in earnest, one thing became apparent — the removal of children from their families was a more complex business than has been thought to be the case. By the time children were school-age, the mission employed highly questionable practices to separate them from their parents.

Missions such as Warburton received children to feed and educate ostensibly with the consent of their parents. The Committee was the first official body to raise doubts about the ethics of this practice. 'It is unlikely that the natives would realise the full import of such consent on their part', the report noted.[6] No officers within the Department of Native Affairs were familiar with the language of the area and only one of the missionaries was in any way familiar with it. Such barriers meant that obtaining consent was extremely difficult 'if we are to be assured that the parent in giving consent has a full realisation of all the implications involved.' However, this was only one of the reasons which made 'the separation of young children from their parents unthinkable from a humane point of view.'

The Committee detailed the circumstances which had led to the removal of children throughout the State. Aboriginal parents placed their children in the Warburton Mission 'almost solely' because of the lack of adequate food on the reserve. 'To take children away from their parents in such circumstances', warned committee members, 'and abandon the parents to fend for themselves savours a form of duress.' The offer of gifts of blankets, clothing and food often enticed parents to place their children in the mission. This was an unethical practice, the Committee argued:

it must be taken into consideration that the natives are living in one of the most arid areas in the world and are eking out an existence where even birds and animals find it difficult to survive. No responsibility is taken for the pre-school age children by the Native Welfare Department and to expect native mothers to bear and raise these children and be

entirely responsible for them under those conditions, only to have them taken away at school age
... to an area where in normal circumstances they
could never hope to visit, would in effect mean that
in many cases the parent would never see the child
again, which would be an unpardonable violation
of human rights.[7]

While these comments refer specifically to the activities
of Warburton Mission, those involved in implementing
the policy of removal would have been only too aware of
their wider application across the State. In the mid 1950s,
the Mission Superintendent at Wandering, Father
Wellems, was able to keep numbers at his mission topped
up by making 'trips into the surrounding districts' where
he 'was able to persuade native parents of the benefits of
a mission education and training for their children.' This
practice was openly acknowledged in the Department of
Native Affairs Annual Report,[8] and grave doubts must
surround the extent to which parents gave their informed
consent. In other cases, children were regularly placed in
missions at great distance from their homes which effectively meant that their parents could not see them again.

The Committee's report contained a striking challenge to
hardened assimilationists. The Committee wrote of the
bonds that existed between mothers and their children. It
argued that nature had made the maternal bond even
stronger for Aborigines than existed between white
women and their children. The sparseness of the environment compelled Aboriginal women to suckle their children
to at least three, and sometimes to six, years of age.

This must assist in creating an even stronger bond
of affection between parent and child than would

apply in the case of whites where the child is bottle-fed or weaned at the age of nine months or so. In addition, the native woman is with her child constantly until it is well beyond school age. She carries the child as an infant wherever she goes when travelling or fossicking for food and later the child is with her constantly in her daily pursuits. This aspect must assist in strengthening the intimate relationship between the parent and the child. It may also be worthwhile pointing out that natives display a great deal of affection towards their children, seldom chastising them. Striking a child is extremely rare, notwithstanding this the children appear to be extremely well-behaved and unspoilt.

However bleak separation was for the parents, the Committee was in no doubt that, for the children, it 'would be intolerable'. Children coming in from outlying parts of the region could only speak a smattering of English and would not have absorbed anything of western life. The Committee expressed its grave worry that such children 'would be lost souls indeed'. They would be 'perplexed in the extreme' and 'without a single stabilising influence on which to orient themselves to the new way of life so inhumanely thrust upon them.'[9] No one had been prepared to so openly champion the virtues of Aboriginal parenting from such a humane point of view.

The significance of this report cannot be overstated. In a few short pages a Committee of Parliament totally condemned as immoral and inhumane the central plank of assimilation. While its investigations had been limited to Warburton, its implications straddled the practice of removing children everywhere. It had demolished as merely a pretext the justification used to remove these children; that their families were poor or their parent's culture was inferior. Moreover, it foreshadowed problems in the years ahead when society would have to face the full enormity of the policy's misguided intent. Yet, children continued to be removed.

Political response to the Report was characteristically indifferent. It was tabled in Parliament at 3 am when Members were 'anxious to get home.'[10] Behind the scenes a bureaucratic campaign was waged to undermine the Report's credibility. In October 1956, Grayden told the House of Assembly that the Commissioner of Native Welfare had been rubbishing the Committee's Report to the Minister by saying it had 'grossly exaggerated' the situation in Warburton and its recommendations 'were not of any practical value.'[11] Thus, an opportunity was passed over to scrap the policy of removing Aboriginal children from their families. Racial attitudes were still too firmly entrenched.

Barely two years later another parliamentary committee on Aboriginal affairs raised concerns about the removal of children from their families and again Grayden took a leading role in its establishment.[12] The 1958 Report of the Special Committee on Native Matters, appointed by the Legislative Assembly, consisted of an influential group of members. It was chaired by F E Gare, from the Department of Native Welfare and had one member each drawn from the Health and Education departments, the Native Welfare Council and the Labor Party. The establishment of this Committee signified recognition that government policy on Aboriginal affairs, over a wide range of issues, was floundering. As the Committee expressed the problem facing it: 'Despite all past efforts to solve it, the 'native' problem remains today the State's most pressing social challenge.'[13] The Committee was also established in the wake of well-founded claims, made in the previous year, that Aborigines in the remote Warburton area were literally starving because of bad seasons and the lack of government provision. According to Grayden, in Laverton, 'we have the spectacle of children fossicking in dust bins behind the Laverton Hotel in the hope of finding a few crusts.'[14] Aborigines had few advocates in Parliament but Grayden pressed the issues with considerable force. He argued that Aborigines in Western Australia were infinitely worse off than those in the Northern Territory, where the Commonwealth Government exercised financial responsibility. He pressed the Minister for figures which, when provided, showed that in the Northern Territory £56 was spent per head on Aborigines, while in Western Australia the sum was little more than £21.

It was Grayden's belief that membership of the Committee should be drawn from relevant Government departments, a decision which shaped the focus of the inquiry. A Committee composed largely of public servants was always going to feel compelled to conform to government. Thus, the prevalence of old, deeply rooted stereotypes about irremediable 'half-castes' easily convinced the Committee to reaffirm the importance of assimilation. This, of course, meant Aborigines had to be 'acceptable to white society' and 'undergo a complete transformation' in their 'whole outlook on life';[15] something best achieved by exposing them to the influences of white society: 'There is little doubt that a native child brought up in a white home from birth with the same rights and opportunities as the white child would in a single generation be white in all but colour'.[16] To do this, however, required children to 'so absorb our Western approach that the inner core and not merely the external customs will change'.[17]

However, as the Committee was forced to acknowledge, the issue was no longer quite so straightforward. It had little choice but to reject the advice of those who suggested the process of assimilation should be expedited by removing all Aboriginal children from an early age and never letting them return home. New thinking on child welfare promoted by academic experts had begun to alter views about the underlying needs of children. The Committee acknowledged, in particular, the work of Dr John Bowlby in guiding its deliberations. Bowlby's work had revolutionised thinking about child welfare in the early 1950s by articulating the concept of 'maternal attachment' to explain the way in which children form deep and affectionate relationships with their mothers. Bowlby drew attention to the dangers of maternal deprivation in orphanages and asylums. In an emphatic acknowledgement of Bowlby's works, the Committee commented that it 'indicates conclusively that the removal of a child from his mother at an early age can cause serious psychological and mental disturbances.'[18] This recognition by the Committee deserves particular emphasis. It shows that the most senior officials implementing the policy of removing children were aware this practice damaged children. However, because of their commitment to the objectives of assimilation, they could not bring themselves to abandon it entirely. The result was a classic bureaucratic compromise. Henceforth, they recommended, no child should be taken from its parents before the age of six years. Unfortunately, no explanation was forthcoming as to why, when a child reached this age, he or she was automatically immune to the damage Bowlby had described.

It was becoming more difficult to sustain uncritically the assimilationist line. The Committee found cause for criticism in the work of missions. In a thinly veiled attack on their methods, the Committee wrote:

> A feature frequently stressed was the necessity for developing in the child removed from his parents at an early age a sense of security — a feeling of acceptance. It was pointed out that too often those who devote their lives to his interests develop an authoritarian approach, denouncing native culture and failing to understand the resulting reactions. In consequence the child's dignity and pride in his cultural background are shattered and he is left in a state of bewilderment which leads him to regard the white man's ways as something imposed on him and hence views him with suspicion and distrust. This insecurity in early life leads in adolescence to defiance and hostility and the youth develops a pride in flouting authority with the results of which we are all too familiar.[19]

These comments are something of a watershed. In all likelihood, they represent the first official acknowledgment that mission life was causing damage to children's behaviour patterns. The 'all too familiar' results to which the Committee referred was the growth in antisocial behaviour among Aboriginal youth, and especially the outbreak of criminal activity. As early as 1966, the Director of the Child Welfare Department alerted missions to the recent trend whereby 'an increasing number of native and part-native children are being placed by the courts in the care of the Child Welfare Department.'[20] Evidence provided to them convinced the Committee that to avoid these problems, an important concession should be made to the principle of assimilation; children must be able to balance pride in their own culture with absorbing 'our Western approach'. Therefore, it recommended children should have access to those 'features of native lore that are worth preserving'. What this actually meant was not elaborated upon but the Committee at least did recognise that special training in Aboriginal culture was necessary for those involved in bringing up Aboriginal children removed from their families.

Failure to develop the building blocks of self-esteem was only one of the substantial criticisms the Committee made of the network of missions straddling the State. It recognised that inappropriate living conditions were contributing to children's failure to thrive. Missions of this era were structured along two basic types. The 'dormitory' model, as the name suggests, congregated large numbers of children in one sleeping area, divided only on gender lines. It had the obvious advantage of costing less to establish and maintain and therefore was found in most missions. Government subsidies to missions were low up until the mid 1950s and the dormitory system was the only option practicably available to mission authorities. The 'cottage' model, developed originally at Sister Kate's, was thought to be preferable but high costs restricted its use. However, the dormitory model, as the Committee acknowledged, was particularly ill-suited to children because 'it lacked the personal touch'.[21] It recommended missions adopt the cottage model.

The care of children was only one aspect of the Committee's deliberations on Aboriginal affairs, however, its critical importance to the future of Aboriginal policy was recognised. At one level it is remarkable that virtually nothing changed in the administration of missions following the release of the Report. After all, the presence of F E Gare should have ensured that the system improve in line with their recommendations. But to implement even the modest changes outlined required commitment of personnel and resources and, sadly, both were lacking. In fact, the Government claimed a special grant from the Commonwealth would be required to implement the recommendations. Such a grant was never formally requested.

Scrutiny of assimilation and the role of missions ceased for many years but the number of children taken from their families continued to grow.[22] Only with the professionalisation of the Child Welfare Department and, to a lesser extent, the Department of Native Welfare, were politicians and senior bureaucrats forced to look again at the plight of Aboriginal children 'exiled' in missions. From the mid 1960s closer supervision and investigation of missions became part of the work of newly recruited social and welfare workers. These professionally trained personnel brought a clear perspective of the needs of children and they managed to expose the extent to which government knowingly turned a blind eye to their systematic abuse and neglect. Only when the case for negligence mounted overwhelmingly did the Child Welfare Department begin to withdraw its subsidies from the missions. This process did not begin until the early 1970s.

The available documents make it quite clear Government agencies were well aware of sub-standard care from at least the mid 1960s. Every aspect of the care at missions which took in Aboriginal children came in for criticism over the ensuing decade. The inappropriate housing of these children at some of the missions attracted the concern of the Child Welfare Department. New Norcia Mission came in for repeated criticism. In 1967 conditions for the hundred boys living at the mission run by the Benedictine Order of the Catholic Church were appalling. New Norcia continued to house children in the dormitory model a decade after the 1958 Special Committee recommended against the use of this form of accommodation: 'The building is extremely old and would no doubt be very cold in winter. Many of the windows were in poor condition and appeared in major need of renovation. This, together with bare floors and damaged paint work contribute to a rather dismal, uncompromising dormitory.'[23] Three years later nothing had changed. A Welfare Officer from Native Affairs described the boys' section as 'still rather depressing, with little more than the bare necessities being available.' While concerned about these shabby conditions, the Department declined to provide a specific purpose grant to improve them. Such an offer would set 'a precedent which may encourage dependency on the Department for any improvement programme.'[24]

Even the newly established missions built in the 1940s such as Roelands, Wandering and Carnarvon quickly had their facilities outstripped by the increasing numbers of children sent to them. By 1958 new buildings at most of the missions housing children were 'badly needed' but the State Government made no new finance forthcoming.[25] In the very remote missions living conditions for children were also poor. At the isolated Forrest River Mission, east of Wyndham, a rare visit from the Native Welfare Department in 1964 damned the girls' dormitory as having 'no privacy for the girls — it is open to the outside, and each girl has a bed in the central space — there are no bathrooms, no change rooms, no mirror, no wardrobes, a most depressing place.'[26] Living in such degrading conditions made a mockery of the justification used in removing these children from homes which were judged to be substandard and the children therefore at risk of neglect.

The poor living conditions endured by Aboriginal children were merely symptomatic of wider neglect. Inattention to the medical needs of children by missionaries was widespread. As early as 1953 a Native Welfare officer wrote a stinging report to the Commissioner about the medical neglect of Aboriginal children in missions:

> Two cases of girls with extreme impairment of vision have recently come to our notice ... both spent several years in Tardun and New Norcia Missions ... Frances' vision is so poor that she can only be assisted with the provision of contact lenses; Margaret is able to read only the top line of the test card of letters. In both cases nothing was done for these girls until they were 16 years of age and had left the mission.

Investigators acknowledged a disturbing truth. Had these children remained with their parents, they would have received better medical attention, because they:

> have the advantage during their school life of at least one, and probably more, routine medical inspections by school doctors. The native child living in at a mission has to my knowledge, no such advantage, and, if suffering from some defect, it is

probable that it will pass unnoticed, with a consequent retardation of the child's progress and a worsening of the defect.[27]

The responsibility of Government, through Native Welfare, could not have been expressed in more stark terms. These children were being grossly neglected by the very authorities who judged their parents unsuitable. However, this stern memo failed to move Native Welfare into action. Missions continued to be criticised for nearly twenty years for failing to meet the basic needs of children. A 1969 Report into New Norcia Mission conducted by social worker, S A Blanchard, from the Child Welfare Department's Midland Division, issued a warning about the need for medical examinations. 'This was much needed,' Blanchard advised, 'as a lot of the children have hearing and vision defects which have not been attended to. From this we can expect a lot of hospital referrals.' In the report, Blanchard noted that the Director of the Department, aware of the seriousness of the issue, was in the process of arranging the School Medical Services to examine the children.[28] This intervention either did not eventuate or was nor properly undertaken because subsequent reports about New Norcia continued to express concerns about medical neglect of children. In 1971 a Welfare Officer from the Department of Native Affairs conceded:

For some time I have been concerned that the children at New Norcia are not being regularly examined. I have been informed that the Doctor in Moora is not very interested, and the time and expense in bringing children to Perth for treatment, is not practicable.[29]

Another inquiry by the Welfare Branch of the Department in 1970 gathered data on the extent of medical neglect. Of the ninety-two children then living in the institution, over sixty had untreated medical conditions ranging from defective hearing — which was common — to nasal discharges, scabies and dental problems. The same report also documented the health of children living at the Mogumber Mission where the situation was similarly shocking. Of the fifty-one children twenty-two were found with untreated medical problems including hearing, trachoma, heart murmur, vision loss and asthma. On one occasion, the Child Welfare Department received a complaint from a family which had fostered one of the children from New Norcia. The child came to the family with an abscess 'about three inches in diameter' which soon burst.

The situation at Wandering was little different, with one important exception — the children attended a nearby state high school. In 1971, the headmaster of the school wrote to the Child Welfare Department informing them teachers had 'noticed small sores appearing on the hands of 2 or 3 of the Mission boys who attend our School.' He explained these boys had been sent to a local doctor who diagnosed 'viral blisters with secondary bacterial infection' caused by poor hygiene. One boy's sores became so serious he was hospitalised. Of this boy, the doctor told the headmaster, 'it was a case of obvious neglect' because 'his hands and arms are covered in blisters, pustules and infected sores and he is suffering from gross hyperidrosis between the fingers of both hands. When two dirty bandages were removed from his hands his skin was mildewed.'[30] This neglect of children at Wandering was known of by the Department of Native Welfare at least as early as 1966 when an internal memo admitted 'many of these children have not been medically examined or seen by a doctor for some years. The same situation applies in regard to dental treatment.' In the same year, the Welfare Superintendent of Native Welfare wrote to the Director of Child Welfare alerting him that 'the physical well-being of every ward should be one of constant review ... as it is too risky not to have children seen, and wait until some situation occurs.'[31] Too often, this is exactly what did occur.

It takes little speculation to imagine the deleterious impact which years of this sort of medical neglect had on the subsequent lifestyle of many of these children. The damage done, in particular, to their education, such as it was, is but one obvious, serious consequence. Only a deep sense that these children were less than worthy human beings could have sustained such indifference from people whose very calling was supposed to be one of Christian compassion. Missionaries were not immune to the racial thinking about Aborigines prevalent in the wider community. As a generalisation, missionaries shared the community's belief that Aborigines belonged to an inferior culture. Typically, they were disgusted by Aboriginal lifestyle and traditional practices. Most thought Aboriginal culture had to go.

The missionaries' self-appointed role was to guide Aboriginal children along the path of spiritual and cultural transformation. Yet the negative characterisations of Aborigines as a race made, for example, by the Benedictines at New Norcia were cast in racial thinking of the firmest conviction. As late as 1972, his missionary work with Aboriginal children about to collapse, Brother Anthony could still proclaim: 'We do not want children to reject their parents because of their low standards of morals but rather to accept them for what they are.' Earlier, Brother Augustine astonishingly told a meeting, convened at New Norcia,to consider ways to improve relations between the mission and Aborigines, that 'natives were basically selfish' and 'many parents subconsciously resent their children being educated'. He made these comments in spite of well-known grievances Aborigines had about the mission, and which were expressed at this meeting. The institution 'has a bad image with some of the parents as a place that "takes kids away".'[32] The private correspondence of the mission is laced with derogatory language about Aboriginal families. In 1972 for example, Brother Anthony wrote of one Aboriginal girl: 'although placement away from her parents will not meet with her approval it may be wise to make an attempt to get her out of the home. Elizabeth is now 13 and quite attractive so there could be sexual problems in the near future in such a lax household.' Such vague and unsubstantiated allegations were driven by the old stereotypes of Aborigines as irredeemably inferior and morally suspect.

In their dealings with children, church missionaries constructed a method of control and management underpinned by harsh discipline. They were not alone in the belief that children required 'a firm hand'. There are many testimonies to the cruel punishment of children who spent their childhood in Government institutions as wards of the State and who went to various boarding schools. Certain Catholic orders earned a reputation for the harsh physical punishment of children. It is therefore hard to quantify whether Aboriginal children were subjected to any greater level of physical abuse than significant numbers of other institutionalised children.

However, Aboriginal children in missions had a different legal status from children whose parents had chosen to send children to particular schools. The State had made itself guardian of many of these children and, in other cases, missions themselves had pressured parents into leaving their children with them. As such, both bodies had a responsibility to ensure their safety and proper care. Moreover, in missions such as New Norcia and Roelands, where children were schooled on the premises, there was no escape from the regime of harsh and, sometimes violent, discipline inflicted on children.

Often Aboriginal parents did not know where their children had been sent and, when they did, distance often prevented regular visits. These factors limited the ability of parents to complain about the treatment the children were receiving. Frank Gare, Commissioner for Native Affairs in the 1960s does not remember many cases of ill-treatment of children coming to the Department's notice but one incident does stand out. He recalled in an interview the case of a boy in Tardun Mission, outside Geraldton in 1958:

> Some boy had offended the Brother in charge of the boys' dormitory and as punishment this child was incarcerated in a sort of gaol. The mission had an enclosed storeroom completely darkened through the absence of proper windows. This child was locked in there overnight. I knew he must have been terrified in this place by himself. Not only was it very dark but there was a constant slow drip from the tank. I hit the roof when I learnt about it and told the person concerned that, with the consent of the parents, I'd bring a charge against him. The next day he was on a plane to Melbourne.

A lack of surviving documentary records prevent an independent assessment of both the level of inappropriate punishment and the Department's handling of those cases which came to its notice. However, one letter to the Native Welfare Department which has survived on the files, was written in 1962 by an Aboriginal mother whose daughter had been removed to Roelands Mission. Her letter is significant for several reasons. It highlights the capricious nature of the daughter's initial removal and the combination of cruelty and sexual deviance at the mission; and it suggests the attempts of Native Welfare to properly address the mother's concerns were not adequate. The mother wrote that the daughter was placed in Roelands, 'because she had missed a bit of school'. It was the 'first time she had ever been in trouble.' The mother complained that the children were being ill-treated at the mission:

> They have a man down at the mission who is a cruel man ... he belted them with a wire whip and when they are changing after their bath this man stands at the door and watches them ... also when you go to see the girls you are only allowed three minutes to talk to her .. she was put there by welfare but what I can see she is not put there to be schooled but to be punished by those people. Don't you think that three minutes is like speaking to people in gaol.[33]

On the back of the letter was a desperate plea: 'if you can't get her out have her transferred to Marribank Mission. I live in Albany ... please I wish I could speak to you.' In its 'investigation' the Department did nothing more than interview the man concerned, whose account was upheld. He was found only to use the cane 'to administer punishment and was adamant that he never went into bathrooms without first knocking or, to maintain discipline as when six girls are in the toilet together, when only two are provided, this is an unnecessary congregation.' Even his own testimony leaves open the likelihood of inappropriate behaviour, but no action was taken.

The Department of Native Affairs continued to hear about the level of physical punishment at Roelands. In 1966 it received a detailed explanation from the mission's supervisor, K G Cross outlining the institution's policy. His convoluted account is noteworthy for its attempt to justify the institutionalised practice of physical punishment:

> As you are quite aware, new Missionaries do find it difficult in the initial stages to obtain the necessary control and discipline of Native children. Instructions are given that all corporal punishment is to be administered by the Superintendent or Assistant Superintendent and as a general principle this has been followed, for the purposes of the control of the Homes and also to give the Home parents a certain amount of opportunity for Home discipline permission has been given to Home parents to give minor Home correction [what this covered is not specified]. Failing this proviso the situation could develop where an overall control would necessitate too much attention from the Superintendent, and could develop out of proportion when considering the overall conduct of the Mission.

Cross' 'explanation' was prompted by an investigation by the Department for Native Welfare into serious allegations of misconduct by one of the 'Home parents'. Apart from this 'serious issue of discipline' the male in question:

has apparently on some occasions entered the older girls' bedroom whilst they were in various states of undress. One of these girls registered her dissatisfaction with this state of affairs with Mr Cross — who took it up with Mr [name blanked out on file]. The reason submitted for [his] action was that on some mornings as Mrs [the man's wife] is not out of bed he, Mr [ ], has to bestir the house.

The officer from Native Welfare did not find this a 'satisfactory arrangement', nor a 'sufficient reason for entering the girls' bedroom — particularly when they are at an age where such action on his part could only cause embarrassment.'[34]

The authoritarian approach to discipline was periodically condemned by the Child Welfare Department in several missions for Aboriginal children. The tone of their comments leaves no doubt that, in the minds of officers, this discipline constituted the gross abuse of children. The Child Welfare Department was fully briefed by its officers about the extent of the routine use of physical discipline. S A Blanchard, the social worker from Child Welfare, wrote to his superiors: 'From conversation with the Nuns and Brother Augustine, it is known that physical punishment is often used, even in cases where, to a person knowledgeable in child care, it would do more harm than good.'[35]

At New Norcia Mission, the harshest discipline was reserved for those children who absconded — in the late 1960s, a frequent occurrence. Children were driven to flee the institution for many reasons, high among them for some was the clear lack of any reason for their being there. In 1969 the Child Welfare Department reported that the 'Nuns state that many of these children [who are not wards] have been admitted through Department of Native Welfare officers who have claimed that the children would later be charged, or by parents who were pressured by Department of Native Welfare officers.'[36] In other words, children were taken from their parents without any attempt to justify the action and literally dumped at the mission. It is no wonder many felt aggrieved and wished to escape.

In May 1968 the Superintendent of the Moora District of the Department of Native Welfare investigated the case of a fifteen year old girl who had absconded twice since being admitted at the beginning of that year, each time returning to her home at Goomalling Reserve. On the second time she absconded she was given a standard punishment for such an offence: her hair was cut off 'in a very short male style.' The Superintendent, even after making allowances for the 'incorrigible' nature of the girls at the mission, could not countenance this action. 'This treatment does not appear to be one generally approved in the Twentieth Century', was his blunt assessment.[37] The Superintendent was deeply unsettled about the impact which this brutality had on the attitudes of the girls. He felt sure that they had 'a deep resentment against society, and emerge from this sort of experience with a feeling often expressed … that 'Anyone can do anything to us, and nobody cares'. The Child Welfare Department was aware of these cruel practices. In May 1968 the Acting Director wrote to the Lord Abbott about his concern over an episode involving several girls who had their hair shorn after running away from the mission:

While I am appreciative of the control and discipline problems coped with by the Sisters, and the shortage of trained and suitable people, nevertheless the Department cannot condone such a method of punishment. If anything it is more likely to have the opposite effect to that desired and reinforce any hostile feelings the girls have.[38]

Absconding was an act of defiance and such acts were a common feature of Aboriginal young people's response to their institutionalisation. In 1948 Bateman had been told of older girls locked in early at night in a particular mission who protested by 'singing "The Prisoners Song" over and over again.'[39] But acts of defiance, as we have seen, were met with stern punishment. In 1964 Native Welfare investigated one girl at the Forrest River Mission whose behaviour the missionaries could no longer countenance. Her report read: 'behaviour satisfactory till during one church service she shouted "Hooray" instead of "amen" at the end of the Prayer, whereupon Rev Hall forced her to leave the church.' Following this incident the girl threatened to kill Rev Hall, 'being generally defiant of authority', for which she was locked in the dormitory for a whole day.[40]

Were these missionaries just overzealous, or were they plain callous? There is no easy answer to explain the institutionalised violence against young people in many, if not all, of the missions. Lack of training was certainly a contributing factor. A Welfare Officer from the Department of Native Welfare admitted the limitations of the missionaries at New Norcia in a 1969 memo: 'From my visits to New Norcia and discussions with the Nuns, they have no awareness of emotional needs and problems of adolescents, and my attempts to make them understand were unsuccessful. They are rigid in their attitude and think that whatever they do is best.'[41]

A similar conclusion was reached about Wandering Mission in 1969:

> There are no trained staff at the Mission, and the motivation is mainly of a spiritual nature. I think it would be of immense value to have a social worker and psychologist to visit this Mission at frequent intervals. It seems quite obvious that there will be some children who will need professional guidance as they graduate from this Mission. The staff, also, should be included in this category as they need guidance to help them to understand the needs of these children.[42]

The Department found itself compromised in its efforts to enforce a more appropriate form of care for mission children. It heavily relied on the missions not only to place children stolen from their families but also to take young Aborigines who had been before the court. It believed the facilities at New Norcia were crucial in solving its problem with delinquent Aboriginal youth. The Director of Child Welfare wrote to the Lord Abbott in 1968 to point out he was 'most anxious that the mission continue and, if possible, extend its work with the care of native children.' Correspondence had been periodically exchanged between the Department and the mission regarding its role. This makes very clear the Department's double standards in its concern for Aboriginal mission children. On the one hand, the Department acknowledged the Brothers were 'well acquainted with the Departmental view that the present set-up is below standard', while, as the same time, supporting the mission to continue its work: 'at present the advantage of New Norcia is that they are prepared to accept a number of delinquent younger children who are not acceptable in other missions.'[43]

It was the same situation at Roelands. Superintendent Cross wrote to Child Welfare pointing out the problems associated with mixing together children admitted because they were classified as neglected, and those showing 'delinquent symptoms'. Cross had a point about the difficulty this caused in the management of the young charges: 'You can visualise the problems that present themselves, when children of both groups are placed together and the House parents endeavour to perform their task to the best of their ability. It requires only one or two delinquent tendencies to influence the whole group.' Cross maintained such children should be placed in a more secure environment but, in reality, the problem demonstrated the complete inadequacy of government's reliance on missions to provide for Aboriginal children. Most of the missions struggled to obtain an adequate number of staff prepared to work in the isolated locations. The Secretary for Roelands once complained to the Commissioner of Native Welfare that 'an acute staff shortage has occurred and our Missionaries are tried beyond reasonable limits to meet the demands of the work.' To overcome the problem, the Secretary wanted the Commissioner to remove a few of the teenage girls who 'have taken the advantage of the greater liberties and are making the lot of the lady missioner almost unbearable to breaking point.'[44] The fate of teenagers who refused to, or were unable to, conform to mission rules is unknown. Left at the mission they were vulnerable to outbursts of routine physical discipline. Removed, especially in the 1960s, they were likely to be fostered out.

The extent of the damage done in terms of the socialisation of children in missions became clearer in the 1960s. As Mrs Morris had observed, Aboriginal mission children were being emotionally deprived. A 1970 memo from Child Welfare made this abundantly clear: 'The smaller boys lack mothering and show signs of deprivation.' Little else could be expected with just two Brothers in charge of seventy boys and because it was not in the Brothers' make-up to be understanding. They were 'extremely authoritarian in their handling of the children and [showed] little understanding and tolerance of the dull child or the child with behaviour problems'.[45] In other words, these children lacked the very thing which, nearly twenty years earlier, John Bowlby had indicated was essential for children to thrive: access to permanent and affectionate parent figures.

Missions such as New Norcia, constructed along the 'dormitory' model and operated on minimal staff, were calculated to stunt the socialisation of their charges. The Child Welfare Department was clear about this from the late 1960s. S A Blanchard's 1969 Report outlined the problems: 'The children who have been in New Norcia for some time are usually inhibited, lacking in social graces and unused to freedom'. The extent of their social isolation is revealed in the following extract from the Report:

> The Sisters at the Mission have seen the need to teach the children social graces in order to help them mix better with the outside world and to gain more confidence. To this end, two 'socials' were held towards the end of 1969, in which young people from outside the Mission participated. Six of the older girls were also taken to dinner at the local

hotel by Brother Anthony. These activities should be greatly encouraged to overcome the isolation of the Mission ... a programme of sports, picnics, and socials should be organised with church groups for weekends ... A programme of deportment and make-up classes and discussions on job opportunities would also be helpful. The lack of table manners and the ability to converse fluently and poor speech of the Mission children has been observed by all their holiday hosts.[46]

Even the faintly approving tone of Blanchard's comments could not hide the reality of life at New Norcia. For decades, these children had been offered nothing to prepare them for life outside the mission; the belated and limited moves to do so in 1969 are an all too transparent attempt to gain the Department's ongoing approval. In fact, it is clear from the evidence that mission life fostered in some of its charges the character of a social misfit. It did so by holding them as virtual captives, isolating them from the broader community, and inflicting regular and violent physical punishment upon them. Native Welfare admitted the extent of the problem in 1964 when an officer visited Forrest River Mission where he found: 'the young ones are antisocial and hostile and very anxious to leave the Mission.'

In fact, when many of them did finally leave Forrest River Mission and headed for Wyndham, they were 'a continual source of trouble ... because of antisocial behaviour; the boys are 'all very reluctant to work' and the girls were found to be regularly 'chasing' married men. 'I find this chasing married men theme cropping up time after time', the Native Welfare officer wrote to his District Office in Derby, 'but it seems to me to be against the law of averages and nature, that so many young girls should behave in the same way.'[47] Three years later it was even clearer to another Native Welfare officer that mission life had been responsible for fostering antisocial patterns of behaviour in too many young Aborigines. 'Difficulties in the handling of teenage children have become apparent,' the officer reported, 'and in a number of instances have contributed to their nonadjustment and unsocial and even delinquent behaviour.'[48]

To overcome the problems in the management of the children, local social and welfare workers from both Child and Native Welfare departments pushed their superiors to establish a training scheme for missionaries. This was considered, and rejected, by the Commissioner of Native Affairs in 1967 who acknowledged that, 'whilst training of mission staff is desirable, there is no practical means of implementing it.'

In addition to the regime of strict, and even violent punishment, the extent of social isolation may be a key to explaining the antisocial behaviour shown by many mission children. As late as 1972, the Child Welfare Department described Wandering Mission as 'a closed institution. It was almost totally severed from the wider society ... there were teenage children who had very limited social experience outside Wandering'.[49] Mission children, especially in those cases where they did not attend state schools, were denied the range of experiences children require to build social competence. It is almost impossible to imagine the belief system held by the missionaries about these children and their needs which drove them to seclude the children from the community.

Compounding the future adjustment problems for these young people was the lack of meaningful education and training they received at missions. Advocates of assimilation such as Bateman argued that Aboriginal children should be trained to fit into the lower echelons of the white workforce — boys as farm labourers and girls as domestics. The missionaries did little more in meeting these basic requirements than to place the young people on the mission farms. On missions such as New Norcia, where children did not attend a state school, 'children are allowed to leave school and receive little preparation for future employment.'[50] In such situations children were open to exploitation as little more than unpaid labour.

The attempts at Wandering Mission to establish some form of vocational training were hampered by the Native Welfare Department. In the early 1960s, Father Mithern started a 'farm course' for the post-primary boys. Held only once a week it included shearing lessons, sheep butchering, ploughing, harvesting, post-cutting and general farm labouring. Boys were instructed by a local farmer. Limited as this training was, the Native Welfare Department opposed it, refusing to subsidise any equipment purchased because it already operated a farm school at Gnowangerup.[51]

Significant as Child and Native Welfare departmental documents are in exposing the extent of abuse and neglect of children in missions, and the knowledge governments had of this, they are silent on one key issue: the sexual abuse of children. The few cases mentioned previously of inappropriate conduct on the part of some male supervisors/home parents only hint at what appears to have been a recurrent practice at many missions. According to one former employee of the Child Welfare Department, there was no general understanding of the existence of sexual abuse of children in the community until the late 1960s, with the consequence that officers from the Department were not actively looking for the signs of it. Many Child Welfare officers of the 1960s were insufficiently trained to detect symptoms of child sexual abuse. It is probable children who suffered this form of abuse were intimidated and/or too shamed to report it.[52]

Considering together all the issues of abuse and neglect compels the question: why did government not act to stop it? To take systematic action against the missions would have required either to cease the removal of Aboriginal children from their families, or increase the resources of the Child and Native Welfare departments to properly supervise the missions. By the late 1950s, government had increased the subsidy it paid to missions for individual children but this applied only to wards of the state. There were also the significant number of parents coerced by the Department of Native Affairs and the missions to place their children in a mission — without being made wards of the state — and for whom the mission had to pay the total cost. Thus, conditions for children as a group improved little, or not at all, in most missions. Governments were not in a strong position to enforce better standards of care on the missions. To stop the removal of children would have required a rethink of assimilation, but government remained committed to it, as evidenced by the 1958 Special Committee. Politically, governments were averse to spending additional resources on Aboriginal affairs and especially on capital works, training and staff. In practice this meant the missions were largely unaccountable.

In the 1950s and early 1960s especially, inspection visits to missions, especially from Native Welfare, were mostly little more than courtesy calls. 'Called at the Mission', wrote one Native Welfare Officer of his visit to Wandering,

> Rev Father Williams, the Superintendent, was away,
> and so I was unable to meet him ... whilst talking
> to one of three native men employed on the
> property I was able to watch the children running
> around and playing and they seemed very happy.[53]

When some pressure came to bear on Child Welfare officers in the mid 1960s to pay attention to the circumstances of individual children, one District Officer wrote to the Director of the Child Welfare Department in 1966, shocked at the new expectations:

> what a colossal task it would be to see 54 children
> individually, in one visit, by the District Officer
> alone, and then to make reports on each child ...
> and keep other work going ... [Nevertheless] acting
> under those instructions I went direct to the
> Mission [Wandering] with the intention of seeing
> each child ... Father Mithern said this had never
> been carried out before by the C.W. Dept., nor had
> it been done by the Native Welfare Dept., when
> they had been responsible. He said he considered it
> would have to be gone into, and given some
> thought. I feel sure that it was the system he
> objected to, not my own personal approach. He told
> me that it appeared that we did not trust them to
> care for the children.[54]

Conflicts over responsibility for supervision between the Native Welfare and Child Welfare departments seems to have impeded proper supervision of children. This, at least was the complaint expressed in 1969 by the Inspector of Child Welfare in Narrogin who wrote:

I am rather concerned as I feel that there are several wards in this district that have not been supervised by the NWD or the CWD in the past. Supervision is very important to the child and in some cases ... the child lacks supervision for months while the two Departments decide who will supervise.[55]

As circumstances showed, the absence of proper supervision allowed neglect and abuse to prevail in the institutions. However, the churches must bear their share of the responsibility for allowing such gross neglect and abuse of children to become institutionalised in missions. The role of the Catholic, Anglican and Church of Christ in particular, in the mistreatment of Aboriginal children is difficult to rationalise. There is little evidence that these children were valued as individuals or that much thought was given to their post-mission life.

However, changing times eventually overcame the resistance of the Child Welfare Department to cease sending Aboriginal children to the missions. A report made out on Wandering Mission in April 1973 explains the Department's emerging policy. In a memo to the Minister for Community Welfare, the senior social worker for the Metropolitan region pointed out that the Department had reduced its usage of Wandering Mission, due largely to an emphasis on foster caring as a preferred alternative, the development of other facilities in locations more suited to the comprehensive care of children, and improved social conditions for Aboriginal parents resulting in fewer children being removed.[56] The era of the mission slowly petered out without any major public scandal arising from its operations in the post-war era or without any parliamentary interest in the fate of the children.

The number of children separated from their parents in the name of assimilation will never be known with any accuracy. It is indicative of the disregard officials had for Aborigines in general, and for children in particular, that they did not feel compelled to keep precise records on numbers. In 1968 the Minister for Native Affairs was asked in Parliament to provide information on the numbers of children in missions, government institutions and 'other' institutions. The curt reply was 'No records are kept'.[57] The statement was not entirely true insofar as records do show several attempts were made to document the number of Aboriginal State wards in the various missions. Records for 1956 and 1957 show nearly 1400 Aboriginal State wards of school age.[58] However, without continuous records showing admissions and discharges the overall numbers remain elusive. Perhaps the most accurate figure available is from the Australian Bureau of Statistics which, in 1994, found that seventeen percent of respondents over the age of twenty-five had reported being taken away from their natural family by 'a mission, the government, or welfare.' With an Aboriginal population in Western Australia of approximately 42,000, this represents over 7,100 individuals.[59] However, this figure is undoubtedly a significant underestimation as it obviously does not include those taken as children but who died before this survey was carried out. With high death rates commonly experienced in the Aboriginal community it is possible that the figure for those taken after the official start of the policy of removal in 1937 may be many thousands higher.

Although the precise figure of those removed remains unknown, the existing record of neglect and abuse is sufficient to raise the query as to the real purpose behind assimilation.

5

Assimilation in Practice

In 1965 'Yvonne' arrived at Wandering Mission. She had been committed by the court 'due to the neglect of her parents and her lack of attendance at school'. She was included as a case history in a 1971 thesis submitted for a Teacher's Higher Certificate which examined the work of Wandering Mission.[1] The details of her case highlight the difficulties in assessing the impact of assimilation. The author is at some pains to construct a 'success story' out of the misery of her family life. Yvonne's father was said to have been 'drinking fuel spirits by the time he was twenty and had over 60 convictions in police courts.' Yvonne was described as 'undernourished, extremely shy, frightened, self-conscious and very moody'. She had little school prior to coming to the mission. For a year she worked at the mission as a domestic, during which time, 'she developed good tastes in personal grooming as well as dress sense.' Through the mission she obtained outside employment as a domestic on a nearby farm. However, she left to rejoin her mother at Narrogin Reserve. Twelve months later she returned looking 'dirty, undernourished and shabbily dressed'. She was again accepted as a domestic and not long afterwards 'she quickly changed to a well mannered, well dressed young girl'. With the help of the Mission's Pallotine Order she was sent to Melbourne to train as a nursing aide and, at the time the thesis was completed, was said to be doing well in her chosen career. She was assessed as capable of doing well 'if she remains in Melbourne. Could possibly meet a suitable male and settle down in that city to a well adjusted domestic life.'

Was this an unequivocal success story of assimilation, as the writer so readily assumes? The 'storyline' is so apparent: mission rescues Aboriginal girl from wretched home life and gives her the skills to enter white society. We will probably never know what this young woman felt about the course her life had taken under assimilation. However, efforts to construct success stories, such as Yvonne's, raise a number of issues. Firstly, she was being constructed as a 'success' only by reference to her external circumstances and, secondly, she was an atypical case. During the 1950s and 60s, when most of the children separated from their families emerged as young adults in the community, Yvonne was one of the very few who managed to obtain vocational qualifications.

Pronouncements in the post-war period ascribed a range of different meanings to assimilation. The official position, as enunciated at the Commonwealth level continued to be, as Paul Hasluck expressed it: 'that, in the course of time, it is expected that all persons of aboriginal blood or mixed blood in Australia will live like white Australians do.'[2] This position assumed a cultural transformation occurring among Aborigines but otherwise gave the appearance of a society striving for material and social equality. It suggested that, eventually, blacks and whites would live side by side albeit with blacks having dispensed with their culture. Some well-intentioned people of the time found this an attractive ideal. It was seen to be an advance on the policy of segregation. It probably explains why some young people like Yvonne were show-cased as success stories. However, as debates within Western Australia show, assimilation was understood by most people in the 1950s and early 60s to involve a much more predetermined set of outcomes. As the Commissioner of Native Welfare wrote in his 1958 Annual Report:

> the policy and the term assimilation postulates a state of mind, our mind, in regard to natives being a people apart — it appears therefore to be a term aligned with the policy referred to elsewhere as 'apartheid'. In its effect it may even be worse because the notion of apartness leads to a belief that we have the right to decide whether they as natives are entitled to share with us certain rights and privileges which we regard and jealously guard as being our birth right.[3]

Hence, assimilation was never really designed to produce many 'Yvonne's' — young Aborigines with an education who could compete equally with whites. There remained an unspoken assumption that assimilation would still confer to white society the ability to exercise social control over the Aboriginal population. This control would be all the more effective if Aborigines could be stripped of their culture. Hence, assimilation involved an explicit understanding about the place of Aboriginal culture. This was acknowledged by the Superintendent of Tardun Mission outside Geraldton who in his 1956 Annual

Report to the Commissioner explained the difference between 'integration' and 'assimilation'.

> We [the mission] use the term 'integrate' designedly, in preference to 'assimilation', the term now in current use. 'Integration' implies the existence of two separate elements which must be moulded to an homogeneous whole at the same time as retaining their individual identity. 'Assimilation', on the other hand, means the absorption of one of the elements, in this case the natives, and their ultimate disappearance.[4]

These comments make the purpose of assimilation during the 1950s, and much of the 1960s, quite clear. At the very time large numbers of young Aborigines were coming out of missions and foster homes to live in the general community, they confronted a society which legitimised racial inequality and cultural destruction while it left the racial attitudes of white society intact and unchallenged. It therefore imposed a double tragedy on those children, now turned young adults, who had been separated from their families. It not only stripped them of their heritage, but it thrust them into a society which never intended to receive them as anything other than inferior beings. Thus, another generation of Aborigines remained firmly marginalised.

Not surprisingly, the missions tried hard to convince themselves they were working towards the social equality of Aborigines. In 1956 the Superintendent at Roelands Mission published figures on the post-release outcomes of the sixty-five children who had finished 'their course of training' since its establishment in 1941. These purported to show seventy-eight percent were living 'in standards equal to the white community', while twenty-two percent have 'gone back to camp conditions.' Of the latter group, nine percent were girls who married husbands who could not provide them with any other accommodation; four percent were 'subnormal and represent special cases' while nine percent 'have of their own choice drifted back into camp life.' Of the larger group, nearly half were domestic and farm workers; a quarter were in 'trades and professions' while just under a quarter were married females.[5] In other words, according to the superintendent of this mission, his efforts had met with significant success. However, his figures are almost meaningless. The categorisation used, that most were living 'in standards equal to the white community', is too vague to make much sense. Which white community? The very poorest or the moderately affluent? Most likely, missions felt the pressure to justify the continued funding they received by placing their work in some sort of vague, unthreatening, but favourable light.

The general pattern of what happened to most of these young people is clear. Lady Jessie Street pointed to the problems as early as 1957 when, in the course of her tour around Australia visiting Aboriginal settlements, she wrote of the mission children in Western Australia.

When they leave school, neither the Mission nor the church to which denomination it belongs take further responsibility for these young people. This is a most difficult period for them. They have led a dependent, sheltered life in boarding school ... When they leave school many of them have to return to aboriginal camps without any facilities. They have not only to adjust themselves to this but as they are unskilled and untrained and coloured they find it difficult to find work. They awaken to the fact that they are regarded as inferior because of their dark skin. They go to towns, as they must to get jobs, and as they can't get proper accommodation on account of their colour they are exposed to all sorts of danger. Many of these young people are exploited and demoralised by the bad elements among the whites against which police seldom take action.[6]

There could be no more concise summation of the realities of assimilation as it was experienced by hundreds of Aboriginal young people. Each of the issues Jessie Street raised — the discrimination, the lack of accommodation, and the difficulty in finding work — are worthy of detailed examination for in them we see the reality of assimilation at work.

At the core of assimilation, as it was understood and practised in Western Australia, was the retention of white attitudes of superiority and political control. State Governments of the period, backed by wider community attitudes, practised massive discrimination against Aboriginal people that was intended to restrict their social advancement. Indeed, Frank Gare remembers the fierce political opposition to Aboriginal advancement throughout the 1950s and 60s. While the occasional minister may have been sympathetic to proposals for Aboriginal social advancement, governments were not. This opposition, and its consequences, were well understood among sections of the educated elite. The members of the 1958 Special Committee chaired by Frank Gare summed up the second-class status of Western Australian Aborigines.

In accordance with Section 10 of the Federal Nationality and Citizenship Act, 1948-1955, every aboriginal person born in Australia is a citizen of the Commonwealth. Western Australia, however, has enacted special legislation which deprives aborigines and most part-aborigines of some of the normal rights and privileges of citizenship, even though it does not absolve them from most of its responsibilities — including taxation. Under this legislation, one of the influential principles of democracy — that there shall be no taxation without representation — is denied the native living in Western Australia. The State Electoral Act deprives him of the right to vote in State elections, and ... disqualifies him from voting in the Federal sphere. In addition, the Licencing Act, the Firearms and Gun Act, a number of other Western Australian Acts and even the Native Welfare (Administration) Act itself, all impose restrictions of varying degree on natives as distinct from other persons. It is obvious, therefore, that although natives in Western Australia may be citizens of the Commonwealth, they are not full citizens of their own State. They suffer under the further disability that the State-imposed restrictions automatically disqualify many of them from certain very important benefits under the Federal Social Services Act.[7]

This body of legislative discrimination, much of which remained in force until the mid to late 1960s, had the effect of entrenching stereotypical attitudes among both whites and blacks, as the Special Committee recognised.

It has the inevitable result, among other things, of implanting in too many minds, native and otherwise, the belief that anyone officially classed as a 'native' must be an inferior being. Anything more calculated to destroy the self-respect and self-confidence of such a people would be difficult to imagine.[8]

One of the core assumptions behind assimilation — that Aborigines could be kept in their place — extended to a reluctance by most governments to provide proper services to them and to grant them civic rights. When, in July 1964, new legislation came into effect removing much of the legal discrimination against Aborigines, the Commissioner noted in his Annual Report that it was passed against a background of considerable social anxiety, of 'fearful and gloomy prophecies of widespread, serious social disorder', which many believed would accompany legal equality.[9]

Keeping Aborigines 'in their place' meant curtailing their social advancement through government sponsored measures. Frank Gare recalls a proposal he backed in the early 1960s to build education hostels for young Aborigines in the bush. When he told his minister of the proposal, the minister said: 'If I am going to get these through Cabinet, you'll have to design hostels that cost half the price of a country high school where white kids go to school.' As Gare explains: 'So we put it to Public Works and they designed cut-price hostels. It was the only way we could get it through Cabinet.'

Backed by community opinion hostile to the integration of Aborigines, governments, throughout the 1950s and 60s continued to drag their feet in providing housing for Aboriginal people. This meant that young Aborigines coming out of the missions were forced back into the same cycle of poor housing that most had experienced prior to their removal. Many went back to the reserves.

Reflecting the continuing preference for segregation of the races, governments continued to expand the reserve system. Their number increased from thirty-six in 1949 to sixty in 1959 and rising to seventy in 1964.[10] For those young institutionalised Aborigines who went back to live in these reserves, conditions remained primitive. Lack of funds from government meant that, by 1959, twenty of the reserves were still without basic water and toilet facilities and only a modest start had been made on housing.[11] Many of the children lacked an electric light to do their homework. Some District Officers from the Native Welfare Department deplored the housing situation facing Aborigines. 'With better facilities for living', the District Officer for the Southern District wrote in his 1958 annual report, 'both on and off the reserves — the lot of the Native People should be considerably ameliorated. But unless the provision of Government finance keeps pace with the needs of the native community and the plans for their advancement, this will remain a pipe dream.'[12]

The double-bind many Aborigines were trapped in became apparent in the early 1950s when the Department of Native Welfare and the State Housing Commission sponsored about one hundred Aboriginal families into conventional suburban housing which failed disastrously. Within a few years, seventy-five percent had been forced to relinquish their properties. The financial commitment involved for rent or purchase payments 'was too much for their insecure economic status.'[13] The Department of Native Welfare expressed dejection in trying to assist these people into housing, reporting in 1957: 'Every consideration has been shown to these people by the State Housing Commission and this office, but in very few cases has the response been worth the effort.'[14] The failure of the scheme fuelled the critics of assimilation. Aborigines were now believed to be incapable of living in the white way. New moves to deal with the housing policy emerged out of the failure of this scheme. These were based on the old desire to maintain segregation: 'until the economic and social standards of the Aborigines reached a level acceptable to the white community, a transitional housing scheme should be provided.'[15]

Far from being designed to promote future social equality, the transitional scheme helped perpetuate Aboriginal marginalisation. Under this scheme, basic houses were built on the reserves grouped around communal facilities. They were designed as an introduction to more sophisticated housing. In reality, the policy could not disguise the harsh reality; these houses were 'little more than rural black slum ghettos', as Henry Schapper vividly described them in his 1970 study of Aboriginal affairs in Western Australia.[16] Most had neither heating nor water for ablutions; inside the houses there were few possessions other than clothing, blankets, cooking and eating utensils. 'All are utterly inadequate for hygienic family living', wrote Schapper.[17] In the mid 1960s, 'Brian' was removed from the Wagin Reserve. His home consisted of 'an old corrugated iron shack', divided into three rooms with 'dilapidated plaster board.' The ceiling was only two metres high and, while there were spaces for windows, there was no glass and no electricity.[18] From these primitive and unpromising conditions, which reflected the ongoing community drive for segregation, Aborigines were supposed to learn the art of 'civilised' white living.

When they were deemed suitably experienced, Aborigines could move from the 'primary transitional' stage on the reserves, to a 'standard transitional' home in a country town. A final stage saw the transition to a conventional suburban house. This scheme gave authorities ongoing power to make judgements on Aboriginal people over their progress through the gateways to white living. By 1967, nearly twenty years after its commencement, the bulk of the building activity had been in the primary stage: 487 primary transitional house had been built; 251 standard transitional houses and only 35 conventional houses.[19] In fact, evidence collected by the Aboriginal Welfare Council in the mid 1960s indicates that shire council's objection to the erection of transition houses in country towns, creating serious difficulties for the building program.[20] These objections were driven by community opposition which feared the presence of an Aboriginal family next door would greatly depreciate property values. One such complainant suggested that 'Aboriginal families should be placed in an area where all the homes were rented and this would not affect people like themselves.'[21] Thus, the reserves remained for many Aboriginal people a place of gloomy impoverishment.

Greatly adding to the problems of poor housing were the bleak employment prospects, especially for young people. In 1964 the Minister for Native Welfare was forced to acknowledge 'the acute unemployment position of teenage natives in south-west towns'.[22] The situation for young people who had gained little, or no, vocational training at missions, was made worse by their lack of access to technical training during most of the 1960s. As late as 1967 only twenty-seven Aboriginal boys were undergoing apprenticeships in any one year.[23] The Aboriginal Advancement Council of Western Australia lobbied government to improve its training efforts for young Aborigines. 'Re-training and rehabilitation of Europeans', the Council argued, 'are undertaken on an increasing scale. Why not raise the standard of skill among the hundreds of Aboriginal men who have missed the opportunity of apprenticeship in their young days through no fault of their own?'[24] However, throughout the 1960s, government efforts, through the Department of Native Affairs, continued to be focused on providing agricultural training to Aboriginal youth. In other words, they were being trained for jobs on the land as farm labourers, a source of employment that had been declining for years.

In 1967 the Department of Native Welfare became concerned at the 'vexing problem' of unemployment among Aboriginal youth, and surveys were conducted in regional areas 'to establish whether an employment market exists for them'.[25] A 1968 employment survey undertaken in Geraldton pinpointed the problems: 'Low education and training standards have made it impossible to place natives in the past. Of several applications for any vacancy, the Aboriginal applicant is generally the least qualified. Even for manual jobs, qualifications are becoming increasingly important.'[26] Contrary to the rhetoric behind assimilation, there is no evidence that Aborigines 'trained' in missions had greater advantages in the labour market than those who had remained in their communities. In terms of skills, they were largely indistinguishable. However, the failure of missions to prepare children for an employment future in white society was never the subject of critical examination until Henry Schapper drew attention to the issue in 1970. In his study of Aborigines in Western Australia he wrote that missions lacked skills and resources for the task.

The result is that it is hardly possible for Aborigines on these missions to learn properly the skills and discipline of sustained work, the skills of household management, and to acquire adequate levels of hygiene, diet and health. Because of these inadequacies and because the school curriculum and methods of education are not geared to the needs of environmentally disadvantaged children, the formal education of school children on mission settlements is largely irrelevant.[27]

Many Aborigines, especially in the South-West, were only too aware that they were effectively locked out of the employment market. In 1966 a group of Aboriginal prisoners in Fremantle Gaol set down their thoughts to prison authorities on 'Why Noongars Can't Get Good Jobs Outside':

1. Because they are unskilled labour.
2. Because they should get more help from Native Welfare from the time they leave school.
3. Because all the money supposed to be spent on Natives is spent on building little two-roomed houses throughout the country.
4. We think the Native Welfare could have done better by building hostels for teen-age boys and girls.
5. Boys should learn carpentry and cabinet making — also metal work like plumbing, engineering etc.
6. Girls should learn secretarial work and nursing etc. (As it is all they do is run around the streets making a bad name for themselves.)[28]

These comments show an acute awareness among the prisoners of the marginalised position of Aborigines in society, and particularly the problems facing the young. They reveal a desire for a better future. Little, however, was done to help provide it. The 1974 Royal Commission into Aboriginal Affairs was forced to concede: 'Opportunities for gainful employment have declined markedly in recent years and it seems to be expected that this decline will increase rather than decrease with the passage of time, as the work load becomes more that of machines than of men.'[29] Two decades of assimilation had succeeded in ensuring few Aborigines competed with whites for employment.

With especially bleak prospects in country towns, Aborigines drifted to Perth in the 1950s and 60s. Here, they congregated in East Perth, a small locale of cheap rents, shabby houses and noisy social interaction. It had the city's seediest wine bars. By the 1960s most people regarded the place as a slum. Many of the houses in which Aborigines lived had been condemned, but not demolished. The only study of East Perth during these years made a number of very interesting observations about the lifestyle of its residents.[30] Jeanette Kidd found a close-knit, if chaotic, and frequently dysfunctional community. Most of the Aborigines who inhabited the area originated from the missions, drawn to the place to be with their own kind. They were indifferent 'as to whether the rest of the community accepts them.' However, they carried with them the legacy of their mission days. 'One downfall of mission training', Kidd observed, 'is the children lead a sheltered life, free from experiences they may meet in the city. And when they come to the city looking for employment and a different way of life, many of them are completely lost.' Here was the full realisation of the consequences of assimilation.

Life was precarious for the Aborigines of East Perth in the 1960s. Unemployment was rife. The men drifted from one poorly paid job to another. Families were continually falling behind in their rent, and landlords showed little sympathy. 'Landlords evict the part-Aboriginal tenants almost as soon as they fall behind in their rent, regardless of the circumstances.' When this happened families moved in together, exacerbating overcrowding. Lack of shower and toilet facilities affected standards of health. Girls became pregnant in their teens, but relationships were unstable.

> Husbands in general show tendencies towards being unable to accept the responsibility of finding permanent employment to support their families. This makes the wife's task very difficult since not many part-Aboriginal women in East Perth are able to find employment due to lack of education and training.

Some young women, recently arrived from the missions, were forced into prostitution. Their clients were the white men who prowled the streets at night. Some had illegitimate children. Drinking and drunkenness were common. Kidd described the habit as an 'escape from the reality of life which the natives feel they have no part in.' However, drinking brought Aborigines under the glare of the police and arrests for drunkenness, vagrancy, and neglect of children were regular occurrences.

The children of these mostly ex-mission adults bore the legacy of their parent's background: problems of adjustment were being transmitted to the next generation. Poor school attendance, the lack of ongoing male influences in households and general poverty made many prone to juvenile crime, the incidence of which was slowly on the rise in the area. These youth, Kidd reported,

> find the society hard to live in, mainly due to the fact that their environment makes it hard for them to adjust and conform. Surveys have shown that Aboriginal youths have no close ties with the 'father' image, which could contribute to their apparent lack of responsibility. There is a high incidence of minor crime which results mainly from boredom or lack of security. Car-stealing is common.

These families were trapped in their poverty. 'Most natives in East Perth', Kidd wrote, 'wanted a better class of home, but these were not available'. Native Welfare was keen for the State Housing Commission to launch a rehousing scheme for East Perth but finance was not forthcoming. However, the problem of poverty was more complex than lack of housing. Kidd's study highlighted, but did not fully explore, a crucial aspect about their backgrounds. Missions had left them without the range of social and vocational skills to make the fullest use of their lives. However, Kidd had come closer than anyone else in understanding the link between ex-mission inmates' tragic backgrounds and their life of unrelieved poverty.

The extent of disadvantage among the Aboriginal community of Western Australia in the mid 1960s was graphically illustrated in a set of data compiled by Henry Schapper in his book *Aboriginal Advancement to Integration*. Contrasting their experiences with European families Schapper found one in three Aboriginal families had someone who was unemployed, compared with only one in ten in European families. Educational disadvantage was even greater with only one family in fourteen who had a member with a junior certificate or higher qualification, compared to Europeans with more than one per family. The extent of welfare discrimination was equally stark. One Aboriginal family in three had a child under the notice of the Child Welfare Department, compared to one European family in thirty-four. However, experience of the legal system between the two races showed the largest gap of all: one Aboriginal family in three had a family member committed to gaol while, for Europeans, it was one in seventy-one. The gap in the rates for juvenile convictions was also large: one in four families for Aborigines, compared to one in nineteen for Europeans.[31]

Compounding the marginalised status of Aborigines in the 1950s and 60s was the existence of widespread community racial prejudice. It is especially hard to measure the extent of racism during the 1960s because it was not, at the time, the subject of systematic study. Undoubtedly, signs of positive changes in some quarters towards acceptance were evident. The state school system, for example, began to take seriously the disadvantage of Aboriginal students in schools and employed specially trained teachers. International trends towards more accepting racial attitudes in general filtered through to influence the educated section of community opinion. However, at other levels, racism towards Aborigines remained entrenched.

Assimilation acted as a facade to perpetuate deeply ingrained racial attitudes. Whites who were disdainful of Aborigines had their views legitimised by the existence of this very policy. Leading advocates of assimilation had long maintained that Aboriginal culture was inferior and unstoppable historical forces would eventually wipe it out. This was the very point Paul Hasluck made in the

Federal Parliament after the States and the Commonwealth reaffirmed their commitment to assimilation in the early 1950s. The 'blessings of civilisation are worth having', he told the House of Assembly:

> The world today ... is coming around again to the idea that inevitable change can be made for the better. We recognise now that the noble savage can benefit from measures taken to improve his health and nutrition, to teach him better civilisation, and to lead him to civilised ways of life. We know that culture is not static but that it either changes or dies ... The native people will grow into the society in which, by force of history, they are bound to live.[32]

No matter how well intended the motives behind such ideas, they were not calculated to inspire acceptance or tolerance for Aboriginal people. The essence of assimilation was the belief in the superiority of white society. It is no great leap from this position to one which seeks to isolate the 'inferior' culture. In country towns throughout the South-West segregation was still widely practiced. At Wagin, for example, the local council erected 'whites only' signs on the lavatories and the rest rooms. In 1963 the *Sunday Times* investigated this discrimination and found that it was being driven by poor housing, poor hygiene and drunkenness. A member of the Wagin Native Welfare Committee explained to the paper that: 'If there is any segregation it is purely because of a need for hygiene'. This 'hygiene bar' was the explanation given by the local cafe owner for refusing entry of Aborigines into her shop. Complaints about abuse of alcohol were also widespread among whites, in particular the frequent sight of Aborigines found drunk in the streets.

Such complaints must be placed in their broader context. Whites were caught in an ongoing and vicious cycle of prejudice. The poor living conditions imposed on Aborigines fuelled the stereotypes which prevented them achieving social acceptance. Some whites could see the process at work. They could acknowledge the causes of the degradation but, seemingly, not to the point of incorporating this understanding into their social attitudes. Social conditions for Aborigines had barely changed in half a century. Maintenance of hygiene was difficult on the reserves and probably impossible in the worst of the 'humpy' tents: 'The humpy has no electricity or cooking area and has an earthen floor covered mostly with ants', reported the *Sunday Times* about one such structure on the Wagin Reserve. This was home to a family of ten including six school children. It had only four makeshift beds for the entire family. The occupant 'said she had been refused a house by the Native Welfare Department because she did not have a priority.' No action was taken by the local health inspector to condemn any of the humpies on the reserve because 'only Native Welfare Officers are allowed in the area'.[33]

Drunkenness had obvious wider causes. Apart from a desire for escapism, legal restrictions meant that alcohol had to be consumed before returning to the reserve or Aborigines faced the risk of prosecution. The Wagin publican knew it was 'a vicious circle that causes so many of them to be found drunk in the streets.' Another publican confirmed that: 'The native has little incentive generally. If he is not working he should be employed by the Native Welfare at the reserve instead of roaming the streets and collecting rations and social service.'

Wagin was by no means an isolated example of poor

race relations. Gnowangerup earned the reputation during the 1960s as an 'Aboriginal-hating town' with attitudes equivalent to those in the American Deep South.[34] Aboriginal opposition to the segregation of the town along racial lines erupted in 1963 when the Superintendent of the South Division of the Department of Native Affairs was called upon to investigate discrimination against Aborigines at the local cinema. It had only been several years since they were admitted at all and, under the prevailing arrangement, a separate block of seats was set aside for Aborigines even though the proprietor had the right to refuse entry to any person not suitably attired. In other words, even those Aborigines who were thought respectable enough to admit to the cinema, were still forced to sit in seats reserved for them only.[35] One of the local service stations refused to serve Aboriginal customers, a practice challenged by one Aboriginal family returning from holiday in Albany in 1972. Driving a 1967 Ford Fairlane and towing a 'fashionable' caravan, the family was told by the owners when they entered the restaurant that 'they did not serve Aborigines in the restaurant.'[36] Geraldton was another town where discrimination was widely practiced. A local firm of furniture retailers had 'a blanket refusal to assist Aborigines with finance irrespective of favourable credit rating.'[37]

The treatment accorded Aborigines in country towns in the early 1960s and 70s was a reflection of wider racially intolerant views. The 'No' vote in the 1967 Aborigines referendum was higher in Western Australia than in any other State: 17 percent in urban areas and 22 percent in rural areas. This contrasted with 12 and 17 percent respectively in South Australia and 7 and 14 percent in Queensland — two other states with high percentages of Aboriginal people living in them.[38] 'A feature of the Western Australian vote', commented the *West Australian* straight after the result was known, 'was the strong 'No' vote in the Federal electoral divisions of Kalgoorlie, Canning and Moore, where the number of Aborigines is higher than in other divisions.'[39] This reluctance to concede the basics of citizenship to Aborigines, in the rural areas especially, indicates the remaining depth of racial antipathy.

The experience of decades of segregation had left its legacy. In the late 1960s a deep racial divide continued to separate most whites from Aborigines, each living in isolation from the other. This was clearly manifest in those few institutions where the two groups unavoidably came together. Schools in the late 1960s saw the entry of larger number of Aboriginal children but this was not accompanied by any breakdown in social barriers. Robert McKeich, a sociology lecturer and former state school teacher in Western Australia, studied the social interaction between Aboriginal students and staff. He found that the school environment failed to put the students at ease and that they were subject to constant teacher reprimands. This was not only a significant cause of school failure among the group, it perpetuated and reinforced their social isolation. Aboriginal students preferred their own company and tended to segregate themselves. Teachers, on the other hand, McKeich found, were ignorant of basic background information on Aboriginal students. 'They tend to play part-Aboriginal educational problems 'by ear', develop stereotyped reasons for retardation, and, with few exceptions, eventually give up any real endeavour to help these children.'[40]

Prisons also formalised racial barriers to social integration. A 1969 study found that Aboriginal inmates employed 'mechanisms of exclusion and segregation'. They placed an emphasis on their Aboriginality to strengthen group boundaries using Aboriginal 'dialect' to swear at prison officers and to exclude other prisoners from conversations. 'On the sports field,' the study found, 'or in other spheres of recreation, Aborigines tend to participate as a group, usually against 'white' prisoners.' This 'closing of the ranks' frustrated prison staff who regarded the 'Aboriginal problem' as an insoluble one. Consequently, 'the staff are accused of apathy and lack of interest in Aboriginal welfare.'[41]

Such barriers were the inevitable result of the racially inspired policies of segregation. They hid even more overtly hostile attitudes which, from time to time, surfaced in public debate. An astonishing outburst of racism was published in a 1971 edition of Western Australia's *Local Government Journal* calling for full racial segregation in Australia. While the journal was a private publication, and not affiliated with the Local Government Association, it was a long-standing publication disseminating much of the news about local government throughout the State. The author of the article, Mr R Hewitt, who had been editor of the journal for thirteen years, evoked the views officially held a generation earlier. It was impossible, he argued, to:

> reconcile the totally different national characteristics of the Nordic-type whites and the aboriginal blacks, you still have the danger of miscegenation, with blacks married to white bringing grey children into the nation, or, worse, a flood of illegitimates of indeterminate colour … The aborigines are being urged to adopt the white man's ways and to live in the white man's houses. But the white people resent it.

Hewitt went on to call for the introduction of apartheid, along South African lines.

Whether the South African system will work in this country, or will even be considered in light of the prejudice that has been fanned up against it, is hard to say, but the idea is worth studying as it represents an alternative to the present method of trying to make the black mind grasp the essentials of white man's living.[42]

Interviewed by the press after the publication of the article Hewitt declared: 'why not give the blacks a tract of country and let them rule themselves. We can select some leaders from among them to guide their development and destiny.'

It is easy to dismiss Hewitt's comments as an isolated outburst from a racial extremist. Just how much support his call for apartheid would have received in the early 1970s is impossible to estimate. However, it should be remembered that the majority of Western Australians had grown up with segregation in the form of the Reserve system for which strong support still existed in the community, especially in country areas. There were places where this system was not all that far removed from apartheid.

The nature and extent of racism towards Aborigines became the subject of academic interest in the early 1970s. Explaining the nature of racist attitudes was the focus of Ronald Taft's 1970 study of 'Attitudes of Western Australians towards Aborigines.'[43] This was a groundbreaking study, providing the first comprehensive picture of racism and its extent, in the State. Reviewing data from opinion polls undertaken in 1954 and 1961, Taft showed that 'States with the largest Aboriginal population had the least favourable attitudes towards spending of more money on Aborigines.' In his own study, Taft conducted in-depth interviews with 286 people in three different settings in Western Australia: a provincial city of 5,000 people with a bad record of racial conflict; a provincial town of 1,500 people and the city of Perth. Colour prejudice was found to play a significant part in overall attitudes towards Aborigines. While extreme racial prejudice was reported to be limited to six percent, or less, of the population, about one-quarter of the respondents would not accept a part-Aborigine as a family friend and one-fifth would not accept one as a table companion in a cafe.

At one level the results were positive, suggesting that 'the trend is for increased feelings of tolerance for Aborigines and greater advocacy of their civil rights'. However, the underlying image held of Aborigines remained unfavourable, particularly in the provincial city and the town featured in the study. Among the examples given were the following:

Smalltown male, aged 50–59 years, brought up in Smalltown. He has had a great deal of contact with Aborigines, having played with them as a child, worked with them and employed them. He has a very unfavourable image of Aborigines and strongly favours their segregation. He reached 7th grade at school and is now a truck driver. He would admit neither part-Aborigines nor full-bloods to any single category of social distance.

Bigtown male, aged 50–59 years, brought up in a Western Australian country town, and has had ten years of education. He has had Aborigines as customers for many years in his capacity as a publican and has an extremely unfavourable image of them ... he favours their segregation from Whites in several spheres of life.

Bigtown female aged 20–29 years. She has had a great deal of contact with Aborigines as customers in the shop where she works. She came from a farm where Aborigines were employed ... she has an unfavourable image of Aborigines in general ... It seems as if her various life experiences have left her with some very specific attitudes in general.

Taft's conclusions were significant and clear cut. Attitudes towards Aborigines were unfavourable, the most frequently mentioned qualities attributed to them being: wasteful with money, unambitious, lazy, dirty and slovenly, drunken, unreliable, and superstitious. These attitudes were held despite widespread support in favour of granting them civil rights. Taft found the driving force behind attitudes towards Aborigines was the extent to which a person had been subject to an unfavourable socially accepted stereotype about them and whether this image was accepted or rejected.

If he lives in Bigtown he will be continually subjected to an unfavourable stereotype and this will dominate his attitudes unless his own personal experience counteracts it. If he lives in the more favourable environment of Perth or Smalltown, it is likely that his image of the Aborigines is less subject to immediate environmental pressures, and is more closely related to his experience.

Stereotypical attitudes towards blacks very frequently translated into overt discrimination which young

Aborigines, coming out of the missions, faced along with all others. In 1971 Professor Leonard Broome, an American sociologist visiting the Australian National University, made a systematic study of census data which gave 'the first true indication of the hopelessness of the Aborigines' employment prospects in a climate of economic and educational black poverty.' The figures showed only two percent of Aboriginal workers occupied the top seven occupation groups. In the press the study was reported as 'nothing less than an indictment of practicing racism.' Professor Broome told the media that 'Australia has run Aboriginal "welfare" on the cheap and it has got what it paid for'.[44]

A unique study into discrimination towards Aborigines was undertaken in 1972. This was sponsored by the Public Interest Research Group and involved the deployment of sixty students from the University of Western Australia's Law School to visit thirteen country towns in the South-West to interview key people in the white community as well as selected Aborigines.[45] The Report documented the attitude and actions of each of the main sections of white population. It showed an interconnected web of discrimination and negative attitudes blocking acceptance and advancement of Aborigines.

Shire councils came in for harsh criticism from the Research Group. While Aborigines were permitted to use shire facilities, 'natives were under closer scrutiny than whites' when using them, even though 'on the whole they did not abuse them.' However,

> With one exception, the Shire Councils in the towns that were visited, had contributed little or nothing towards helping Aborigines. The individuals on the Council interviewed mirrored this action by

generally displaying either apathy or antipathy towards Aborigines.

Police in country towns came into frequent and close contact with Aborigines and exercised a controlling influence over their activities. In some of the towns visited by the law students police refused to answer all the questions asked, claiming the information was classified. In other towns cooperation was more forthcoming. This attitude was a reflection of the town's broader relationship with the Aboriginal population. In towns which enjoyed relatively good Aboriginal living conditions and little racial discord, police were more tolerant than in towns where these conditions were not met. At much the same time as this study, the State Labor Government expressed its concern about relations between police and Aborigines. Allegations of plainclothes police 'creating fear in Aborigines by badgering them', were made at a public forum by Mr Arthur Tonkin, a Member of the Legislative Assembly.[46]

The Public Interest Research Group also showed Aborigines were grossly over-represented in the prosecution rates in country towns. These varied from as high as ninety percent of all prosecutions to as low as about one half, but in no cases were there fewer prosecutions than against whites. The proportion of successful prosecutions was even higher, 'since there was almost 100% success rate for Aboriginal prosecutions in every town'. These shocking figures seem to indicate the magistracy itself practiced discrimination. In a few of the towns visited, magistrates were interviewed. They 'seemed to have either a patronising or even prejudicial attitude against Aborigines.' Problems with the relations between the magistracy and the Aboriginal community were raised in a separate forum. In 1969, Carnarvon's stipendiary magistrate told a conference of Justices of the Peace that such was the prejudice against Aborigines among magistrates in the north of the State that those who knew themselves to be prejudiced should disqualify themselves from sitting on cases involving Aborigines.[47]

In their visits to schools, the Public Interest Research Group found relations between whites and Aborigines to be a complex mix of partial acceptance and underlying discrimination. On the positive side, Aboriginal children were well integrated into school life and played an active part in school activities, especially sport. However, Aborigines usually formed their own sub-groups within each school. Teachers were generally less negative about Aborigines than much of the general population, but few took any active role in helping them. Most of the Aboriginal children left school at the minimum leaving age of fifteen and most often before qualifying for their Junior Certificate. 'Not one instance was given of an Aborigine in one of the schools that was visited being educated beyond this standard.'

Both country doctors and priests were found to vary widely in their attitudes towards Aborigines. In some cases they showed genuine interest in Aborigines while others avoided contact. Some doctors in particular, 'seemed to have opted out of trying to alleviate the problem [of poor health] and had become almost totally apathetic towards them.' In a few cases doctors had developed very negative attitudes, referring to Aborigines as 'the lowest scum of the earth':

We were told that a doctor in one town had declined to treat two native children on the grounds that they did not require it, but that when taken to another doctor, they were immediately hospitalised. Other similar allegations were also received.

Similarly, priests 'tended to be either patronising or apathetic' or both, in their relationships with Aborigines. In most towns where there was two priests; 'only one of them usually had much to do with the Aborigines'. However, the practical support offered by priests could be crucial in assisting Aborigines to negotiate the welfare and legal systems.

The picture of discrimination towards Aborigines painted by the Public Interest Research Group, together with the studies carried out by academics, is indeed grim. However, one area ignored by all commentators was the prison system. In 1966 prisoners at Fremantle prison complained to the Native Welfare Department that a system of segregation was in place at the prison. 'Why can't Native Welfare stop this segregation in gaol', the prisoners complained:

> Because of segregation the yard is a breeding ground for trouble, and because of this also a Native seldom in a lifetime gets to have a proper sensible conversation with a white man. Assimilation could well begin in prison ... as well as gleaning news from white men, Natives might also gain a clue or two on how to speak and express themselves better.

These comments show a strong desire on the part of the Aboriginal prisoners for racial harmony. It is extraordinary that they could be expressed in such a demanding environment and amid overt discrimination. Among their complaints, Aboriginal prisoners highlighted the fact that they had no supervisors in their yards, a situation which led to the outbreak of fights. They protested the overcrowding in cells for Aborigines.[48] Complaints surfaced again in 1972 when five Aboriginal prisoners in Fremantle gaol signed a statutory declaration alleging racial intolerance and discrimination. 'In the declarations the prisoners tell of fights between whites and Aborigines and say that warders have made it possible for whites to bash Aborigines.'[49]

It had become fashionable to explain the social degradation suffered by most Aborigines as a 'culture of poverty'. This was an American-inspired concept to explain persistent and unrelieved poverty among disadvantaged groups. As Schapper argued in his influential book:

> This is not the poverty of merely being without adequate income. It is way-of-life poverty. Aborigines are born into it, reared in it, and remain in it. They are psychologically attuned to it and are probably reasonably content in it. Their poverty is inherited and self-perpetuating.[51]

There is no evidence that these assertions are accurate ones. In fact, when people bothered to listen to Aborigines, the desire for better housing and opportunities for their children was widely heard. Some had achieved these conditions and were held up as examples of assimilation being achievable.

In 1970 Henry Schapper surveyed the current conditions of Aborigines and noted five major problem areas. Most Aborigines appeared to suffer from emotional depression; they did not understand the meaning of school experience; children were socially isolated and many adults had not developed the values of responsibility or dependability. Consequently, family failure was common. His concluding comment reads almost as a throwaway line: 'Many children are institutionalised and without appropriate models for stable family formation.'[53] While the difficulties Schapper identified were the result of complex processes of colonisation, the impact of removing children from their families was the common thread connecting all of them. By the 1960s two generations of families had been removed, as Trish Hill-Keddie's family story outlined at the beginning of this book shows.

By the 1970s new thinking about the Aboriginal 'problem' was exercising the minds of officials. The 1974 Royal Commission highlighted the destructiveness of assimilation. It acknowledged that the religious convictions of missionaries broke down traditional Aboriginal culture. It stated there was no satisfactory replacement for Aborigines in Christianity, and it affirmed the role missions had played in destroying the Aboriginal family. When it came to the policy of removing children from their families, one brief but pointed acknowledgement was made. The practice was, the Commission wrote, 'the result of policies designed to weaken the race'.[54] It was a legacy of almost unbelievable social tragedy but the full realisation of its impact had not yet begun.

6

Living with the Aftermath

In an outer suburb of Perth a group of Aboriginal men and women, all in their fifties and early sixties, meets occasionally to provide mutual support. They have been united in the common bond of friendship, having together experienced Roelands Mission as stolen children. Few Australians would be aware of the emotional intensity of such gatherings. Forty years after emerging from this institution their anguish remains unresolved and some are unable to recall parts of their experience without breaking into tears. When one succumbs to quiet sobbing, others are drawn in to provide close physical comfort. They have never forgotten their experiences and the despair of 'crying for home.' In the course of researching this book we spent some time with members of the Roelands Mission group. The years they have spent caring about each other has an inspiring quality except it is all too clear that the bonds they have forged are those of survivors of a shocking personal tragedy.

The struggles of people like the ex-Roelands inmates show that the vision of the assimilationists was largely realised. These people have lost much of their Aboriginal heritage but few have been able to compete equally with whites for jobs and lifestyle. In significant ways they have been disempowered.

As soon as they take you from your family the indoctrination begins. Those in control of you, white foster parents, schools, the welfare all set out to crush and demoralise you, they try to change you, to whitewash you and force you to fit into a world that is alien to you. It's interesting because they don't try to make you fit into relationships, they always let you know that you don't belong, you remain on the fringes of the 'family' pretty much all your life. This total disregard for your humanity and your identity is part of the 'assimilation' process. They dehumanise you by denying you the right to be who you really are.

This instills in you a deep level of resentment in regard to your Aboriginality and towards those who 'failed' to protect you. People often say to me: 'You might not have been where you are today if you had been left with your parents'. What they are saying is that I would be nothing without my 'white' upbringing, that I'm worthless and doomed to failure as an Aborigine. This is such an insult to me.

What people fail to recognise is that this is the kind of thinking that formed the racial stereotyping that created the policies that took us from our families in the first place. They still say it was 'for our own good'. How can anyone justify taking small children away from families who love them? The best intentions in the world can never compensate me for the pain and loss that I have experienced and continue to experience. We all have a right to our Identity, it's something that most white people take for granted. For more than thirty years I didn't have this basic right and that will always continue to cause me great anguish.

Acknowledging the damage and the hurt inflicted on the stolen generations has only recently begun in Australia. Unresolved grief and psychological dysfunction still plague the Aboriginal community. Many have died early and untimely deaths resulting from the underlying problems associated with their forced removal from their families. Others have undertaken journeys of personal healing and have managed to move their lives on. Yet, a great many have never recovered. An altogether separate group claim to have mostly fond memories of their time in missions and claim not to have been adversely affected by the experience. Generalising is therefore difficult. However, all the evidence suggests that a great many — perhaps most — of the stolen generations have experienced a range of emotional, social and psychiatric problems.

The various dysfunctions associated with the after-effects of forced separation have been summed up in a Canadian Report into the removal of its native children as 'the inner despair of individuals'.[1] In fact, the Aboriginal Legal Service in Western Australia argues that the great hurt suffered by the stolen children is a significant factor in the over representation of Aboriginal people in the justice system; physical, mental and emotional health problems; domestic violence; welfare dependency; substance and alcohol abuse; the breakdown of traditional family structures; a loss of cultural and spiritual identity; and the loss of individual self-esteem, security and happiness.[2] In other words, an almost limitless toll of human misery, most of which is ongoing, and untreated. Much of the mental distress is 'acted out' in antisocial ways but the underlying grief has not generally been recognised.[3]

While there are difficulties associated with disentangling the effects of removal and institutionalisation from the wider causes of mental illness among Aboriginal people, research has highlighted the central role played by separation and institutionalisation.[4] The 1991 New South Wales Aboriginal Mental Health Report gathered information on 1501 consecutive adult patients visiting the Redfern and Taree Aboriginal Medical Services; 25 percent of these patients were diagnosed as having a mental health problem. There was 'a very strong association between a history of childhood disruption, employment difficulties in adult life, and having a mental health problem.'[5] Similar conclusions were reached in a 1992 Victorian study of psychological distress among urban Aboriginal people visiting the Melbourne branch of the Aboriginal Medical Service. Of the 112 individuals selected at random, over fifty percent were found to have the likelihood of a psychiatric disorder. Childhood experiences were assessed. It was found that many respondents had been separated from their families for significant periods before the age of fourteen years, with forty-nine percent being separated from both parents and nineteen percent from one. Twenty percent had been brought up in children's homes and ten percent adopted or fostered by non-Aboriginal parents. Conversely, 'a significantly lower proportion of respondents who grew up with their Aboriginal families, who learned their Aboriginal identity early in life, and who regularly visited their traditional country, were psychologically distressed'.[6]

The Aboriginal Legal Service in Western Australia has attempted to document the ongoing impact of separation and institutionalisation in a recent questionnaire given to 483 individuals who suffered separation from their families. While the results of the study are revealing, caution is needed in interpreting them in light of the high non-response rate (up to one-third) to many of the sensitive questions, indicating the possibility that many did not want to present as someone who had experienced ongoing problems in their lives. However, almost a quarter stated they had physical problems and fourteen percent stated mental problems. About one-fifth reported they had abused substances while sixty-two percent were currently unemployed.[7]

Surviving this traumatic ordeal in childhood has very often involved years of painful struggle. The experience of Trish Hill-Keddie is illustrative: 'There was a time when I wanted to go and neck myself, because it was all too hard. I got to rock bottom, a feeling of absolute hopelessness.'

How are such crisis points reached? The simplest and clearest explanation for the social and emotional pain among the stolen generations is the concept of trauma. There needs to be recognition that these are a traumatised people. Trauma is an overwhelming experience of terror and helplessness. It is an 'affliction of the powerless'.[8] It can seep into the personality, affecting personal development. Severe or repeated trauma is not easily dislodged. As Trish Hill-Keddie explained: 'The experience of removal never leaves you. No matter how hard you try or how many times you talk about it, you always remember something different, something triggers up your memory.' For some, the intensity of their emotional pain remained with them throughout adulthood. Frank Gare still remembers a forty year old Geraldton woman who had been taken away as a child. In the 1960s, she was a happily married, educated woman approaching mid-life. However, from time to time she 'got drunk and would wander around weeping and wailing, crying for her mother.'[9]

According to one prominent psychiatrist, the symptoms and behaviour of stolen children are similar to those of holocaust victims.[10] This comparison is unpalatable to some Australians. The scale and horror of the Nazi crimes against the Jews and the Gypsies — and the central fact of physical extermination — should not diminish the similarities with Australia's policy to assimilate Aboriginal children. These were all races victimised by the belief in racial superiority. The Jews, the Gypsies and the Aborigines all had many family members forcibly torn from their communities and isolated from the outside world. Among each group are survivors left to pick up the pieces when social and political circumstances changed.

The children caught up in the Holocaust form the most direct parallel with Aboriginal children living under assimilation. They, too, suffered abrupt, and often permanent separation from parents and families. Important insights into the impact of their sudden loss of family can be found in recent studies among the adult survivors. These show that the moment of separation is one of the 'most powerful, and in many instances still psychologically unresolved' events in their lives.[11] Moreover, it exists at a very deep level, 'perhaps the most difficult trauma to cure.'[12] Common knowledge about childhood tells us that children who have the opportunity to make strong bonds with their parents have the best chance to grow into well-adjusted adults while those who do not are more likely to experience mental health problems. As Haas explains in relation to the children caught up in the Holocaust: 'When we lose a loved one, we lose a part of ourselves. When so much of the self is removed at once, a disorientation ensues, an emotional paralysis follows.'[13]

The moment of separation was the first, and possibly deepest, trauma many of the stolen generations suffered. As Phillip Prosser reflects on his own experience of removal: 'It was traumatic as far as I was concerned because I was being torn away from my loving strong family environment.' He was being raised by his grandparents; his mother having died and his father working in the North-West. They lived in a three-bedroom house with a well-kept garden and picket fence at the front and vegetable garden and fruit trees at the back. A request by his grandmother to adopt him was turned down by Native Affairs. Consequently, 'I was torn from an environment that was the equivalent or better than the environment I was transported into.'[14]

Trauma was an inevitable accompaniment to removal because, as the Human Rights inquiry extensively documented, 'invariably they were traumatically carried out with force, lies, regimentation and an absence of comfort and affection.'[15] For many, the trauma of their separation generated ongoing feelings of insecurity. Why had parents allowed this to happen? Would they visit? One woman explained to the Aboriginal Legal Service: 'During my whole time at the mission [Forrest River] I used to wonder about my mother and family. I missed them terribly and used to cry a lot for them. I thought they had forgotten me.'[16]

While the trauma of removal embedded itself in many of its childhood victims, their subsequent experiences in institutions and foster homes added new layers of emotional distress. 'Trauma compounded trauma', the Human Rights inquiry confirmed. Studies on the importance of attachment theory, in the wake of John Bowlby's pioneering work in the early 1950s, show institutionalised children were typically not provided with a replacement caregiver with whom they could form a loving relationship. As one woman reflected to the Human Rights inquiry about her time in Sister Kate's in the late 1940s: 'we were brought up in various stages by various house mothers — who were usually English ladies who were not really interested in us.'[17]

The ongoing symptoms of trauma suffered by the stolen generations should come as no surprise in light of longstanding studies which show that childhood is a particularly vulnerable time in which to be exposed to emotional distress. Wolff believes that, on their own, children cannot master their anxieties.[18] Fears about personal safety or impending danger cannot be dispelled because of the child's limited capacity to reason what is going on in any situation. In the presence of a mother and/or father, the child naturally leaves this function to them: 'he trusts them to put things right.' Of course, Aboriginal children stolen from their parents had no such comforts.

In very many cases repeated trauma was compounded by the isolation of many of the institutions and by the lax supervision exercised by the Departments of Native and Child Welfare. So cut off were many of these children that they existed in a state of virtual captivity. From a psychological perspective, a state of captivity exists where there are barriers to 'escape' and where there is 'despotic control over every aspect of the victim's life'.[19] A state of captivity is also associated with fear, coercive control, capricious attempts to enforce rules, the need for absolute compliance and attempts to reshape an individual. Many of the personal testimonies provided to the Aboriginal Legal Service in their survey of the stolen generations bear witness to children's realisation that they were being confined against their will. Memories of missions 'being like a prison', of being confined without the freedoms of normal children; of not being able even to go down to the local shop, are commonplace.[20] Confining children in such a manner increases the chance of trauma. One ex-inmate, for example, remembers the practice at the United Mission of locking children in at night so they couldn't leave: 'Even now I find it distressing to be in a closed environment.'[21]

Institutional life provided the conditions for repeated trauma. Many children were both witnesses to, and victims of, unconscionable acts of abuse and cruelty. The following testimony given to the Aboriginal Legal Service of life in Roelands Mission is illustrative:

> there was a lot of cruelty by the missionaries. I used to hate seeing other children belted by the mission-aries. I hated any form of cruelty. I felt so frustrated that there was nothing I could do to stop it. We mission kids had to hold in our feelings, if we didn't we would suffer from physical abuse ... When I was about six years of age I experienced sexual abuse at Gnowangerup Mission. One missionary tried to penetrate me but he was unsuccessful. However he did play around with my genitals. This still affects me very much today. I am trying as much as possible to block it out.[22]

The struggle to repress, to 'block out' the intrusive

memories of a traumatic experience is widely associated with people who have suffered deep emotional distress. It is a key finding in studies of Holocaust survivors. Interviews with these survivors showed that 'memories involuntarily intrude with even great frequency in recent years'.[23]

The uncertainty and unpredictability of parents' visits was another cause of emotional distress. The very purpose of the institutional experience was to cut children off from their Aboriginal families. However, some institutions allowed infrequent contact between children and their parents, contact which was often made very difficult by the distances frequently separating parents from the missions. For children, not used to seeing their parents, visits could be traumatic. One woman told the Aboriginal Legal Service:

> The most enduring memory that still causes so much pain for me is the time I saw my mum once while I was in the orphanage and I wanted to go out and see her but one of the nuns was holding me back. I wanted to go with my mother ... My mother was crying and I was being held back by the nun. The image on my mother's face sticks vividly in my mind and it is very upsetting — it still causes me much grief and sorrow. When I think about it I still cry a lot.[24]

The deepest scars were on those subjected to abuse. As we have seen in previous chapters, the scale and extent of physical abuse was often extreme. In such cases, it has left lasting psychological damage.

In about 1990, when I was about twenty-one years

old, I began having occasional memory flashbacks of the incidents from my life at the Smiths [the foster family], in particular, some of the beatings I used to receive. Some of the memories of events in the past were like looking at myself being hit. These experiences were very frightening.[25]

A woman told how in 1960 when she was five years old she was taken away with six brothers and sisters from their parents who lived in Narrogin. Carol was placed in Sister Kate's Children's Home which she described as 'a horrible nightmare'. Not only was she frequently hit for crying about her mother and father, for three years she was subject to regular sexual abuse by the sons of cottage parents running the home. She told the Aboriginal Legal Service she 'is still deeply traumatised' by the experience of being forced to 'sit on the laps' of cottage boys from where they would 'finger' her 'private parts' and also 'penetrate her with their penis'. The long-term impact of this experience has been severe. Carol feels 'confused', and 'used' and suffers from low self-esteem and a hatred of life; every day she 'cries about the pain and suffering of her childhood.'[26]

Sexual abuse of mission children also occurred when they were sent to work or live with foster families. One account given to the Human Rights inquiry is revealing about the social attitudes to children who made complaints about such ill-treatment:

While I was in first year high school I was sent out to work on a farm as a domestic. I thought it would be great to get away from the home [Sister Kate's] for a while. At first it was. I was made welcome and treated with kindness. The four shillings I was paid went to the home. I wasn't allowed to keep it, I didn't care ... The first time I was sent to the farm for only a few weeks and then back to school. In the next holidays I had to go back. This time it was a terrifying experience, the man of the house used to come into my room at night and force me to have sex. I tried to fight him off but he was too strong. When I returned home I was feeling so used and unwanted. I went to the matron and told her what had happened. She washed my mouth out with soap and boxed my ears and told me that awful things would happen to me if I told any of the other kids. I was so scared and wanted to die. When the next school holidays came I begged not to be sent to that farm again. But they would not listen and said I had to.[27]

It is impossible to tell how widespread such terrible experiences were for Aboriginal children in missions or foster homes. From the testimonies collected for this book, and from those given to the Aboriginal Legal Service and the Human Rights inquiry, it is clear sexual abuse was a disturbingly common experience. There is extensive literature now available explaining the legacy of such abuse, especially the sense of personal struggle victims often face:

Many abused children cling to the hope that growing up will bring escape and freedom. But the personality formed in an environment of coercive control is not well adapted to adult life. The survivor is left with fundamental problems in basic trust, autonomy, and initiative. She approaches the task of early adulthood — establishing independence and intimacy — burdened by major impairments in self-care, in cognition and memory, in identity, and in the capacity to form stable relationships. She is still a prisoner of her childhood; attempting to create a new life, she re-encounters the trauma.[28]

According to Alice Miller, an expert on child psychology, 'it is not the traumas we suffer in childhood which make us emotionally ill but the inability to express trauma.'[29] She says children prevented from expressing pain and anger will learn to be silent and it is in this silence that lie the seeds of future psychological problems. This perspective may help explain the extent of the severity of psychological problems which many of the stolen generations continue to experience, as well as point positively to the role appropriate counselling services can provide.

If trauma represents the thread running through many children's experience of institutionalisation it also comes with other, identifiable effects. Prominent among these is the legacy of identity confusion. This is not surprising given that the explicit aim of assimilating these children was to provide them with a new cultural identity. To this end, their Aboriginal identity was widely, and often cruelly, denied. One of the common recollections of the stolen generations is the length to which missionaries and foster-parents went to denigrate their Aboriginal heritage and to forbid any practice of it. The attitude of these people was frequently motivated by more than belief in the superior virtues of white civilisation; there was a corresponding contempt for anything Aboriginal.

Racial identity is a large component in the development of personal identity which, in turn, leads to feelings of self-esteem and confidence. This natural path of development was broken for the stolen generations. Not only did they endure the heightened anxiety of being separated from their parents, the transracial experience of being placed in an institution, or fostered out, created widespread confusion over the fundamental issue of identity. Of course, the institutions were designed to effect cultural transformation. The regimented, doctrinaire, and harsh routine adopted by missions were calculated to ensure that some of their objectives were achieved.

Little research has been carried out in this area of identity confusion among Australia's stolen generations. However, there is substantial evidence of identity confusion from psychiatric work conducted among Native Americans who suffered similar experiences. These people, particularly in their adolescence, 'had higher suicidal tendencies; had trouble forming intimate relationships; had trouble with violence, theft, truancy, and substance abuse and developed a mistrust of other Indian people.'[30] Similarly, Aborigines taken from their families and institutionalised in a culturally alien environment report the effects as akin to profoundly fragmenting their sense of identity: 'That has an impact on people's sense of who they are, how you fit into the world and where you're going — what in technical terms people call your sense of coherence.'[31] As the Aboriginal Legal Service has explained:

> The Aboriginal person who is brought up with non-Aboriginal values and without any reinforcement or recognition of their Aboriginality may suffer an identity crisis when faced with non-Aboriginal attitudes in the outside world, where racist attitudes are prevalent. They may be spurned and rejected because they are Aboriginal yet have

values and expectations that set them apart from Aboriginal people. Thus they feel they don't belong anywhere.[32]

Frequently, stolen children told the Aboriginal Legal Service that 'a big problem with myself and other mission kids is that we feel we are in between a white society and an Aboriginal society and don't really fit in either.'[33] Even more directly, some pointed to an inability to feel comfortable living in either culture. One ex-Roelands inmate explained: 'Because I was taken away from my parents I really did not know who I was, where I was heading. I felt really lost. I felt no one cared.' Failure to develop self-esteem is a well-recognised component of mental health problems and is linked to behaviours such as depression and substance abuse. For Aboriginal children, few opportunities existed to develop self-esteem in foster homes, children's homes and missions. Commonly these children experienced being 'spoken down to' or denigrated because of their Aboriginality.

Problems over identity have only been compounded by the barriers in the way of reuniting with their families. For some, the barriers are language. Children taken from parts of the State where parents spoke Aboriginal languages as their primary mode of communication were unable to bridge the communication barrier. For others the difficulties are cultural; they feel assimilated into the white way and cannot rebond. There are others who cannot overcome the emotional bitterness and the feeling that their parents rejected them. Whatever the reason, the consequence for many is a loss of their Aboriginal heritage and the wider family connections this embraces.

In the 1940s and 50s knowledge of child psychology was in its infancy, though this lack of knowledge cannot justify the cruelty and abuse many stolen children received. However there is little evidence that institutionalised Aboriginal children benefited much from the greater understanding of children's needs that slowly spread in the post-war years. Right up until their closure in the early to mid 1970s, institutions continued to be run along the kind of strict and depersonalised lines which denied recognition of individual differences among children and failed to foster their sense of self-worth and competency. Such a regime may not have been experienced by all children in all the many institutions that looked after them, but it was sufficiently common for pertinent generalisations to be made.

The enforcement of strict and frequently coercive discipline, which we have described as commonplace in many of the missions, characterises them as autocratic institutions. As long ago as the early 1940s, a study on the effects of different kinds of group leadership identified three types: autocratic, democratic and laissez faire. The study showed how techniques of institutional organisation can have profound effects on children. Summing up the study Wolff writes:[34] 'It was found that groups of boys react either with submission or rebellion to an autocratic leader', and that children of such leadership display 'a lack of initiative and individuality, and of ... discontent.' While some caution is obviously needed in directly applying such findings to mission life, they do offer some compelling insights. Mostly, the missions were unconducive to the development of individual responsibility, social development and personal goals, as the accounts given by the Department of Child Welfare and discussed in Chapter Four amply demonstrate. A recollection by Frank Gare about life for children in New Norcia Mission emphasises this point: 'I remember going into the girls' dormitory once and seeing about forty toothbrushes all the same colour and all lined up at exactly the same angle in their small beakers. The place was regimented to the nth degree.'[35]

For many of the stolen generations, the lack of development of basic competencies persisted into their adult lives. One woman explained that when she left Roelands as a teenager she was too frightened to catch a bus. Others have spoken of the sense of helplessness they felt at sixteen when they typically left missions for the wider world. This could be a time of great confusion leading to early dependence on alcohol. Some were prone to involvement in crime and periods of imprisonment. In the Aboriginal Legal Service's survey of the stolen generations, twenty-five percent of respondents reported they had been imprisoned, although the non-response rate of more than thirty percent to this question indicates that this figure might be an understatement. The connection between a background of removal and the likelihood of imprisonment involves a range of causal factors — such as low levels of education and poor employment prospects — applying more generally to the Aboriginal community. However, a study of survey data on the circumstances of two groups of Aborigines — one which had experienced removal and one which had not — revealed higher levels of unemployment and poorer levels of education among those who had been removed. The authors of the study concluded that these poorer outcomes are 'a testimony to the total failure of child removal policies.'[36]

When the numbers of Aboriginal prisoners began its steady climb in the late 1960s, contemporaries searched for deeper causes. A connection was drawn between imprisonment and a mission background by Mike Robinson, an honours graduate in anthropology, whose work focused on the problem of law and Aborigines. In 1969 he wrote an article heavily influenced by Erving Goffman's book, *Asylums,* published in the early 1960s. Goffman had postulated the idea of the 'total institution' characterised by regimentation and restrictions on individual liberties. Drawing on this concept, Robinson noted that many Aborigines came to prison from a background in missions and/or reserves, the structure of which he likened to 'total institutions'. He concluded that many Aborigines were not deterred by the thought of prison. Because of their

> frequent involvement in other 'total institutions', Aborigines tend to develop a 'matter of fact' attitude towards imprisonment which does not make a prison term as catastrophic for them as it might be for others. Previous institutionalisation may enable the Aboriginal inmate to make a smoother adjustment to the prison environment, and this adjustment is aided by the presence of other Aborigines in the goal.[37]

How valid these conclusions are for the majority of Aborigines is open to question. Subsequent evidence of the rate of deaths of Aborigines in custody has revealed that many Aborigines with a background of removal from their parents find prison an unbearable experience: nearly half of those who have died in custody came from such a background. Equally disturbing are estimates showing the high rate at which Aborigines removed as children are imprisoned: at least half of those thirty years and older were removed as children, while an equal number below this age group have parents who were removed.[38]

Whatever the mix of factors predisposing Aborigines from the stolen generations to imprisonment, it represents the continuation of the vicious cycle of institutionalisation. As the Aboriginal Legal Service has commented:

> Because of the profound psychological effects of being removed and abused as a child, a person may commit offences as an adult and end up in prison. These prisoners have children too, but as a consequence of their imprisonment, the next generation of children are denied the love and care of a parent and the parent is denied the chance of bringing up his or her children.[39]

Family life can be disrupted by problems the stolen generations may experience in sustaining intimate relationships. Some find that they cannot settle down and form stable relationships because they do not want to get close to people. The difficulties in relating to people across a range of settings are well illustrated by Trish Hill-Keddie:

> I'm extremely protective of my own children. I don't trust a lot of people. I'm very outspoken simply because of the disempowerment at such an early age and I've had to re-gain that. I've had dysfunctional marriages and relationships. People say that you've just picked the wrong partners. It's nothing to do with that. I felt I could never keep a family together because that's what I've been taught; my family went in all directions. I didn't try very hard to keep things together because I thought

that is what you're supposed to do. The disempowerment was something that was very hard to grasp. It took a lot of years and a lot of hard work to stand on your own two feet.

Children who experienced repeated dislocations by spending time in foster families in between stints in institutions are particularly vulnerable to the inability to form continuous, stable relationships. Research around the world has identified the specific consequences stemming from repeated family disruptions. Each separation breaks attachments generating insecurity that impairs the ability to form future attachments. Later in life, the learned insecurity about forming attachments affects the development of love relationships.[40]

This loss of basic trust can affect their relationship with broader society. Difficulty in coping with authority after being brought up in an authoritarian institution is one manifestation. Some have linked this with their inability to hold down employment.[41] For others the experience of removal has hardened into a bitterness towards white society and white people. The feeling of being badly treated by white society extends into a lack of trust towards white institutions. Most obviously, there is a residual distrust against 'the welfare' as it is mostly closely associated with the policy of removal.[42] The historically bad relationships between police and the Aboriginal community in part stem from the role police officers played as 'protectors'; that is, agents of the Department of Native Affairs. Schools and teachers are also the focus of widespread distrust because of the policies of exclusion meted out to Aboriginal people.

Feelings of bitterness and resentment are not confined to the children who were taken. They are also found among the parents who suffered the pain of losing their children. The plight of these parents has been much over-looked even in the recent rush of interest and concern generated by the Human Rights inquiry and the publication of its Report *Bringing Them Home*. Most of the parents are now elderly or have passed on and, therefore, much will never be known about the effect of removal on their lives and their communities. It is clear that fear and anxiety were generated in Aboriginal communities by the policy of removal. Before their children were born many parents knew the fate that might await them. There are a number of stories of the elaborate measures that were taken by parents to protect any lighter-skinned children. The most common seems to have been darkening the skins of children with dust or charcoal in an effort to fool authorities that the children were 'full-blood' and, therefore, might be spared.

The effect on those parents who had their children removed could be devastating. Very often it resulted in a rapid emotional disintegration. The case of a Cue family who had their children removed in the 1960s illustrates the impact. The father was a railway worker with a steady job and the family lived in a modest miner's house. The parents were in the habit of spending their afternoons drinking in one of the local hotels. The regional Child Welfare officer believed something had to be done about the family because the children were missing a lot of school and because it was felt they were spending too much time playing around the streets outside the hotel waiting for their parents. Eventually the children were committed to Tardun Mission. 'That family fell apart straightaway', remembers Frank Gare who was familiar with the case. 'The fellow tossed in his job and became derelict. It just ruined the family.'[43] A cycle of despair, ill-health, heavy drinking and mental illness afflicted many such parents. 'In some instances', notes the Aboriginal Legal Service, 'the removal of children created a downward spiral of alcohol abuse. Other children were neglected and the relationship of parents broke under the strain.'[44] In other cases parents gave up hope; the removal of their children robbing them of the incentive to struggle against otherwise adverse conditions. It contributed to a sense of powerlessness within Aboriginal communities; there was nothing they could do to stop the 'welfare' taking their children in the face of the dominance of white power. The loss of so many of their children caused people 'to lose confidence in what they know and their own value as human beings.'[45] Thus, it further weakened and undermined the perpetuation of Aboriginal culture.

The struggles of many Aboriginal people who were taken away as children challenges one of the dominant views about Aborigines still held today: that the current generation of Australians bears no responsibility for the actions of past generations. The severing of past from present is rarely so neat. For many of the stolen generations past and present continue to be closely entwined. Trish Hill-Keddie expresses this connection:

> There are many issues that I must deal with today arising out of the forced removal from my family: The child within me remains frightened; I am unable to maintain a close relationship with one person and I still fear being abandoned. I know in time to come that I will not hide behind the door, for there will be no more strangers to frighten me. I have come such a long way since I was removed, yet I also know some of my issues will not be

resolved. They are ongoing. There are moments when I badly want normality, but what is normality? I know I have become a strong and empowered Aboriginal woman who is enormously proud of who she is today but, without the kindness, understanding, prompting and encouragement of many non-Indigenous people, I may not have reached this point.

As Trish so clearly conveys, there is an ongoing journey of self-discovery for many of the stolen generations. Finding their Aboriginal identity, resolving trauma, reuniting with family and dealing with sadness— these are daily responses to the painful legacy of assimilation. That so many manage to hold their lives together during this journey is testimony to their courage and strength.

7

THE INTER-GENERATIONAL EFFECTS

'We buried a girl the other day,' Phillip Prosser explained
to us in interview. She

> died from an overdose. Her brother was shot trying
> to escape from Canning Vale Prison. The mother of
> these two children spent her childhood in Roelands.
> If she had had parenting skills and counselling she
> would not have lost her two children in the way she
> did. If she'd had the knowledge to impart to her
> kids when they were growing up, things may well
> have been different.

The loss of these two children in such tragic circumstances may seem, at first sight, to be an extreme and
isolated case with which to illustrate the impact of
removal on the next generation. However, this mother's
difficulties are at one end of a continuum of parenting
problems linking the stolen generations with their
children.

Since the Second World War, two generations of
Aboriginal children have been raised into adulthood as
the offspring of the stolen generations. Children of a third

generation are still in their teenage years. In a great many cases these young people have experienced a range of emotional, behavioural and adjustment problems. Together they represent the ongoing legacy of assimilation. Its effects are felt in the difficulties parents face in raising their children and in the manner in which contemporary institutions replicate the experience of institutionalisation for Aboriginal children.

In many instances parents from the stolen generations have been unprepared for their role in raising children. As the Aboriginal Legal Service acknowledges: 'For many Aborigines, family and parenting skills have never had the opportunity to develop, the family environment being foreign to many of them.'[1] Understandably, this is a very sensitive issue to discuss. To cast judgement on parents in this way risks the unfair stereotyping of all Aborigines who are part of the stolen generations. Not all have experienced difficulties in raising their children. As evidence to the Human Rights inquiry acknowledged: 'despite all the odds and despite the pain ... [m]any parents from the stolen generations are very good parents. Some have been able to reconstruct their sense of self worth and commitment to their children.'[2] These are important acknowledgments, yet they do not alter the fact of the sad parenting experience arising from assimilation of a significant number of Aboriginal families. For this group, childhood experiences of removal and institutionalisation have had crippling effects on their ability to parent effectively. It is not surprising many of the stolen generations have experienced these problems. The same phenomenon has been noted in research among Holocaust victims. One writer noted: 'The price of survival for these people may have been deep rooted disturbances within the families they formed after liberation.'[3]

A range of possible factors have been identified linking removal with parenting difficulties. Most obviously, those who were institutionalised lacked a family model around which to develop understanding of the parenting role. It is within the family that children learn the skills essential to effective parenting. By removing the children, white society broke their link with Aboriginal child-rearing practices, and gave them no other family model. As evidence to the Human Rights inquiry noted, the stolen generations 'have not had a history of socialisation which includes processes of being nurtured, so that they have difficulty in sustaining and developing good constructive family relationships with their own children.'[4] Specifically, they were denied the basic affection accepted as necessary to the normal path of personality development. The personal stories of the stolen generations collected by the Aboriginal Legal Service in 1995 affirm this. Many told how they felt distant from their children, which limited the development of close intimate bonds and actual physical care.[5] Unresolved trauma, the lack of family role models and the effects of mission life all contributed to these problems.

The poor self-esteem common to the stolen generations has made some vulnerable to unplanned pregnancies, as parents they 'are often disorganised, impatient, capricious and ultimately demoralised, feeling unable to provide for their children what they missed out on'.[6] Allied to poor self-worth can be an inability to accept family responsibilities. A prominent Aboriginal community worker has observed: 'the missions have created a handout mentality which was totally foreign to our past society ... Those children, today's parents, have learned a dependency, preferring to pass on responsibility than to take charge of the situation.'[7]

The relationship between parenting styles and the experiences of removal remains a largely unexplored area, and generalisations are very hard to make, but it does appear from the interviews conducted for this book that some Aborigines, at least, have internalised the mission experience and expressed it in the way they parent their children. Some are extremely worrying and overprotective of their children. Others replicate the strict corporal discipline of missions. At the other extreme are parents who are compelled to avoid all forms of discipline because of their exposure at the hands of various missionaries. Still others struggle with unresolved trauma which hinders their ability to parent effectively. Unresolved destructive emotions can be passed from parent to child. As psychologist Alice Miller has written, if children exposed to trauma become parents 'they will then often direct acts of revenge for their mistreatment in childhood against their own children, whom they use as scapegoats.'[8] For these reasons, there is a crisis of parenting in sections of the Aboriginal community and a large unmet need for culturally appropriate programs in parenting skills.

Problems with parenting combined with ongoing poverty have made Aboriginal children, and especially those whose parents are from the stolen generations, vulnerable to being removed into substitute care or to incarceration for juvenile crime. These are new forms of institutionalisation that have become so pervasive in recent decades and the active support given to them by successive state governments are seen by Aboriginal people as mirroring the practices earlier generations endured. The strongest of Aboriginal misgivings are towards the juvenile justice system. This is not surprising.

The operation of this system evokes the powerlessness and injustice Aboriginal people suffered under assimilation. The number of children removed from their families by the justice system and the physical distance it frequently puts between them replicates what happened to Aboriginal people under earlier regimes. In fact, the removal of children under assimilation and by the justice system are the product of very similar social forces. Even though the justice system purports to be non-racial in its operation, its disproportionate application to Aboriginal children and families opens it to the criticism that it is a modern-day version of breaking up Aboriginal families and subjecting Aboriginal children to white control. Undoubtedly, the closest analogy between the two systems lies in the lived experience of the stolen generations who are very vulnerable to having their own children taken and locked away in detention. One mother told her story:

> Sean is my son. He is sixteen years of age. He is in gaol at the moment. He has been in and out of gaol since he was twelve years of age. He does not know how much it hurts me to see him locked up. He needs his family. I need him.
>
> When I go and visit him he tells me that he is very sorry for what he has done to me. He just cannot seem to help himself. He just cannot help getting into trouble with the cops.
>
> Sean has been in and out of gaol for a number of offences. He does not know what he really wants in life. It is very hard for him and for me, not having him around. I have to look after five children who are all younger than Sean. That has been very hard.
>
> What is even harder is the fact that Sean is away

from me. Things have not changed that much from when I was taken away from my parents and placed in a mission at Norseman. By the time I got out, my mum had died and I could not find my father. I think he had gone somewhere over east and from what I heard he hit the bottle pretty badly.

Sean's father had also been taken away from his parents. He had gone to Mogumber Mission. He left me when Sean was only two years of age. The other kids' father is another man who also left me now. Sean's dad just could not cope with his childhood. He was subjected to sexual abuse and made to work really hard.

No wonder Sean is the way he is. I and Sean's dad have had our own problems and I suppose they have rubbed off on Sean.

It really hurt me being taken away from our family and culture.[9]

There could be no more tragic illustration of the link between past and present. Both systems represent a form of legal discrimination against Aboriginal families and their children. Under assimilation this discrimination was often overt. In the case of juvenile justice, it is underlying, but none the less real.

Until the early 1980s, the 'welfare' model of juvenile crime gave great power to white welfare workers to incarcerate young people for antisocial behaviour. However, it did give some emphasis — often very misguided — to rehabilitation. The alternative to this system has been characterised as the 'justice' approach and was introduced in Western Australia in the latter part of the 1980s. This shift in policy from 'welfare' to 'justice' also involved a shift in the status of young people within the system:

from a 'vulnerable' group to one which has 'just deserts' coming to them.[10] The adoption of the 'justice' model has caused a skyrocketing in the number of young Aborigines removed from their families and incarcerated. Under this new approach, police officers became the 'gatekeepers' of the system. They make the initial decision on who is to be charged and with what crimes. In Western Australia, their power to make initial contact with any citizen has no legal limits. Arguably, this power has been used in a highly discriminatory fashion against Aboriginal youth. Partly, this has been a result of entrenched racism within sections of a police force with its historic roots in controlling the lives of Aboriginal people. Recent Australian Bureau of Statistics figures show that thirty-one percent of all Aborigines between fifteen and forty-four years report being arrested in the last five years, while sixty-two percent of this group report being arrested more than once.[11] This over-representation occurs in a police service which pays too little attention to cross-cultural training.

In addition to the cultural vacuum existing between police as gatekeepers and Aboriginal youth the justice system intervenes with its culturally ignorant legalism. Many Aboriginal youth coming before the Children's Court are culturally disadvantaged by its proceedings. It is an alien forum even to those living in urban areas. A Queensland study undertaken by Diana Eades, a sociolinguist specialising in Aboriginal issues, has presented unique insights into these cultural disadvantages. She studied the case involving three Brisbane police officers who faced charges of depriving the liberty of three Aboriginal teenage boys. These boys had been approached by the police officers in the inner city of Brisbane and instructed to get into the police car even though they had not been informed of any charges being laid against them. It was a spontaneous, cruel trick. The police took the youths fourteen kilometres away to an industrial wasteland, dumped them, and told them to find their own way home. It appeared a straightforward case of police harassment of Aboriginal youth, like much of which had gone unreported in the past. On this occasion, however, the youths pressed charges relating to deprivation of their liberty. Their case was dismissed by the magistrate but in such a way as to give rise to grave doubts about the justice of the proceedings.

Eades pointed to a range of ways in which the court process disadvantaged the boys. They spoke Aboriginal English, a recognised and distinct dialect. They also used other, non-verbal ways of Aboriginal communication. However, neither the magistrate nor the prosecutors were aware of these cultural differences. Eades found that, like other Aboriginal people who do not have bicultural skills necessary to participate successfully in interviews,

> the boys were culturally disadvantaged by the pressured and prolonged question–answer sessions. Repeated direct questions, especially in a situation where silence is not allowed as part of the answer, are not an effective means of eliciting information from many Aboriginal people.

This form of question can lead to what Eades defines as 'gratuitous concurrence'; a tendency to say 'Yes' to any question regardless of whether or not the person agrees with the question, or even understands it. This is 'a characteristic Aboriginal strategy for dealing with interviews, particularly in situations of serious power imbalance.' Other cultural differences ignored in the court proceedings included the misinterpretation of silence as a normal part of Aboriginal communication which, in this instance, was taken to mean 'No' as answers to questions. Further problems arose in the misinterpretation of the boy's disinclination to engage in direct eye contact. As Eades points out, in many Aboriginal societies throughout Australia, children learn it is disrespectful to make eye contact with an older person with whom they are speaking. However, the cross-examining counsel for the police officers:

> repeatedly insisted that one of the witnesses should look at him when answering questions. When this counsel suggested that the boy's refusal to look at him was because he was thinking that 'we'll see lies written all over your face', the court seemed totally unaware of the cultural issues involved, and again no objection was raised.[14]

In effect, the juvenile justice system perpetuates a form of legal discrimination similar to the one their parents found during the assimilation era. It is discrimination based on extreme social disadvantage, a gross imbalance of power and unacknowledged cultural differences. In such circumstances the whole notion of 'justice' blurs.

Although forming only 4 percent of the state's population, in August 1995, 61 percent of youth in police custody in Western Australia were Aboriginal, the second highest rate in Australia. One in five of these young people was fourteen years or younger and over 90 percent already had an arrest history.[13] The picture in detention centres is depressingly similar. In Western Australia, 57 percent of inmates were Aboriginal. The degree of over-representation is only fully revealed by a comparison with the number per one hundred thousand. For Aboriginal youth the detention rate is 734 youth per hundred thousand; for non-Aboriginal youth it is 23. The injustice inherent in the system is exposed by Michael Dodson, Aboriginal and Torres Strait Islander Social Justice Commissioner:

> In Western Australia, Aboriginal juveniles are 4.1 times more likely to be imprisoned, if convicted of a crime, than the next non-Aboriginal kid to stand in the same dock and get the same guilty verdict. The average number of charges per Aboriginal kid at each court appearance in Western Australia is 8.6, more than twice that per non-Aboriginal offender. It rises to 12.5 in metropolitan areas.[14]

At all levels of contacts with Aboriginal youth, the criminal justice system in Western Australia rates among the highest of any State. This, in itself, reflects discrimination in operation, as Michael Dodson has so pointedly explained:

> The differential likelihood of Aboriginal kids being held in detention in different jurisdictions is a direct reflection of the intensity of systemic discrimination in each jurisdiction. The greater the prejudice in the police force, the more aggressive the police tactics, the deeper the systemic discrimination in health, housing, education and employment, which shape 'neutral' discretionary decisions by the police and judiciary, the deeper the alienation and hostility felt by Indigenous youth, the deeper their despair and recklessness, all factors that conspire to inflate the negative, punitive results of the juvenile justice system.[15]

Dodson's reference to the police is worth emphasising in more detail. The wide powers and considerable discretion at their disposal is frequently used to target and harrass Aboriginal youth. Despite their renewed official anti-discrimination stance, police are not immune to the racism in the broader community. In fact, entrenched racism has a long history in sections of the Western Australian police force. Consequently, relations between many Aboriginal youth and police are conflict orientated.[16]

The absence of community outrage against such a range of injustices is eerily reminiscent of attitudes towards Aborigines during the decades of assimilation. It represents a very similar 'out-of-sight-out-of mind' approach to the presence of Aboriginal children in our community. Under assimilation great power was given to the state to banish these young people to missions; now the 'justice' approach to their behavioural problems has sanctioned state power to remove many hundreds of them to detention centres over the past several decades. In both cases the removal process has been backed up by community opinion unsympathetic to its effects on these young people. The clamour of public opinion in Western Australia, as elsewhere, about juvenile crime has well-documented racist undertones,[17] just like the attitudes which, from the 1930s, unquestioningly tolerated removal to missions. In each case, too, the aura of legal sanction has served to legitimise a process which lacks clear criminological or moral foundation.

The assimilation laws created the myth of the 'neglected' child whose parents were unfit to keep it. The juvenile justice laws have created the 'myth' of the deviant Aboriginal youth who requires locking up in large numbers to ensure the public safety. Both are social creations born of racial attitudes which, if not openly hostile to Aboriginal people, are blithely indifferent to the causes and effects of their disadvantage.

There are still deeper parallels between the justice and

assimilation systems in their effects on Aboriginal youth. Both systems undertook the removal of children while turning a blind eye to the underlying causes of Aboriginal social disadvantage, a disadvantage which has its historic roots in government policies towards Aboriginal people. In the era of assimilation the shocking conditions of the reserves, which made parenting such an unrelenting battle, were never systematically addressed. Instead, it better suited the purposes of government to remove the children. It is the same with contemporary Aboriginal juvenile crime.

Crime is common among some Aboriginal young people, as it is among other socially disadvantaged groups. However, as one of the most marginal of all social groups, Aboriginal youth are particularly prone to involvement in crime, although the proportion is not known. Of great concern is the group of predominantly Aboriginal repeat offenders.[18] Their way of life creates a self-perpetuating tendency towards criminal behaviour and requires sympathetic and insightful understanding. On the one hand, the forces of racial discrimination undermine the self-confidence of many young Aborigines making them liable to acts of retaliation while, on the other, endemic poverty breeds a spirit of despair which may be expressed in vengefulness.[19] Inextricably linked with this is the destruction of their cultural heritage, which of course, is the very outcome the architects of assimilation had in mind. Today's Aboriginal youth, and especially those living in urban areas, are the direct inheritors of the post-war drive for cultural destruction. As the Aboriginal Legal Service has explained:

> The assimilation and integration policies denied
> Aborigines their culture, and taught them to be

ashamed of and renounce their race and traditions ... Aboriginal youth suffer ... cultural disempowerment. Many young Aborigines have never been exposed to, or have rejected the controls and authority of their own culture. Similarly many have been rejected by and reject the impositions and restrictions of non-Aboriginal society. For some Aboriginal children laws of neither society control them and as a result they consider themselves to have absolute freedom and apparent independence. That is until they come into contact with the justice system.[20]

While it is very difficult not to see these young people as victims of broader social injustice, they are by no means helpless victims. Crime among the repeat offenders group can be seen as a form of retaliation against authority, especially the police, but also against white society in general. These young people know they are poor so they take 'a piece of the action' for themselves. Crime is a source of pride for many within their own subcultural group.[21] However, by embodying in the juvenile justice system a legalistic notion of crime as an individual act of choice deserving of punishment, it is inevitable that socially marginalised groups will bear the brunt of its application. The system perpetuates the notion that it is founded on impartial legal justice in the face of all the evidence to the contrary. Weighty evidence from studies in most States guarantees one thing: that Aboriginal youth will be over-represented in arrest, court appearance and detention rates. This reflects a legal process unable to deal with juvenile crime in its holistic, social and historical context.

State governments have never seriously asked themselves why so many Aboriginal youth are involved in crime in the first place. To do so would be politically unpalatable. It would involve taking the side of Aboriginal people; of acknowledging the injustice and committing the considerable funds needed to bring hope to these young people. It would involve tackling police practices and attitudes. There is simply no tradition in Western Australian politics for this kind of action to be taken on behalf of Aboriginal young people.

Neither State nor Commonwealth governments have been prepared to develop preventative programs of sufficient scope to keep young Aborigines from entering the system in the first place. One of the known effective ways to prevent juvenile crime is to encourage education and school attendance. Yet, for decades in Western Australia school participation rates for Aboriginal youth have been significantly below the national average which, in itself, is half that of non-Aboriginal youth. Howard Groom, a specialist in Aboriginal education, outlines the complex set of factors behind the high drop out rate of young Aborigines from school.

The academic problems of Aboriginal adolescents are rarely related to their intelligence and ability. The causes lie in a range of issues. Many involve unsatisfactory relationships and feelings of insecurity and not belonging in the classroom, false expectations held by teachers and racism from teachers and peers ... Aboriginal students may come to the point of feeling that to achieve in school terms they have to give up their Aboriginal identity and forfeit their acceptance by the Aboriginal peer group ... They may realise that too few Aboriginal adolescents have succeeded and found a good job; they may see school as a waste of time, or irrelevant to their lives.[22]

The backdrop of the assimilation experience gives these issues further significance. The parents of many of these children were themselves denied an adequate education. In Western Australia, only 13 percent of seventeen year old Aborigines were participating in education (31 percent nationally). Keeping young people out of crime depends on providing them with employment. Yet, in Western Australia 52 percent of fifteen to nineteen year olds and 53 percent of twenty to twenty-four year old Aborigines in the labour market are without jobs.[23]

In 1994, the House of Representatives Standing Committee on Aboriginal Affairs was critical of the failure of Western Australian governments to produce evidence of positive outcomes of programs to reduce the rate of involvement of Aboriginal youth in the criminal justice systems, or the rate at which they are separated from their families and communities.[24] The Committee questioned the sincerity of the Western Australian Government in making a genuine commitment to bring about a reduction in the rate of Aboriginal young people entering the criminal justice system. In fact, governments in Western Australia had willingly sponsored measures which were calculated to increase this rate.

Since the early 1990s successive Western Australian governments have responded to ill-informed community opinion about the causes of juvenile crime and introduced several waves of 'get tough' legislation, which predominantly target Aboriginal youth. In 1992 the Lawrence Labor Government introduced the Crime (Serious and Repeat Offenders) Sentencing Act which laid on the statute books minimum mandatory sentences for repeat offenders. Later, changes to the Bail Act were made whereby juveniles could only be bailed to a responsible adult. These changes were made without consultation with the Aboriginal community and in the face of persistent criticism that they 'would impact predominantly on youth, leading to increased numbers of young indigenous youth being held in custody.'[25] In addition, proposals for increased penalties for assaults on police officers has attracted criticism from legal circles because such charges often 'escalate from interventions by the Police in the lives of non-offending Aboriginal youth through routine questioning and asking for names and addresses.'[26]

Most recently, the State Government has added the United States-inspired 'three strikes and you're in' to its 'get tough' legislative armoury. This measure, which imposes a mandatory one-year gaol term for third-time home burglars, was recently investigated by a Senate inquiry into legal aid. Evidence to the inquiry indicated 600 youths were sitting on their 'second strike' — 75 percent of them Aborigines. Responding to these figures, inquiry member Senator Nick Bolkus commented: 'It seems to me that we are talking about the next generation of young Aborigines growing up in prison.'[27]

The State Government's response to a recent case involving a fourteen year old boy from Broome indicates its determination to pursue this new form of removing Aboriginal children from their families. Before the boy appeared in the Perth Children's Court he had already spent forty-two days in custody thousands of kilometres away from his family. He had pleaded guilty to burglary, his third offence. Therefore, he came under the Government's new legislative regime. The President of the Court sentenced the boy to twelve months imprisonment but released him immediately into an intensive supervision program in the community.

Not surprisingly, the Attorney-General was quick to publicly denounce the President's decision and equally quick to state the intention of the Government to block such a loophole with amending legislation. Assessments of this legislation point out its potential danger to Aboriginal people and particularly to Aboriginal youth living in remote regions. If these young people are given a mandatory sentence by the Court it must be served in a juvenile detention centre, all of which are located in Perth. Thus, Aboriginal children from remote areas will be separated from their family, customs and lifestyle for a considerable period. Mandatory detention 'will prove to have lethal consequences and neglect any true form of culturally appropriate rehabilitation.'[28]

The 'three strikes and you're in' legislation runs the risk of increasing the numbers of Aboriginal youths in custody. This in turn will feed into the adult prison system because, once Aboriginal youths enter the treadmill of the justice system, most find it hard to extricate themselves.

Where reforms are made to the system of juvenile justice in an attempt to divert children and youth away from the formal court system, such innovations apply less often to Aboriginal young people. As Michael Dodson has pointed out, Aboriginal young people are less likely to receive a caution, more likely to be arrested than receive a summons, more likely to be refused bail and more likely to receive a detention order. Reflecting on these figures, Dodson brings to light their underlying meaning. The figures, he writes, are not a matter of bad luck but of systemic, underlying racism.

Even if the discretionary decisions of police, magistrates, judges, prosecutors and correctional officers may not be made on the basis of race, the context of their decisions are shaped by race. The family circumstances, education and employment history of young Indigenous offenders — the product of other established and predictable forms of systemic discrimination — are marshalled against our kids. Even when their 'best interests' are uppermost in the minds of those exercising judgement, the end results of their judgements serve to deepen and add another level of knock-on oppression to young lives.[29]

Thus, removing the children continues unabated. It is the convenient, politically acceptable way of dealing with the problems associated with extreme social disadvantage and racial marginalisation widely experienced by Aboriginal youth.

What about the young people who emerge from the justice system's 'correctional' facilities? Are they better prepared for getting on with life in constructive ways than before they went inside? Here again, the parallels with assimilation are stark. Another generation of Aboriginal children is growing up without the benefit of close contact with their families. A New South Wales study of young Aboriginal detainees found many worried about the lack of contact with families; over one third claimed they missed their families. Some were eight or ten hours drive from their homes, making visits from their families difficult. Even telephone contact was difficult because some families did not have immediate access to one.[30]

Just as the missions rendered so many of their young Aboriginal charges dysfunctional, so can the detention centres, and for very similar reasons. Young people cannot develop social competence in a closed facility removed from their communities. Social Justice Commissioner Michael Dodson has written of young life being 'diminished by contact with the juvenile justice system'. It is, he writes further, 'a crude system of prohibitions and punishments. Beneath the rhetoric of 'rehabilitation' carried out in 'correctional' centres lies the reality of a system that most often deepens the damage to kids who are already in trouble.'[31] In some, it sparks an angry aggression against a society in which they feel they are offered no legitimate place. Some become institutionalised. They accept periods of incarceration in terms of its positive benefits of providing food and shelter and as a respite from the grinding realities of living at the margins.

Just as the indiscriminate removal of Aboriginal children under assimilation had a destructive impact upon wider Aboriginal society, so does the ongoing detention of significant numbers of these young people today. As the Aboriginal Legal Service has highlighted: 'Incarceration as a response to crime is fraught with its own problems, including the collectivisation of criminal attitudes resulting in the indirect development of criminal careers and social alienation.' Michael Dodson has expressed much the same point: 'Alienation and disaffection, in turn, becomes a further source of negativity and aggression.'[32] These are the very characteristics of an underclass; a poor, marginalised group living on drugs and crime, with a value system alien to mainstream society. Assimilation was instrumental in creating the conditions for such an underclass to exist in today's society. Juvenile justice mimics its approach in taking away these children. In each case white society has, and uses, the legitimacy of the law to sanction its actions and to provide a convenient mask to cover the racial attitudes which have supported this practice.

The removal of Aboriginal children from their families will only increase unless significant steps are taken to address the underlying causes of their disadvantage. The Aboriginal population is overwhelmingly young: 50 percent of the Aboriginal population is under fifteen, compared with 22 percent of the overall population; 15 percent of the Aboriginal population is under five, more than double that of the whole nation. If these figures are overlaid onto the current imprisonment rates of Aboriginal youth, there will be a 15 percent increase in the number in detention by 2001.[33]

Similar trends can be noted for those removed because of reasons of 'neglect'. In Western Australia, 35 percent of all children in foster care are Aboriginal, the second highest in Australia after the Northern Territory. Overwhelmingly, the neglect is a manifestation of the impact of poverty and dispossession on parenting. Fewer Aboriginal children are removed for reasons of emotional, sexual or physical abuse than is the case in the non-Aboriginal community. There is a general recognition that the underlying causes of this over-representation include 'the intergenerational effects of previous separations from family and culture, poor socioeconomic status and systemic racism in the broader community.'[34]

Since assimilation officially ended in the early 1970s, the Western Australian welfare department has struggled to deal with the issues of Aboriginal child poverty. In 1974, the Royal Commission into Aboriginal Affairs recommended that the [then] Child Welfare Department should avoid the removal of Aboriginal children from home and make efforts to assist them in improving their domestic arrangements. The Welfare Department itself was aware of these criticisms, and especially the objections raised against its policy of cross-cultural adoptions. It justified this policy in a submission to the Royal

Commission on the basis that it could not recruit enough 'suitable' Aboriginal foster-parents. However, the departmental submission to the Commission acknowledged concerns that it applied the 'European yardstick and standards' to Aborigines, which were not appropriate.[35] Consequently, and in spite of its spirited defence of its practices to the 1974 Royal Commission, little changed. In 1980 a report into child welfare found that 56 percent of the children in the care of the Department were Aboriginal, two-thirds of whom were placed with non-Aboriginal caregivers. Another decade elapsed and another report was undertaken. It found 46 percent of children in substitute care were Aboriginal, however a high proportion were now placed with relatives or with Aboriginal caregivers. Problems of ensuring the quality of the services for children removed from their families and taken into substitute care remained. In 1992 the Department's handling of this issue was roundly criticised in a report to the Minister for Community Services. Services were judged as being poorly coordinated and without a 'visible plan'. Moreover, 'Departmental workers appeared under pressure and under-resourced, and often seemed to have little understanding of, or regard for, the principles of good placement practice.'[36]

Arising out of these developments is an obvious, but important question: what have governments learnt about the damage done to the Aboriginal community by policies which tolerate the removal of large numbers of their children from their families? The principles of the assimilation era appear to be firmly lodged in the attitudes of Western Australia's political elites, not to mention sections of the community at large. The strength of this legacy became all too apparent when, in September

1996, the Minister for Education, Colin Barnett, announced that the Government was contemplating setting up a system of hostels to enforce better educational standards for Aboriginal children. Under the plan, children would live in rural hostels during the week, to ensure they attended school, but would be allowed to go home on the weekends. Media reports of his statement sent a chill through those familiar with assimilation:

> He warned that the Government's answers to the problem [of Aboriginal education] might not be politically correct. 'We are going to grab hold of these kids', he said. 'I am not sure how. We might break a few rules but we are not going to let another generation of children be lost'.[37]

The Minister was sternly rebuked, not least by the head of the Human Rights Inquiry into the stolen generations, whose hearings were still in progress. His plan was stillborn but he left every indication that the attitude of white dominance — however well intended — still had strong advocates. His comments illustrate, too, that a much deeper appreciation is needed on the problems facing Aboriginal children and young people. The *West Australian* put this in very succinct terms in an editorial following the release of the Human Rights and Equal Opportunity Report into the stolen generations. 'The report should help us to understand', it wrote, 'how the wrongs of the past are visited on the socially alienated Aboriginal children of today. They put the antisocial activities of some Aboriginal children into a historical and psychological context.'[38]

8

THE POLITICS OF REMOVAL AND RECONCILIATION

The stolen generations' struggle for recognition has been a long one. Their struggle for justice is ongoing, especially because the issue has become embroiled in the resurgence of right wing politics in Australia. While several Aborigines believe the policy of removing children from their families has haunted the conscience of white Australia,[1] the outward signs are few. Neither the 1974 Royal Commission into Aboriginal Affairs nor the 1994 Report of the Task Force on Aboriginal Social Justice — the two landmark official investigations in Western Australia in recent times — engaged in more than passing reference to the assimilation era or its long-term impact. This failure to hold the policy to account left Aborigines to cope alone with its effects and their sense of outrage and loss.[2]

In the meantime, Aborigines themselves mobilised public recognition. In 1990 Patrick Dodson's investigation into the Underlying Causes of Deaths in Custody documented some of the effects of removal and mission life on contemporary Aboriginal disadvantage. In 1995 an even more concerted effort to uncover the truth about the fate of these people was undertaken by the Aboriginal Legal Service. It interviewed 600 Aboriginal people and documented their stories in a way which highlighted the connection between their removal from their families and their subsequent life experience.

National prominence was finally given to the issue with the establishment in 1995 of the Human Rights and Equal Opportunity Commission Inquiry by the Keating Labor Government as part of its commitment to reconciliation. Two years later, in May 1997, Patrick Dodson launched the Human Rights and Equal Opportunity Commission's Report (HREOC) of its investigation into the stolen generations at the National Reconciliation Convention in Melbourne. By this time, considerable publicity had been given to the work of the Commission in gathering the harrowing personal testimonies of those who had been taken from their families. Dodson touched a raw emotional nerve among the 1800 people attending the Convention which included Aborigines and many whites. Pausing momentarily, he said, 'one thing missing from this report are the mothers' stories — but how could a mother possibly bear to tell of her loss?' The comment stunned the audience. 'Those listening sat numb, with tears staining their faces.'[3] Their reactions seemed to symbolise the broader awakening slowly taking place among Australians to the suffering Aboriginal people have experienced at the hands of government policy. However, it soon became clear that not all Australians — or even a majority of them — shared this understanding.

Reaction to the Report became politicised by the actions of the Prime Minister, Mr Howard, in quickly rejecting most of its principal recommendations, including those for a national apology and compensation. Mr Howard refused to go beyond issuing a limited statement of personal regret. Much of the press coverage of the Report centred on Howard's refusal to offer a national apology. This tended to overshadow the importance of the act itself and what it symbolised for the future of black/white relations. At least two profound issues were at stake. Firstly, from an Aboriginal perspective, an apology represents part of the healing process. 'At present,' an Aboriginal health adviser explains, 'there are large numbers of Aboriginal people who are either yet to confront or acknowledge their past, or who have undergone this painful process but do not have access to a healing process which is capable of understanding and addressing their specific needs.'[4] An apology is an important starting point for these people. The experience of the South African Truth and Reconciliation Commission has shown that acknowledgment of the suffering of black people 'lifts a burden from their shoulders.'[5] Secondly, there are the broader needs of the nation. The ability to deal with the legacies of the past requires an acknowledgement of its impact. American psychiatrist Aaron Lazare has highlighted the wider significance of apologies for historic wrongs. 'It's the absence of an apology which lets the issue smoulder and stops people from ever trusting each other again … It is only by remembering, and honestly addressing something, that anyone can really forgive.'[6]

Government attempts to justify their refusal to issue an apology reveal, at best, a disturbing lack of understanding about the history of the policy of removal. At worst, these attempts represent a blatant attempt to rewrite the history of this policy. In a media interview on 16 December 1997, the Minister for Aboriginal Affairs, Senator John Herron, attempted to draw a distinction between governments which had apologised to victims of wartime atrocities and the Australian Government's response to the stolen generations. The former group, he said, were victims of the 'deliberate killing of people. That was an attempt to exterminate them.' The removal of Aboriginal children was very different — and by implication — did not warrant an apology. 'This was taking children away — the churches were doing it because they believed it was in the best interests of the children.' This distinction is artificial. It completely overlooks the role of government in establishing forced removal as official policy and the racial ideas of extermination upon which it was originally founded.

Very different sentiments on apologising for the historic wrongs of racial policies gathered pace internationally during 1997. In the United States President Bill Clinton spoke of the need for Americans to apologise for slavery. 'Surely every American knows,' Mr Clinton explained to a recent television audience, 'that slavery was wrong and that we paid a terrible price for it and that we had to keep repairing that ... and just to say that it's wrong and that we're sorry about it is not a bad thing. That doesn't weaken us.'[7] Most recently, the Canadian Government apologised to its indigenous people for the forced removal of children and their institutionalisation in residential schools.

Undoubtedly, the establishment of the South Africa Truth and Reconciliation Commission is the most far-reaching example of a country confronting its past racial policies. Its Deputy Chairman recently explained that 'part of the truth in our reconciliation commission is for the nation to say we're sorry for what we did to you even when people aren't directly involved in it.'[8]

Why has the Australian Government been unwilling to

acknowledge the stolen generations as part of the reconciliation process? In many ways this is the most tragic part of the entire issue. Having inflicted such suffering on large sections of the Aboriginal community, the nation, as a whole, is not willing to respond appropriately. Howard's refusal to offer an apology was based on advice he received indicating such a gesture could open a 'Pandora's box' of litigation.[9] However, fear of possible compensation payouts did not prevent state parliaments, including Western Australia, from apologising for the impact of this policy. In fact, the Federal Government's rejection of the Commission's findings is bound up in a larger agenda, partly politically motivated. The government sought to represent contemporary majority opinion about Aborigines as undeserving of so called special rights, thereby showing favour with its newly won electoral following. In addition, the Federal Government also wished its response to the HREOC Report to serve an even larger goal: to refocus reconciliation away from consideration of past injustices suffered by Aboriginal people to a more narrow provision of practical measures of material assistance. These responses represent a shift to the right in Australian politics, which has been accompanied by an apparent resurgence of mainstream conservative thinking about race and race relations in Australia. This needs some explanation.

Racial attitudes in any society are notoriously difficult to analyse and explain. As has been demonstrated throughout this book, ideas among whites about race are often tied up with their fears about threats to racial purity and the cultural and economic domination of whites. The history of race relations in Australia has been dominated by such fears for much of the twentieth century. However, positive signs of change occurred in States such as Western

Australia from the mid 1960s and symbolised the shift away from authoritarian control over Aborigines lives. The resounding vote in favour of the 1967 Referendum on Aborigines in which over ninety percent supported the proposals to change the Constitution to give the Commonwealth power, concurrently with the States, to make laws for Aboriginal people and that they be counted as citizens in the census, is usually taken as indication that most Australians had made a decisive break with the worst features of its racist past. Australians were thought to have embraced a more sympathetic, compassionate and accepting attitude towards Aborigines. Yet, with the benefit of hindsight, it is not entirely clear that a majority of Australians ever had in mind in the late 1960s that significant new rights would or should be given to Aborigines as a result of the change to the Constitution.

Even if the 1967 Referendum did mark a high point in positive race relations, there is some evidence that attitudes steadily slid backwards thereafter. Throughout the 1980s, opinion poll data tended to show declining levels of support for Aboriginal issues among the Australian population. This data became evidence for a 'backlash' hypothesis. The public at large, it was argued, had rejected Aboriginal causes. This is a particularly difficult point to prove because there is only one poll question which has been asked in the 1960s and the 1980s — 'whether we are doing enough to house and educate Aborigines'. Limited as this question might be, responses show that over this period the proportion answering 'spend more' declined from 77 percent to 41 percent. A similar question — 'Whether governments are spending the right amount of money on Aborigines' — was asked four times from 1974 to 1986. The 'too much' answer rose from 15 percent (1974) to 42 percent (1984), although it fell back to 21 percent in 1986.[10]

In 1984 the Department of Aboriginal Affairs commissioned Australian National Opinion Poll (ANOP) to conduct a poll on land rights, the results of which are supposed to have convinced the Hawke government to abandon its promise of national land rights. Half the sample were described by ANOP as 'soft racists', opposed to land rights. However closer analysis showed a marked division within this group, with approximately 30 percent supporting the need for Aborigines to be compensated by giving them land rights because of the way they have been treated. In the early 1990s, these figures were interpreted by Groot and Rowse as evidence of the growing complexity of public opinion on Aboriginal issues. They suggested a three-tiered structure of public opinion. One group was defined as openly hostile to any notion of Aboriginal rights while those who supported rights were divided into two blocks of opinion. One block, which inherited its views from the assimilation era, showed commitment to notions of 'equality' and 'fairness' but in a way which precluded recognition of any 'special' rights. The second group, representing more recent attitudes 'is organised around such notions as respect for Aboriginal culture [and] a sense of the need to restore both resources and dignity to Aborigines damaged by non-Aboriginal actions.'[11]

While supporters in this second block have undoubtedly grown in recent years, there is evidence that public opinion at large shows declining support for Aboriginal causes. This, at least, is the finding of the Council for Aboriginal Reconciliation. In 1994 it concluded that a plateau had been reached in public support for reconciliation. From 48 percent of people saying they were in favour of reconciliation in November 1991, the percentage climbed to 53 percent in February 1993 and 55 percent in September 1993. However, by March 1994 it had slipped back to 52 percent. According to Patrick Dodson, Chairman of the Council, 'this fall was linked to the increased political debate on the native title decision and land claims.'[12]

The points to draw from the available figures on contemporary public opinion towards Aborigines are, basically, twofold. There has been a steady climb in compassionate recognition of Aboriginal rights but the number of people holding such views does not yet appear to have reached a majority. Most people still hold hostile views on Aboriginal rights, although the degree of hostility varies. The number in this group is likely to rise in a period marked by assertive claims by Aborigines for those rights. The structure of this broadly unsympathetic group continues to be founded on the following principal components, identified in the 1994 Task Force on Aboriginal Social Justice: negative stereotyping, a denial of past injustices, a 'we' versus 'they' attitude and resentment over supposed privileged 'handouts'.[13] The Task Force was compelled to acknowledge the existence of deeply entrenched racist attitudes in the Western Australian community; attitudes that regard 'Aboriginal people of less value than others — and consequently requiring a lesser level of service from the community.'[14] The Task Force also held a number of community workshops for white and Aboriginal participants at which racism was regularly raised. Reports from these workshops show how the interaction between community ignorance of history and the perpetuation of negative stereotypes impedes recognition of Aboriginal rights.

There was much concern about the portrayal of Aboriginal people in the media which both reflects the current negative perceptions in the community, and reinforces and perpetuates them. Many workshop participants suggested the need to re-educate the Australian public about Aboriginal people. Community knowledge about Aboriginal people and culture and history was felt to be lacking, as is their understanding of contemporary Aboriginality, the relative recency of paternalistic practices such as the widespread removal of Aboriginal children from their families and the consequences this had for contemporary Aboriginal families, and their culture as a whole.[15]

The climate of public opinion worsened in the lead-up to, and immediately after, the 1996 election. Evidence of a backlash against Aboriginal rights was now clear cut. A significant component of Australia's so-called race debate at this time became focused on allegations raised by Pauline Hanson, a Liberal turned independent candidate for the Federal seat of Oxley, that Aborigines were given too many special privileges unavailable to whites. As Race Discrimination Commissioner Zita Antonios has written, this 'new wave of racism has been bubbling under the surface for some time but has erupted in the past year [1995] quite publicly. It manifests itself in the view that policies, legislation, and even funding for Indigenous Australians and people of non-English speaking background have gone too far.'[16]

Thus, on the eve of the establishment of the Human Rights and Equal Opportunity Commission inquiry into the stolen generations, public opinion towards the rights of Aborigines was a mixture of long-standing ignorance and stereotypical attitudes which had gradually been hardening in opposition to Aboriginal rights. This climate represented less a 'backlash' than a continuity of thinking about Aborigines as undeserving of 'special' privileges. What are perceived to be special privileges represent in real terms, however, basic human and sovereignty rights. As the *Age* newspaper recently commented: 'Each of the milestones that has marked the reconciliation process since the 1967 referendum — the Mabo and Wik judgements, the creation of ATSIC and the land councils — has been greeted with fear and resentment by significant sections of the non-indigenous community.'[17] This reaction is, of course, indicative of more deep-seated prejudice towards Aborigines. It is often overlooked how the deep antipathy to Aborigines as a people and culture perpetuates itself with each new generation. Experience of overt racism remains a common feature in the lives of many Aboriginal youth growing up in Western Australia. The *West Australian* recently reported the experience of one talented young Aboriginal footballer, Steven Garlett:

> Out of school and out of work, Garlett does not go out much any more because racism in the wider community gets him into too many fights ... But racism is infiltrating the game at the most junior levels. Garlett said that he had been called names for years but the worst incident of all was when he was spat on last year ... [Garlett's coach] said many young Aboriginal players, who were often shy and reserved, bottled up years of abuse, then exploded. Others simply dropped out of the game that could give them self-esteem, pride in their team and club, a place in their community and, perhaps the ultimate, the chance to play at national level.[18]

Within the broader climate of racial antipathy, the issue

of an apology to the stolen generations was inevitably going to arouse significant public opinion. However, one crucial fact emerged from the opinion poll data on this issue: a larger number of Coalition supporters were unsympathetic towards an apology and, by implication, compensation. A Newspoll, taken on 3 June 1997, which asked 'Should the Government apologise for the 'stolen children'? showed that 50 percent of respondents favoured the issuing of an apology and 40 percent opposed it; 43 percent of those opposed were Coalition supporters and 37 percent ALP supporters. Interestingly, this poll showed that support for an apology dropped with age, with 55 percent of the eighteen to thirty-four year old age group in favour of an apology and 42 percent of those fifty years old and over. Western Australians registered the highest number of people opposed to an apology (51 percent) followed by Queensland (46 percent). (The Northern Territory was not included in the poll.) In other words, those States with the highest proportion of Aborigines in their populations were the least sympathetic.[19]

The *Bulletin* published the results of a Morgan Poll in the first week of June 1997. The poll had asked a more pointed question, requiring a 'Yes/No' response to the following statement: 'No formal apology to Aborigines [is needed] as present generations are not accountable for misdeeds of past generations.' Fifty-seven percent of respondents agreed with this statement, of which a massive 71 percent were Coalition voters, leading the magazine to conclude the obvious: 'John Howard's veto of a national stolen generation apology has received firm public support.'[20] The significant difference in the results of the two polls may well be explained by the manner in which the second question was asked: 'accountable for misdeeds of past generations' taps into a long-held attitude of many Australians towards Aborigines that a clear separation exists between past and present. It is an attitude born of a reluctance to confront the racism experienced by Aborigines. The Prime Minister has been one of the most forceful exponents of this view. 'Australians of this generation,' he told the National Reconciliation Convention, 'should not be required to accept guilt and blame for past actions and policies over which they had no control.'[21] The implications of such a view are, of course, to limit the degree of responsibility people are prepared to accept for the wrongs of the past, even though, in this instance it represents the very recent past, with on-going effects.

The letter pages of major newspapers give some flavour to the findings of the opinion polls by revealing some of the reasoning behind opposition to the HREOC Report. For some of these letter writers, there was never anything wrong with assimilation in the first place. As far as the following letter writer to the *West Australian* is concerned, the original ideals of assimilation have never been questioned. 'I am amazed', the writer noted,

> that there is no reference to the reasons why these children were taken from their families. Was it not to give them better opportunities in the white man's world — better health care, better education and better employment opportunities? If this had not been done and accepted by them, would not the children have tried to return to their families and would not these families have tried to assist them to do so? I know of no such cases.[22]

The rhetoric behind assimilation — that it was in the best interests of the children — continued to hold sway among sections of the public. Aboriginal children, many letter writers argued, were not only given 'opportunities', they were positively 'saved' by assimilation. As one correspondent wrote to the *Bulletin*, the 'sad fact is that the "stolen generation", whatever emotional scars are nourished, were the saved generation. That so many survived and are living well attests to the good intent of the program.'[23] This, too, was the theme of an angry correspondent to the *West Australian*. 'The stolen children is another slander which distorts the effort to save some of the mixed-race Aborigines from the benighted and abysmal conditions which seemed a never-ending cycle of failure by the Aboriginal culture to adapt to modern society.'[24] Claims that Aboriginal children somehow benefited from the policy of removal were made by prominent Liberal Party backbencher, Mr Wilson Tuckey. 'In any materialistic sense, most Aboriginal children who were removed to mission schools or adopted by white parents have benefited substantially and many were no worse off socially than those white children who went to boarding school.'[25] How such wild claims could be made by such a prominent politician is worrying enough, but the purpose such comments serve in deprecating the claims of justice for these people, is particularly unfortunate.

A variant of the 'for their own good' theme is the attempt by opponents of the HREOC Report to support the motivations of those who were involved. If these can be judged as well-intentioned, as the following correspondent indicated, then the policy itself is not at fault. The correspondent recalls having had:

long conversations with a white married couple in the 1940s at Huskisson, near Nowra. They had been in charge of a Government institution for fostering;

I was absolutely convinced of their genuine concern for the children and their conviction that the children were being given a better start in life than their parents could offer.[26]

These attempts to uphold the merits of assimilation as justification for not apologising to the stolen generations, reveal a mixture of ignorance and cultural superiority. Common to all these commentators is classic assimilationist thinking: Aborigines had to be integrated into white society because of the inferiority of their family and/or cultural background and this attested to the noble motives behind the policy. Moreover, those involved in the policy were known to be compassionate people. By implication, therefore, no apology is necessary. As this book has tried to show, the facts are more complex and unpalatable. The motivation of assimilationists may have been presented as compassionate concern, but beneath this lay deeper hostilities to Aborigines as a race. As to providing opportunities for Aboriginal children, thereby 'saving' them from their impoverished backgrounds, there is too much evidence of the obverse being the case. It was the policy of segregation, with the sanction of the community at large in States like Western Australia — which found expression in the reserve system, in opposition to Aboriginal children attending school, in discrimination in employment, and in the refusal to grant citizenship and social security — which represented the real origins of the endemic poverty among Aboriginal people and especially those who, because of dispossession, were forced to live on the fringes of white society.

The intentions of those involved in the policy of assimilation, and the pre-war policy of absorption, were not always so high minded as some now attempt to portray.

The widespread abuse of Aboriginal children in missions and foster homes and the coercive power which the State exercised over their lives amply demonstrates the racial hostility which continued to drive this policy at all levels in the community, if not by all individuals. In any event, the very notion of 'good intentions' implies a value judgement. It so very frequently meant 'good' according to a white perspective. To 'save' these children from poverty was a 'good' intention; to offer them a white culture was judged equally 'good'. However, no similar moral worth was attached to the need to end their poverty, to value their culture and to let them exist in their own way. Claims that these judgements reflected the different standards of the time is to confirm that the standards were racial. This may be unpalatable to those who lived through the assimilationist era and who now claim today's standards should not be applied to that earlier generation. However, it is important to recognise the conscious choice behind Aboriginal policy in the decades covered in this book. Segregation, discrimination and removal of children may have represented majority opinion, but there were contrary views voiced which were ignored. Moreover, in the post-war period, evidence suggests that many people who held unsympathetic views towards Aborigines were aware of the moral wrong involved.

Opposition to the HREOC Report was also evoked by the framework of human rights in which it was presented. The Commission called for reparations, including acknowledgment and apology; guarantees against repetition; measures of restitution; measures of rehabilitation; and monetary compensation. This framework conflicts with the views of many people who remain hostile to Aboriginal 'special rights'. Greatly compounding hostility to the Report was the finding of genocide implicit in the policy. Political attempts to undermine the Report on this basis were spearheaded by the Minister for Aboriginal Affairs who told ABC radio:

I don't believe we ever attempted genocide ... Do the Australian people as a whole believe that our forebears committed genocide? I don't believe the Australian people support that either ... This practice could not be described as genocide as it did not involve an intentional elimination of a race.[27]

From correspondence to newspapers the Minister appeared to be correct in his assumption that many people would disagree with this finding. One wrote to the *West Australian*:

The comparison with the Holocaust is an intemperate slander. The worst that can be attributed to white settlement is that of neglect and of assuming too easily that a Stone-age culture could be shed after having led a hunter-gather existence for thousands of years.[28]

Another wrote:

I must protest about the use of the word 'genocide' by Sir Ronald Wilson and his ilk to describe what happened to the stolen Aboriginal children. In recent history this word has rightly been used to describe events such as the Holocaust, Pol Pot's regime and the ethnic cleansing in the former Yugoslavia. All these were times of unspeakable cruelty, perpetrated by grossly evil men and women. What happened in Australia was, without doubt, paternalism of the worst kind ... There was never an intention to destroy the Aboriginal race and any attempt to equate this policy with the events listed above, by using the word 'genocide' is historically, intellectually and morally dishonest.[29]

Taking as benchmarks the Holocaust and Pol Pot' regime to define the term 'genocide' is understandable enough. However, the resistance to incorporating forced removal of Aboriginal children as genocide shows an unwillingness to grapple with the notion of genocide in international law. It is, in effect, an attempt at denial of the racist past. As the HREOC Report carefully documents, Australia was a member of the United Nations when the General Assembly declared genocide to be a crime against humanity in 1946, and that Australia also supported the 1948 Convention on the Prevention and Punishment of the Crime of Genocide.

Those who were quick to denigrate the Report and its findings clearly have little working knowledge of the origins of assimilation. Neither have they examined the details of the United Nations conventions or even the analysis on them provided in the HREOC Report. The latter would have made clear that the United Nations' adoption of the conventions on genocide was based on the work of Raphael Lemkin who, even before the full horrors of the Nazi regime were made apparent, defined genocide as 'the coordinated and planned destruction of a national, religious, racial, or ethnic group by different actions through the destruction of the essential foundations of the life of the group with the aim of annihilating it physically or culturally.'[30] In its definition, the United Nations included the criteria that genocide amounted to a policy based on planning and intent to destroy an ethnic group. The following actions were covered: (a) killing members of the group, (b) causing serious bodily or mental harm to members of the group, (c) deliberately inflicting on the group conditions of life calculated to bring about its physical destruction in whole or in part, (d) imposing measures intended to prevent births within the group and forcibly transferring children of the group to another group.

What is the evidence that assimilation amounted to genocide, according to this convention? As stated in Chapter One, Neville's clear intention was to wipe out the Aboriginal race. As he informed the 1937 Conference of Commonwealth and State Aboriginal Authorities, his long-range plan would make it possible to 'eventually forget that there were ever any Aborigines in Australia.' The dovetailing of this long-range plan with the establishment of Sister Kate's to exert control over the marriage of inmates constitutes, in total, a clear breach of sections (b), (c) and (d) of the Convention.

The post-war transformation of the policy shared several components in common with its earlier version. Bateman, the architect of the post-war policy, envisaged the large-scale removal of Aboriginal children because their parents, as well as their living conditions, were perceived to be deficient. 'It is abundantly clear in my mind', he wrote in his report to the State Government, 'that the only chance of successfully training the children is to segregate them from the adults.' Further, 'education must be made to fit these people into our own economic and social structure. They must be changed from a nomadic, idle and discontented race to a settled, industrious, contented section of the community.'[31] These statements confirm that the foundation of post-war assimilation, at least as it was practiced in

Western Australia, was based on the clear intent to remove large numbers of children from their 'inferior' environment to a more 'civilised' white one. In this, it breached the United Nations Convention on genocide. While in the popular imagination, the idea of genocide remains fixed on the episodes of mass killing of ethnic groups, those who drafted the Genocide Convention 'understood that the destruction of culture and a people need not be so crude.'[32]

Given the finding on genocide, it is not surprising Aborigines regard this issue as a litmus test for reconciliation. In its broadest definition, reconciliation involves building closer relations between Aboriginal and non-Aboriginal people. Since 1991, when the Council for Reconciliation was formed, this objective has been pursued through identifying eight key issues around which to build better relationships. These include greater recognition of land and culture; greater awareness of the causes of Aboriginal disadvantage; a sense of shared Australian ownership of history; and greater opportunities for Aboriginal people to control their own destinies. The issue of the stolen children relates to many of these objectives. Out of the tragedy of these people's lives could come a positive focus on reconciliation, and especially developing a richer understanding of our past and the role that racial ideas have played in it. Yet, the signs of this taking place are not encouraging. Since the election of the Coalition Government relationships between it and Aborigines have deteriorated markedly.

The battleground for this change has been a struggle over Australian history and the efforts by some conservative thinkers to endorse what John Howard has labelled as the 'black armband' view of Australia's history. According to this conservative view, Australia's history is being portrayed 'as little more than a disgraceful record of imperialism, exploitation and racism.'[33] It is an attempt to assert a counter view of Australian history as an essentially heroic struggle marked by impressive achievements in which 'blemishes' are acknowledged but do not intrude on the larger story. Its effect is to downplay injustices to Aborigines. The Prime Minister, for example, is reported to have informed Lois O'Donaghue, (at the time, the Chairperson of ATSIC) that: 'while non-Aboriginal Australians are more than willing to do their bit to bring about reconciliation, they do not want to dwell on the past and are simply unwilling to take upon themselves the burden of previous generations' supposed wrongdoings.'[34] Thus, any extended opportunity for Australians to reflect on this policy and its impact on victims, runs a grave risk of being ignored by government.

On another front, the legal fight for justice by the stolen generations has received a set-back. Only two months after the release of the HREOC Report, the High Court handed down a decision that the 1918 Northern Territory Ordinance, which facilitated the removal of Aboriginal children, was not constitutionally invalid. Commenting on the decision, Matthew Storey, from the Northern Territory Aboriginal Legal Service, argued that the Court's decision 'means that the legislative basis to the program of genocide was not unconstitutional.' The Legal Service had argued that the legislation which authorised the removal of children violated certain implied freedoms in the constitution, including freedom of movement, association and religion. A Bill of Rights, it is argued by Aboriginal groups, 'would ensure that the sort of program that led to the Stolen Generations could never happen again.'[35]

Contrary to some opinion, the High Court decision

does not prohibit future court action to obtain compensation for the survivors. Aboriginal legal opinion interprets the High Court decision as having said 'there will be no compensation for the violation of Constitutional Law. They haven't said that there will be no compensation in other Common Law rights.'[36] In other words, the Court was not asked to rule on the effects of the policy of removal on those subjected to it. In consequence of this interpretation, Aboriginal Legal Services around Australia have already, or are about to, file hundreds of cases for compensation. It is hoped that this move will force the Commonwealth Government to come to a country-wide agreement on compensation.[37]

Response to the HREOC Report reveals much about current social attitudes towards Aborigines. The available data show that a significant section — perhaps up to one half — of Australians are prepared to respond sympathetically to the stolen generations' claims for justice and recognition. Overwhelmingly these are younger and politically progressive Australians. Another large group remains hostile to Aboriginal claims for so-called 'special privileges' and acknowledgment of rights. The politicisation of the Report in a right-wing fashion ensured the views of the latter prevailed. In addition to being predominantly older Australians, this group is overwhelmingly politically conservative. In Prime Minister John Howard they found a receptive voice; someone who sees little value in delving too deeply into whether the racial beliefs of the past continue to find some voice in the present. Sadly, the available evidence suggests the attitude of many whites continues to be driven by racial mythology.

CONCLUSION

THE STOLEN GENERATIONS AND RACISM

Today, explanations of the three-decade long policy of removing children are commonly couched in one of two ways. The first seeks to dismiss any connection with racial thought by claiming removal was in the best interests of the children, as perceived by the authorities at the time. The second seeks to diminish any potential connection with racism by excusing the policy as being based on a different set of standards from today. In other words, it may have been misguided, but only because people of the day thought about the problems of Aboriginal disadvantage in ways that are no longer accepted. Both of these popular explanations are inadequate for understanding the origins of the policy and the ways in which it was sustained through more than three decades.

In this book we have shown how the policy of assimilation affected Sandra Hill, Trish Hill-Keddie, Rosalie Fraser, Phillip Prosser, and many other people like them. We have argued that the policy which stipulated the removal of such children was an outcome of a set of racial ideas about Aborigines and their place in the broader community. The highly discriminatory ways in which they were removed, the limited expectations held for Aborigines and the treatment they received in many of the missions and foster homes illustrate the operation of this set of racial ideas. It remains to explore the nature of this racism in more detail. What was it about the power of racial ideas, as they were manifest in Australia from the 1930s to the 1970s, that could sustain such a fundamental abuse of human rights? Moreover, what light is shed on the character of this racism from the implementation of the removal policy? These questions are fundamental to our account.

Racism operated as official government policy for the first seventy years of Australian nationhood. In the case of the Immigration Restriction Act, the racial intent was explicit, as were the attempts by national governments to defend it. As is well known, the intention of the nation's immigration laws was to keep out of Australia people from cultures perceived to be alien and whose presence would threaten the desire to create in Australia a culture of British civilisation. Writers such as Andrew Markus have characterised this policy as representing the attempt at creating an 'Anglo-Australian superiority'.[1] It was shaped around the idea of a mono-culture with its attendant intention that no 'pure' non-European could be granted permanent residence in Australia.

Invariably, this racially motivated attempt at nation-building had to overcome the problem of indigenous, black Australians. How were they to fit into white Australia? The removal of Aboriginal children was their answer. A O Neville's absorptionist scheme in the 1930s held out the promise that the race could be genetically bred out of existence. When this later became officially unacceptable, assimilation proposed that Aborigines could, and should, be encouraged to enter the mainstream of Australian life, but only on the basis that they renounced their Aboriginal culture. In all the rhetoric about assimilation and its so-called generous offerings of Aboriginal access to the trappings of 'civilised' life, it is perfectly clear that assimilation was a vehicle for cultural genocide: to make Aborigines lose their culture and become more acceptable to white Australia. Those, like anthropologist Ronald Berndt, who could see through the cant, knew this to be the case. His 1958 remark, that assimilation represented unequivocal opposition to Aboriginal cultural and social life is a more realistic appraisal of community attitudes than is the attempt to couch the policy in humanitarian terms.[2]

The removal of children was the key instrument of this drive for cultural destruction. As the Commissioner for Native Welfare explained in his 1958 Annual Report: 'The social development of any race lies in its children and it is through them that the Department hopes chiefly to guide and direct the cultural change taking place among Aborigines.'[3] What else explains why Aboriginal children were denied access to their culture and to their families? Once separated from their Aboriginal culture every effort was made to ensure that they were not to be reconnected with it. The implementation of this policy came with the power to exercise cultural control over Aboriginal communities. 'I know of many cases where the parents have asked for their children to be returned to their care,' wrote a District Officer of the Department of Native Affairs in 1958: 'In some instances', he continued, 'I have refused outright, but mostly the parents were told that if they provided the child or children with a decent home, etc, I would favourably consider obtaining permission of the Commissioner for the child's discharge from the

Mission.'[4] In other words, the white standards of decency acted as a form of cultural control; when 'they' became more like 'us', they could be trusted with their children.

This is the broader racial context within which the removal of children must be placed if it is to be fully understood. Alongside restrictions on immigration, it represents a pillar of official policy aimed at ensuring that Anglo-Australian superiority remained unchallenged. The determination with which Australian governments of this period articulated and defended their policy of racial discrimination needs some emphasis. Australia's efforts, from the early years of the twentieth century, to establish human rights in international law is well-documented. Less well known is the selective morality which lay behind these efforts: Australia's commitment to human rights did not extend to racial equality.

Although heavily involved in developing international law to protect human rights following the First World War, including those of minorities, Australia was not prepared to recognise the human right of racial non-discrimination.[5] The first real test came at the Versaille Peace Conference in 1919 when the Japanese representatives suggested a clause on racial equality be inserted in the Covenant of the League of Nations. The Australian delegation, led by the Prime Minister, William Hughes, was most uncomfortable, arguing such a clause would encroach upon the right of countries to determine their own domestic policies. Hughes outlined Australia's opposition in these words: 'Our White Australia policy would be a pricked bladder. Our control over immigration laws would be so much waste of paper.'[6]

Australia's discriminatory attitude continued into the period following the end of the Second World War when the contemporary human rights protocols were developed. During this period, Australia's eagerness for greater observance of human rights was counterbalanced by a tenacious defence of her racially discriminatory White Australia Policy and law. London describes this tenacity and its implication thus:

> at the San Francisco Convention in 1945 Dr Evatt as Deputy Prime Minister vigorously argued for a Charter resolution which prohibited United Nations authority from interfering in the domestic policy of member states. His argument — a reaction to the possibility that pressure would be exerted to change the White Australia policy — unwittingly forced Australia into 'the racialist camp'.[7]

Subsequent events, well into the 1960s, gave Australia the tag of being a human rights activist blinkered by racism. For instance, in order to save Australia's immigration policy from scrutiny and denunciation, her representative in the United Nations General Assembly vehemently protested an attempt to put South African apartheid on the agenda in 1952. The Menzies government insisted that the UN respect the principle of non-interference in domestic affairs. When pressures forced South Africa out of the Commonwealth, Menzies had this to say:

> Even though there has been a great deal of international agitation this is still a matter of domestic policy in South Africa ... It is as much a matter of domestic policy as Australian immigration policy is a domestic matter for us. And to have a member of the Commonwealth virtually excluded on a matter

of domestic policy presents, in my opinion, a rather disagreeable vista of the possibilities for the future.[8]

Such an official attachment to racism helps explain why the policy of removing children was so readily endorsed by government: Aborigines were not thought of as having rights. Rather, they were subjected to the broader racial aims of government and the nation. However, this broader connection to official racial policy is only part of the explanation for the persistence of the policy of removing children from their families. It could not have been sustained but for the character of Australian racism.

As a mode of human behaviour, racism has always defied easy explanation, as does its persistence in a wide-range of societies. In recent years a vast literature has grown around the concept of racism to try and explain its workings. Examination of the major theories about racism is valuable for shedding further light on the deeper motivations for policy-makers' persistence with removing Aboriginal children.

One explanatory theory categorises racism into two main types: dominative racism and aversive racism. Together, they produced the uniquely troubled legacy of black-white relations Australia has witnessed to date. Dominative racism is the desire by some people to dominate or subjugate members of another group. Whites, for instance, would live and work in close proximity to blacks, even assigning black women to nurse and care for their young. White men might visit black women for sexual purposes, a practice producing the 'mixed blood race'. Whites do not mind associating or having contact with blacks on a daily basis — 'as long as they know their place! They were not to get uppity or self-assertive.'[9] Aversive racism, on the other hand, is expressed in the desire to avoid contact with blacks, thus restricting them to isolated areas — beyond the boundaries of white interests. Settlement reserves, mission homes and other forms of 'caste barriers' in Australia owe their origins largely to this racial concept.

Comte Gobineau, commonly cited as the father of modern racism, popularised the claims of dominative and aversive racism in his *Essay on the Inequality of Human Races* in the 1850s, a period during which both forms of racism were jockeying for dominance in Australia. As the experience of the stolen generations shows, the white attitude to Aborigines became simultaneously subjugatory and repelling from the second half of the 19th century, peaking arguably in the 1930s-60s. (In this regard, the Australian experience of racism stands apart from the United States of America where the dominative form has been more common in the southern states and the aversive form in the northern states.) During the era of the stolen generations in Australia, the two forms of racism drove official policy in a mutually reinforcing way. Aversive racism removed Aborigines off their land or out of the cities, to make way for European possession, and dominative racism turned them into cheap labourers and domestic servants. The result was a more systematic and long-standing implementation of white-on-black racism than in any other part of the Western world.

Giving effect to this fusion of dominative and aversive racism required that its aims become built into the operation of society's institutions. It is only here that it can be transformed into official policies. This process involves formulating a vision and designing mechanisms to give effect to this vision. The aim of institutionalised racism is the subordination of one racial group by another and to render them as inferior beings. This process is crystallised around policies and laws designed to ensure subjugation. In Western Australia this included the raft of legal sanctions denying citizenship to Aborigines, using legal powers to determine where they could live, how they could work, and who they could marry. Reviewing this body of legislative restriction in 1953, the Commissioner for Native Affairs wrote:

> It approved of their pauperisation on the one hand and on the other directed a form of control which bordered on unwarranted interference of personal liberty unparalleled in the legislative treatment of any other people in the Commonwealth. Its effect on Aborigines was to create in their minds a state of degradation, or at least inferiority.[10]

The removal of Aboriginal children from their families was an expression of the institutionalised racism in Australia. It was to play a significant role in this process of subordination. Alongside the contribution this policy made to destroying Aboriginal culture for the purposes of white Australia, it served several other purposes as well. It signified to Aboriginal people their inferiority as parents and it ensured the future economic marginalisation of generations of Aboriginal people. The frank admission made in 1958 by the Commissioner for Native Welfare — and discussed on page 160 — that assimilation was, in some respects, worse than apartheid because it gave to whites the right to decide whether Aborigines could share in their jealously guarded privileges, is the clearest possible demonstration that removal and assimilation were tools to perpetuate Aboriginal disadvantage. Moreover, the meagre preparation these children received in missions and other institutions to which they were sent condemned most of them to unskilled worker status. Neville alluded to this outcome in the 1940s. Of children in missions, he wrote, 'only a very few are taught how to handle modern farming machinery correctly, indeed much of the plant is obsolete, and as such would not be found on any up-to-date farm.'[11] This was not just a product of neglect, it represented a choice; a decision not to train Aboriginal teenagers in any way that they might compete with white interests in the skilled trades. This was acknowledged by authorities at the time. It is in this context that the 1945 admission — discussed on page 91 — by the Commissioner of Native Affairs is so significant. The aim of education, he said, was to bring Aborigines into employment in ways which 'will not bring them into economic or social conflict with the white community.' In other words, Aborigines had to be kept, as much as possible, out of the skilled trades.

To characterise the removal of children as an example of institutionalised racism is to beg one further question. What perpetuates the institutionalised racism where expression is given to schemes to both segregate and subjugate Aboriginal people? While no general theory can account for this process, it is the product of several interacting forces. Importantly, it is a reflection of the determination of whites to protect their economic interests from any challenge by Aborigines. As Castles has argued, economic exploitation played a part in the emergence of racism throughout the world.[12]

Dispossessing Aborigines of their land and exploiting them as a cheap labour force have been central themes in black/white relations since the earliest days of settlement. Nowhere are these intentions clearer in Western Australia than in the report of a 1927 meeting at which the struggle for land was discussed. Archbishop Riley, A O Neville, together with several of the State's large land owners were present:

> the native and the European, the missioner and the squatter, both [sic] wanted the same thing ... The meeting was held in view of the fact that the native was suffering under the impact from the white man ... and that the future of the squatter depended upon getting rid of the native, even though he represented cheap labour, if only by segregation.[13]

Little more than a decade later, the desire to prevent Aborigines from becoming numerically strong enough to threaten white economic interests was an important part of the motivation behind the adoption of absorption among delegates attending the 1937 conference. There is little doubt, too, that it suited the purposes of whites to have a pool of marginalised Aboriginal workers to labour on the farms in times of high demand. The desire to institutionalise the removal of Aboriginal children thus suited the wider economic interests of white society. By removing the children's culture they were unlikely to feel connected to their land; indeed many were not to know the location of their 'country'. The almost universal acceptance that they should be trained as domestics and farm labourers reflects the future economic role envisaged for them.

Institutionalising racism in order to dominate and control Aboriginal people was also underpinned by the need for whites' to protect their feelings of psychological superiority which, in racial terms, was manifest in prejudice. The depth of prejudice shown towards Aborigines by almost every level of society is one of the central themes running through this book. It was prejudice that lay behind the creation of the policy of segregation in the form of the disgraceful network of reserves. It was prejudice that justified the low wage levels paid to Aboriginal people and banned their entry into Perth city for so many years. The policy of removal was also a product of a mentality of prejudice. Those who planned the policy openly paraded this prejudice which they objectified in the form of 'half-castes': a group of people stereotyped as lazy, drunken, and lacking morality. From such prejudice it easily followed that their children should be taken from them. Those prepared to sanction this, and other policies of discrimination, closely represent the category identified by Rose as 'prejudiced discriminators': 'These are people who embody the commonly held assumption that prejudice and discrimination are mutually dependent. [They do] not hesitate to express the basic attitude — 'all whites are superior to coloured people' — or to convert it into overt behaviour.'[14]

The longevity of whites' belief in their own superiority also owed much to the replication of this belief among succeeding generations. Racism is learnt attitudes and behaviours and, once ingrained into the fabric of social thought, it can easily become the accepted way of dealing with minority groups. The socialisation of succeeding generations into ways of thinking about Aboriginal families as inferior helped institutionalise the response of removal as a justifiable policy. As Rose observes, 'if the agents of socialisation — parents or peers or community leaders — are themselves prejudiced people, they are apt to be effective teachers of group antipathies whether the objects of their attitudes are immediate neighbours or distant groups.'[15] We have shown government officials, community leaders and ordinary members of the public openly seeking to segregate Aboriginal people from schools, workplaces and suburban areas; signalling to younger generations their belief in the inferiority of Aborigines. It was this well of community prejudice socialised into succeeding generations, which partly explains why removal lasted for more than three decades.

Considering the economic, psychological and sociological manifestations of prejudice, it is clear that the racism which Aborigines suffered cannot be seen merely as a product of some 'fallen human nature' or an aberrant human quirk. Nor should it be dismissed as the work of wrong-headed 'scientists' who come and go in the history of ideas. Moreover, we should not tell ourselves that its worst manifestations are only in the past. As this book has shown, the policy to separate Aboriginal children from their families was a deliberately constructed choice supported by many sections of Australian society. Other forms of removal exist today and are widely supported Periodic opposition to this policy then, and now, underlies the choice available to policy-makers. Why has this policy persisted? The experiences of the stolen generations, their parents and, subsequently, their own children show it is the three-century phenomenon of white-on-black racism, grounded in a historically skewed world view on race and material exploitation.

ENDNOTES

ALS	Aboriginal Legal Service.
NAAR	Native Affairs Annual Report.
NWAR	Native Welfare Annual Report.
HREOC	Human Rights and Equal Opportunity Commission.
V&P	Votes and Proceedings, Western Australian Parliament.

INTRODUCTION
1   Speech by the Hon. Prime Minister, P J Keating, Australian Launch of the International Year for the World's Indigenous People, Redfern, 10 December 1992.
2   933/77/1949.
3   933/306/1938.

CHAPTER 1
1   Initial Conference (1937), p 1.
2   Ibid., p 12.
3   P Jacobs (1990), pp 15–22.
4   A T Vaughan (1995), p 5.
5   C Fyfe (1994), p 72.
6   M Kohn (1996), p 34.
7   C Wilson (1996), p 109.
8   Fyfe, op cit., p 73.
9   R Littlewood and M Lipsedge (1989), p 43.
10 Royal Commission (1905), p 25.
11 Ibid., p64.
12 Ibid., p 26.
13 A Haebich (1992), p 85.
14 Ibid., p 111.
15 Jacobs, op cit., p 25.
16 Ibid., p 67.

17 For a general discussion on Moore River and Carrolup settlements see Jacobs (1990), pp 123–125; Haebich (1992), chapter 6.
18 ALS (1995), p 15.
19 Jacobs, op cit., p 68.
20 Royal Commission (1935), p 12.
21 Ibid., p 3.
22 P Hasluck (1939), p 1.
23 Ibid., p 2.
24 Ibid., pp 4–6.
25 Royal Commission (1935), p 8.
26 Ibid., p 9.
27 Ibid., p 8.
28 *West Australian*, 18 April 1930.
29 993/709/42.
30 993/804/40.
31 Cited in ALS (1996), p 27.
32 993/305/1930.
33 993/77/1949.
34 S Dubow (1995), p 214.
35 K Malik (1995), p 114.
36 Kohn, op cit., p 71.
37 A P Elkin (1937), p 486.
38 Initial Conference, op cit., p 14.
39 Ibid., p 16.
40 Ibid., p 10.
41 Ibid., p 17.
42 Ibid.
43 Initial Conference, op cit., pp 10–11.
44 A O Neville, op cit., p 68.
45 Ibid., p 57.
46 Ibid., p 47.
47 Initial Conference, op cit., p 11.
48 Neville, op cit., pp 61; 63.
49 Royal Commission (1935), p 8.
50 Initial Conference, op cit., p 8.
51 993/817/1939.
52 Ibid.
53 Neville, op cit., p 62.
54 993/898/43.

55 Cited in T Buti (1996), p 8.
56 993/1306/46.
57 Canadian Royal Commission (1996), vol 2, chapter 10.
58 *Hansard* 1936, p 2382.

CHAPTER 2
1   Malik (1995), p 124.
2   NAAR 1945, *V&P* 1947, vol 2, p 11.
3   Survey of Native Affairs (1948), p 25.
4   Ibid.
5   NAAR 1945, *V&P* 1947, vol 12, p 11.
6   1733/692/1951.
7   Neville (1947), p 76.
8   Survey of Native Affairs, op cit., p 31.
9   Ibid., p 26.
10 993/970/43.
11 1733/277/1949.
12 Neville, op cit., p 139.
13 Ibid., p137.
14 Survey of Native Affairs, op cit., p 27.
15 993/678/43.
16 P Biskup (1973), chapter 7; and Haebich (1988), chapter 3.
17 NAAR 1935 *V&P* 1935, vol 2, p 151.
18 Hasluck (1938).
19 NAAR 1945 op cit., p 8.
20 NAAR, *V&P* 1954, vol 3, p 5.
21 1525/76/1949.
22 993/965/43.
23 NAAR 1954, op cit., p 7.
24 Survey of Native Affairs, op cit., p 16.
25 No author (1967), *A Place in the Sun*, p 29.
26 Special Committee on Native Matters (1958), p 25.
27 NAAR 1945, op cit., p 10.
28 NAAR, *V&P* 1955, vol 3, p 40.
29 993/313/44.
30 *A Place in the Sun*, op cit., p 23.
31 NAAR, *V&P* 1956, vol 3, p 28.
32 993/1137/42.
33 993/32/53.

34 993/140/49.
35 NAAR, *V&P* 1938, vol 1, p 2.
36 NAAR, *V&P* 1952, vol 3, p 9.
37 993/1147/42.
38 NAAR, *V&P* 1959, vol 3, p 28.
39 NAAR, *V&P* 1952, vol 3, p 5.
40 NAAR, *V&P* 1952, vol 3, p 15.
41 Survey of Native Affairs, op cit., p 22.
42 993/14/49.
43 NAAR, *V&P* 1938, vol 1, p 13.
44 993/222/43.
45 Survey of Native Affairs, op cit., p 25.
46 993/222/43.
47 Survey of Native Affairs, op cit., p 23.
48 Ibid., p 23.
49 993/140/49.
50 993/140/49.
51 993/490/49.
52 993/134/45.
53 *Hansard* 1944, vol 113, p 826.
54 Ibid., vol 114, p 825.
55 Ibid., vol 113, p 1176.
56 Ibid., vol 114, p 1021.
57 NAAR, *V&P* 1956, vol 3, p 12.
58 993/140/49.
59 993/140/49.
60 *Cyclopedia of Western Australia*, vol 1, 1985 edition, Hesperian Press, p 51.
61 Neville, op cit., p121.
62 *Cyclopedia of Western Australia*, op cit.
63 Survey of Native Affairs, op cit., p 24.
64 993/262/50.
65 NAAR 1945, vol 2, p 8.
66 Survey of Native Affairs, op cit., p 10.
67 NAAR, *V&P* 1952, vol 3, p 26.
68 Interview, Frank Gare, 1997.
69 Hansard 1947, vol 1, p 514.
70 HREOC, p 33.

CHAPTER 3

1   This section is based on an extended interview with Phillip Prosser, 1996.
2   NAAR,*V&P* 1952, vol 3, p 28.
3   *West Australian,* 5 May 1950.
4   Interview, Phillip Prosser.
5   Cited in ALS 1996, p 28.
6   Some information on Roelands was obtained from non-Aboriginal sources close to the institution who did not wish to be identified.
7   NAAR, *V&P* 1952, vol 3, p 28.
8   *West Australian,* 5 May 1950.
9   This section was based on an extended interview with Rosalie Fraser, 1997.
10 D Sweeney (1995), p 5.
11 Ibid.
12 *Australian,* 11 November 1995.

CHAPTER 4

1   2532/302/4.
2   Ibid.
3   *Hansard* 1956, vol 1, p 1108.
4   Ibid., vol 3, p 1105.
5   Ibid., p 1111.
6   Select Committee into Native Welfare in the Laverton–Warburton Range (1956), pp 12–13.
7   Ibid., p 12.
8   NWAR, *V&P* 1956, vol 3.
9   Select Committee into Native Welfare in the Laverton–Warburton Range, op cit., pp 12–13.
10 *Hansard* 1956, vol 3, p 3820.
11 Ibid., vol 2, p 2467.
12 Ibid., 1957, vol 2, p 2465.
13 Report of the Special Committee on Native Matters (1958), p 7.
14 *Hansard* 1957, vol 2, p 2467.
15 Report of the Special Committee on Native Matters, (1958), p 15.
16 Ibid., p 16.
17 Ibid., p 29.
18 Ibid., p 28.

19 Ibid., p 16.
20 993/59/1949.
21 Report of the Special Committee on Native Matters (1958), p 29.
22 HREOC (1997), p 112.
23 2532/302/4 A403, vol 1.
24 Ibid.
25 NWAR, *V&P* 1958, vol3.
26 1733/200/64.
27 1733/277/1949.
28 2532/320/A403, vol 1.
29 Ibid.
30 2532/320/A413, vol 1.
31 Ibid.
32 2532/320/A403, vol 1.
33 993/1493/45.
34 Ibid.
35 2532/320/4A403, vol 1.
36 Ibid.
37 Ibid.
38 Ibid.
39 Survey of Native Affairs (1948), p 11.
40 1733/200/64.
41 2532/320/4A403, vol 1.
42 2532/320/4A413, vol 1.
43 2532/320/4A403, vol 1.
44 993/1493/45.
45 2532/320/4A403, vol 1.
46 Ibid.
47 1733/200/64.
48 1733/277/1949.
49 993/59/1949.
50 2532/320/4/A403, vol 1.
51 E Gallagher (1971), p 59.
52 Interview 1997.
53 993/59/1949.
54 2532/320/A413, vol 1.
55 2532/320/4A326, vol 1.
56 993/59/1949.
57 *Hansard* 1968–9, vol 3, p 2858.

58   1733/277/1948.
59   Australian Bureau of Statistics (1994), p 1.

CHAPTER 5
1   Gallagher (1971), p 123.
2   Hasluck (1953), p 16.
3   NWAR, *V&P* 1958, vol 3, p 5.
4   NWAR, *V&P* 1956, vol3, p 27.
5   NWAR, *V&P* 1956, vol 3.
6   1733/692/1951.
7   Special Committee on Native Affairs (1958), p 9.
8   Ibid.
9   NWAR, 1964.
10   *A Place in the Sun*, p 24.
11   Ibid.
12   NWAR, *V&P* 1958, vol 3.
13   *Place in the Sun, p* 25.
14   NWAR, *V&P* 1957, vol 4.
15   *A Place in the Sun*, p 25.
16   H Schapper (1970), p 42.
17   Ibid., p 41.
18   Gallagher (1971), p 130.
19   *A Place in the Sun*, p 26.
20   *Aboriginal Welfare News*, April 1965.
21   2559/320/6 A1 852, vol 1.
22   *Hansard* 1964 vol 3, p 3163.
23   *A Place in the Sun*, p 29.
24   *Aboriginal Welfare News*, April 1967.
25   NWAR, *V&P* 1967, vol 4, p 40.
26   1724/138/68.
27   Schapper, p 64.
28   1724/451/64.
29   Royal Commission on Aboriginal Affairs (1974), p 254.
30   J Kidd (1967).
31   Schapper (1970), p 192.
32   Hasluck (1953), p 17.
33   *Sunday Times,* 24 February 1963.
34   Gallagher (1971), p 59.
35   1724/191/62.

36 *West Australian,* 10 June 1972.
37 1724/191/62.
38 S Bennett (1989), p 54.
39 *West Australian,* 29 May 1967.
40 R McKeich (1969), p 22–23.
41 M Robinson (1969), p 18.
42 1724/451/64.
43 R Taft (1970).
44 1724/191/62.
45 Public Interest Research Group (1972).
46 *Daily News,* 7 April 1971.
47 *West Australian,* 20 September 1969.
48 1724/451/64.
49 *West Australian,* 10 June 1972.
50 Schapper (1970), p 56.
51 Ibid., p 42.
52 Ibid., p 58.
53 Ibid., p 75.
54 Royal Commission on Aboriginal Affairs (1974), p 299.

CHAPTER 6
1 ALS (1995), p 46.
2 Ibid., p 5.
3 Ibid., p 44.
4 P Swan and B Raphael (1995), Part 1, p 3.
5 Ibid., Part 2, p 36.
6 Ibid., p 37.
7 ALS (1996), pp 54–57.
8 J Herman (1992), p 34.
9 Interview Frank Gare, 1997.
10 ALS (1996), p 64.
11 A Hass (1996), p 13.
12 D Wardi (1992), p 9.
13 Hass, op cit., p 41–42.
14 Interview Phillip Prosser, 1996.
15 HREOC (1997), p 196.
16 ALS (1996), p 69.
17 HREOC (1997), p 173.
18 S Wolff (1981), p 70.

19 Herman (1992), p 75.
20 ALS (1995), pp 3, 125; (1996) p 198.
21 Ibid., p 3.
22 ALS (1996), p 199.
23 Hass (1996), p 108.
24 ALS (1995), p 237.
25 Ibid., (1996), p 328.
26 Ibid., (1995), p 62.
27 HREOC (1997), p 117.
28 Herman (1992), p 110.
29 A Miller (1983), p 7.
30 ALS (1995), p 36.
31 HREOC (1997), p 31.
32 ALS (1995), p 39.
33 Ibid., p 264.
34 S Wolff (1982), p 187.
35 Interview Frank Gare, 1997.
36 G Majchrzak-Hamilton and N Hamilton (1997).
37 Robinson (1969), pp 17–18.
38 Estimates based on information provide by the Aboriginal Visitors scheme.
39 ALS (1996), p 236.
40 ALS (1995), p 43.
41 Ibid., p 30.
42 Task Force on Aboriginal Social Justice (1994), vol 2, p 495.
43 Interview Frank Gare, 1997.
44 ALS (1995), p 31.
45 Ibid.

CHAPTER 7
1 ALS (1996), p 338.
2 HREOC (1997), p 223.
3 Hass (1996), p 7.
4 HREOC (1997), p 222.
5 ALS (1995) Telling Our Story, pp 214–47.
6 HREOC (1997), p 222.
7 J Winch (1992).
8 Miller (1990), p 168.
9 ALS (1996), p 336.

10   Ibid., p 339.
11   Australian Bureau of Statistics (1994), p 39.
12   D Eades (1995).
13   HREOC (1997), pp 492–93.
14   M Dodson (1995), p 18.
15   Ibid., p 20.
16   Q Beresford and P Omaji (1996), Chapter 4.
17   Ibid., pp 23–27.
18   Select Committee on Youth Affairs (1991), no 3, p 8.
19   Beresford and Omaji, op cit., Chapter 6.
20   ALS (1996), p 338.
21   Beresford and Omaji, op cit.
22   H Groome (1995), p 20.
23   Australian Bureau of Statistics, op cit., p 23; 31.
24   House of Representatives Standing Committee on Aboriginal and Torres Strait Islander Affairs (1994), p 292.
25   Ibid., p 295.
26   Ibid., p 294.
27   *West Australian*, 17 April 1997.
28   D Saylor (1997).
29   Dodson, op cit., p 17.
30   B Howard (1995), p 50.
31   M Dodson, op cit., p 13.
32   Ibid., p 19.
33   Ibid., p15.
34   HREOC (1997), p 432.
35   Department for Community Welfare Submision to the Royal Commission on Aborigines, pp 12–18.
36   Cited in ALS (1996), p 279.
37   *West Australian*, 9 September 1996.
38   Ibid., 27 May 1997, p 11.

CHAPTER 8
1   ALS (1995), p iii.
2   Ibid.
3   Council for Aboriginal Reconciliation (1997), p 20.
4   *Australian Medicine* (1996), p 13.
5   *Age*, 2 June 1997, p A25.
6   *Australian*, 21–22 June 1997, p 18.

7   *Australian*, 21–22 June 1997, p 18.
8   *Australian*, 21 May 1997.
9   *Age*, 2 June 1997, p A15.
10   M Groot and T Rowse (1991), pp 4–5.
11   Ibid., p 6.
12   Council for Aboriginal Reconciliation, Annual Report, 1993–4, p2.
13   Task Force on Aboriginal Social Justice (1994), vol 2, p 551.
14   Ibid.
15   Ibid., Appendix L, p 4.
16   HREOC Annual Report 1995–96, p 73.
17   *Age*, 29 May 1997, p A14.
18   *West Australian*, 28 July 1997, p 3.
19   *Australian*, 3 June 1997, p 12.
20   *Bulletin*, 4–10 June 1997, p 14.
21   *Australian*, 27 May 1997, p 4.
22   *West Australian*, 30 May 1997, p 12.
23   *Bulletin*, 22 July 1997, p 9.
24   *West Australian*, 17 June 1997, p 13.
25   *Australian*, 7 October 1996, p 1.
26   *Age*, 29 May 1997.
27   *Australian* 27 May 1997, p 5.
28   *West Australian*, 17 June 1997, p 12.
29   *West Australian*, 31 May 1997, p12.
30   K Jonassohn and F Chalk (1987), p 6.
31   Survey on Native Affairs (1948), p 13; 26.
32   W Morgan (1997), p 26.
33   *Australian*, 27 May 1997, p 4.
34   Ibid., 8 July 1996, p 11.
35   *Australian*, 1 June 1997, p 21.
36   *Aboriginal Independent Newspaper*, 3 September 1997, p 7.
37   Ibid., 20 August 1997, p 5.

CHAPTER 9
1   A Marcus (1994), p 157.
2   NWAR 1957, *V&P* vol 3, p 115.
3   Ibid., 1958 *V&P* vol 3, p 5.
4   1733/418/51
5   J Starke (1984), p 139.
6   Ibid., p 140.

7   London, p 209.
8   Ibid., p 210.
9   A Fleras and I Elliot (1992), p 332.
10 NWAR 1954, *V&P* vol 3, p 3.
11 A O Neville (1947), p 161.
12 S Castles (1996), p 21
13 Cited in F Gales and A Brookman (1975), pp 57-58.
14 S Rose (1997), p 117.
15 Ibid., p 130-31.

BIBLIOGRAPHY

STATE ARCHIVES

993/32/53	Infant Welfare Matters
993/59/49	Wandering Mission Patrol Report
993/77/49	Sister Kate's Children's Home
993/134/45	Inquiry Regarding Departmental Policy
993/140/49	Native Attitudes Towards Whites
993/196/46	Forrest River Mission — Reports of Inspection
993/222/43	Exclusion of Half Caste and Native Children from Schools
993/262/50	Hostel for Natives
993/305/38	Home for Quarter Caste Children
993/313/44	Gnowangerup Mission. Reports of Inspector
993/423/38	Absorption of Half Castes into the White Population
993/490/49	Education — Irregular Attendance of Native Children
993/678/43	Native Girls as Domestics and Nurses
993/817/39	Gnowangerup Mission: Native Matters General
993/844/40	Sister Kate's Home for Quarter Caste Children
993/898/43	Native Children — Secondary Education
993/904/40	New Norcia Mission — Education
993/904/42	Homes for Half Caste Children
993/965/43	Agricultural and Pastoral Workers
993/970/43	Carrolup Native Settlement
993/1137/42	Post War Housing for Natives and Half Castes
993/1306/46	Department of Native Affairs — Inspector's Journal, 1946
993/1493/45	Roelands Mission — Native Matters
1525/76/49	Employment Permits
1724/138/68	Employment Survey
1724/191/62	Discrimination Against Natives
1733/1493/45	Roelands Native Mission
1733/200/64	Forrest River Mission

1733/277/49   Missions: Policy Regarding Control
1733/416/51   Missions: Policy Re Discharge
1733/692/51   Private Tours and Inspections of Natives
1417 A2738   Sister Kate's Children's Homes: Educational Matters
2532 320/4 A403 Vol. 1   New Norcia Mission
2532 320/4 A326 Vol. 1   Native State Wards
2532 320/4 A413 Vol. 1   Wandering Mission

OFFICIAL PAPERS

Annual Reports, Department of Native Affairs/Native Welfare (WA) 1930-1970.

Australian Bureau of Statistics (1994). *National Aboriginal and Torres Strait Islander Survey: Western Australia.*

Canadian Royal Commission on Aboriginal Peoples, 1996.

Australian Council for Aboriginal Reconciliation (1997). *Walking Together*, No. 19.

Australian Council for Aboriginal Reconciliation, Annual Reports 1991-96.

Department of Child Welfare (WA), Annual Reports 1940-1960.

Department for Community Welfare (WA) (1974). *Submission to the Royal Commission on Aborigines*, unpublished.

Dodson, M (1995) *Third Report: Aboriginal and Torres Strait Islander Social Justice Commissioner*, AGPS, Canberra.

Dodson, M (1996). *Fourth Report: Aboriginal and Torres Strait Islander Social Justice Commissioner*, AGPS, Canberra.

Hansard (WA) 1940-1980.

House of Representatives Standing Committee on Aboriginal and Torres Strait Islander Affairs (Commonwealth) (1994). *Justice Under Scrutiny.*

Human Rights and Equal Opportunity Commission (1997). *Bringing Them Home,* Human Rights and Equal Opportunity Commission, Sydney.

Human Rights and Equal Opportunity Commission, Annual Report 1995-96, Human Rights and Equal Opportunity Commission, Sydney.

Report of the Royal Commission into the Conditions and Treatment of Aborigines (WA) (1935). *Votes and Proceedings* Vol. 7.

Report of the Royal Commission on the Conditions of the Natives (WA) (1905). *Votes and Proceedings* Vol. 1.

Report of the Select Committee into Native Welfare in the Laverton-Warburton Range (WA) (1956). *Votes and Proceedings* Vol. 3.

Report of the Special Committee on Native Affairs (WA) (1958). *Votes and Proceedings* Vol. 3.

Report on Survey of Native Affairs (WA) (1948). *Votes and Proceedings* Vol. 2.

Royal Commission on Aboriginal Affairs (WA) (1974). unprinted.

Select Committee into Youth Affairs (WA) (1991). *Discussion Paper No. 3 Youth and the Law.*

Swan, P and Raphael, B (1995). *Ways Forward: National Consultancy Report on Aboriginal and Torres Strait Islander Mental Health* Parts 1 and 2, AGPS, Canberra.

Task Force on Aboriginal Social Justice (1994). *Report of the Task Force* Vols 1 and 2, Government of Western Australia.

BOOKS AND ARTICLES

Aboriginal Legal Service (1995). *Telling Our Story*, ALS, Perth.

Aboriginal Legal Service (1996). *After the Removal*, ALS, Perth.

Bennett, S (1989). *Aborigines and Political Power*, Allen and Unwin, St. Leonards.

Beresford, Q and Omaji, P (1996). *Rites of Passage: Aboriginal Youth Crime and Justice*, Fremantle Arts Centre Press, Fremantle.

Berndt, R and C (1980). *Aborigines of the West: Their Past and Their Present*, University of Western Australia Press, Perth.

Biskup, P (1973). *Not Slaves, Not Citizens: The Aboriginal Problem in Western Australia*, University of Queensland Press, St Lucia.

Buti, T (1996). History That Must be Told: The Removal of Aboriginal Children From Their Families in Western Australia, *Hindsight*, Vol. 7, No. 2.

Castles, S (1996). The Racisms of Globalisation, in Vasta, E and Castles, S *The teeth are smiling: The persistence of races in multicultural Australia*, Allen and Unwin, Sydney.

Dubow, S (1995). *Scientific Racism in Modern South Africa*, University of Cambridge Press, Cambridge.

Eades, D (1995). Cross Examination of Aboriginal Children: The Pinkenha Case, *Aboriginal Law Bulletin*, Vol. 3, No. 75.

Elkin, A P (1937). Education and the Australian Aborigines, *Oce*, Vol 7, No 4.

Flevas, A and Elliot, J (1992). *The nations within: Aboriginal-state relations in Canada, The United States and New Zealand*, Oxford University Press, Toronto.

Fyfe, C (1994). Using Race As An Instrument of Policy: A Historical Review, *Race and Class*, Vol 36, No 2.

Gale, F and Brookman, A (1975). *Race Relations in Australia: The Aborigines*, McGraw Hill, Sydney.

Groome, H (1995). Towards Improved Understandings of Aboriginal Young People, *Youth Studies Australia*, Vol 14, No 4.

Groot, M and Rowse, T (1991). The Backlash Hypothesis and the Land Rights Option, *Australian Aboriginal Studies*, No 1.

Haebich, A (1992). *For Their Own Good: Aborigines and Government in the SouthWest of Western Australia 1900-1940*, University of Western Australia Press, Perth.

Hasluck, P (1939). *Our Southern Half Caste Natives and Their Conditions*, Native Welfare Council, Perth.

Hasluck, P (1953). *Native Welfare in Australia*, Perth.

Hass, A (1996). *The Aftermath: Living with the Holocaust*, Cambridge University Press, Cambridge.

Herman, J (1992). *Trauma and Recovery: From Domestic Abuse to Political Terror*, Harper and Collins, London.

Howard, B (1995). Different Coloured Skin: The Experiences of Aboriginal Young People in the Juvenile Justice System, *Youth Studies Australia*, Vol 14, No 4.

Jacobs, P (1990). *Mister Neville: A Biography*, Fremantle Arts Centre Press, Fremantle.

Jonassohn, K and Chalk, F (1987). A Typology of Genocide and Some Implications for the Human Rights Agenda, in Walliman, I and Dobkowski, M *Genocide and the Modern Age: Etiology and Case Studies of Mass Death*, Greenwood Press, New York.

Kohn (1996). *The Race Gallery: The Return of Racial Science*, Vintage, London.

Littlewood, R and Lipsedge, M (1989). *Aliens and Alienists, Ethnic Minorities and Psychiatry*, Unwin Hayman, London.

London, H (1970). *Non-white Immigration and the White Australia*

Policy, Sydney University Press, Sydney.

Majchrzak-Hamilton, G and Hamilton, N (1997). Socio-economic Deprivation of Australia's Stolen Generation, *People and Place*. Vol 5, No 41.

Malik, K (1995). *The Meaning of Race: Race History and Culture in Western Society*, MacMillan, Basingstoke.

Marcus, A (1994). *Australian Race Relations*, Allen and Unwin, Sydney.

McKeich, R (1969). Part Aboriginal Education, in Berndt, R *Thinking About Australian Aboriginal Welfare*, University of Western Australia Press, Perth.

Miller, A (1983). *For Your Own Good*, Farra, Straus, Girovx, New York.

Miller, A (1990). *The Untouched Key: Tracing Childhood Trauma in Creativity and Destructiveness*, Doubleday, New York.

Morgan, W (1997). Review: Bringing Them Home, *Aboriginal Law Bulletin*, Vol 4, Issue No 6.

Neville, A O (1947). *Australia's Coloured Minority*, Sydney.

Robinson, M (1969). Imprisonment of Aborigines and Part Aborigines in Western Australia, in Berndt, R *Thinking About Australian Aboriginal Welfare*, University of Western Australia Press, Perth.

Rose, P (1997). *They and We: Racial and Ethnic Relations in the United States*, McGraw and Hill, New York.

Rowse, T (1994). Middle Australia and the Noble Savage: A Political Romance, in Beckett, J (ed.) *Past and present. The construction of Aboriginality*, Aboriginal Studies Press, Canberra.

Saylor, D (1997). Three Strikes by the Burglar: The Police and DCJ, *Indigenous Law Bulletin*, Vol 4, Issue No 2.

Schapper, H (1970). *Aboriginal Advancement to Integration: Conditions and Plans for Western Australia*, Australian National University Press, Canberra.

Starke, J (1984). Australia and the International Pprotection of Human Rights, in Ryan, K (Ed.) *International Law in Australia*, Law Book Company, Sydney.

Swain, T and Rose, D (1988). *Aboriginal Australians and Christian Missions: Ethnographic and Historical Studies*, The Australian Association for the Study of Religions, Adelaide.

Sweeney, D (1995). Broken Promises: The Crown's Fiduciary Duty to Aboriginal Peoples, *Aboriginal Law Bulletin*, Vol 3, No 75.

Taft, R (1970). Attitudes of Western Australians Towards Aborigines, in Taft, R, Dawson, J and Beasley, P *Aborigines in Australian Society: Attitudes and Conditions*, Australian National University Press, Canberra.

Vaughan (1995). *Roots of American Racism: Essays on the Colonial Experience*, Oxford University Press, New York.

Wardi, D (1992). *Memorial Candles: Children of the Holocaust*, Routledge, London.

Wilson (1996). *Racism: From Slavery to Advanced Capitalism*, Sage Publications, London.

Wolff, S (1981). *Children Under Stress*, Penguin Books, Ringwood.

UNPUBLISHED MATERIAL

Department of Native Welfare (1967). *A Place in the Sun*, Department of Native Welfare, Perth.

Gallagher, E (1971). Wandering Mission as Part of the Pallotine Mission Effort in Assimilating the Aboriginal, Teacher's Higher Certificate, Perth.

Kidd, J (1967). Aborigines in East Perth, Graylands Teacher's College Thesis.

Public Interest Research Group (1972). Aboriginal Survey, Law School, University of Western Australia.

Winch, J (1996). Aboriginal Initiatives in Aboriginal Health, Proceedings: Children of Indigenous People of the Asia Pacific Region. An Agenda for Academic Public Health. Curtin University.

NEWSPAPERS/JOURNALS

Aboriginal Independent Newspaper 1997
Aboriginal Welfare News 1963-68
Age 1997
Australian 1997
Bulletin 1997
West Australian 1997

INDEX

Aboriginal culture, 46
 not valued by mission and carers, 101, 107, 108
  see also missions
 strength of, 46, 65, 66, 68, 71, 83
Aboriginal Legal Service
 survey, 193, 195, 197-9, 202-3, 205, 214, 235
Aboriginal rights, 248
 white support for, 54, 59-60, 63, 125-6, 128-9, 131
Aborigines
 classification by colour, 14-15, 21
 dying race concept, 46-7, 48
 'half caste' problem, 33-6, 39-42, 48-50
 living conditions, 18-19, 41, 65, 70
 measures of disadvantage, 173-4, 218, 231, 232
 population statistics, 40, 64, 231
 standing in law, 38, 97
 as threat to white society, 16, 38-9, 47-8, 62, 64, 89
Aborigines Act (1905), 15, 37
absorption policy, 48, 51-4, 61
 targeted 'half castes', 44-5, 47, 53-4
Apology
 opposition to, 236, 237-8, 244-7
 symbolism of, 236, 237
 by WA Government, 238
assimilation policy, 12, 17, 61, 256-7
 discriminatory, 63, 99
 opposition to, 63, 89
 purpose of, 89-92, 160-1
 racist base, 64, 92, 99
 removal of children legalised, 62, 67, 90, 93-5
 segregationist, 100, 161, 163, 174-5
 under resourced, 92-3
Australia
 Aboriginal policies *see* absorption policy; assimilation policy
 cultural genocide practised, 257-8

history, 252-3
international record on racism, 258
racist laws, 256, 258-60
white superiority, 163, 164-5, 256, 258

Bateman, F E A, 66-7
attitude to Aborigines, 64, 66-8, 91, 153
reforms needed, 92, 93-4
removal policy, 67-8, 251-2
Berndt, R, 257
Blanchard, S A, 138, 150-1
Bordern Reserve, 77-8
Bowlby, J, 132-3, 196
Bray, F I, 55, 56, 68

Calgaret, Doreen *see* Hill, Doreen
Canadian Natives *see* Native American children
Chief Protector *see* legal guardianship; names of individuals
Child Endowment, 76, 80
Child Welfare Act, 15, 67
Child Welfare Department
abuse in care known, 135-6, 138-40, 146-7, 153-4
failure of duty of care, 117-18, 122-4
foster care, 115, 156
Hill family file, 17
importance of family, 56-7
neglect charges, 93, 96-7
vs. Native Welfare, 98-9, 155-6
Church of Christ missions, 84, 105-6
citizenship, 87-8, 163-4
restrictions, 16, 87, 88, 164
Clutterbuck, Katherine (Sister Kate), 43-4, 60
Commonwealth Conference on Aboriginal Affairs (1937), 29-30,45
absorption policy, 53-4
white interests protected, 47-8
Cook, Cecil, 47-8
Council for Aboriginal Reconciliation *see under* reconciliation
country towns, 168, 175-8, 183-4
Coverley, A A, 59
Cross, K G, 104-7, 144-5

cultural genocide *see* genocide
cultural transformation *see* purpose under removal of children

Darwin, Charles, 33
deaths in custody, 206, 234-5
Department of Native Affairs, 98
    attitudes of staff, 65-6, 96
    duties in conflict, 98, 155-6
    practice of removal, 57-8, 96, 125-8, 146
    racist practices, 55, 56, 98
    relationships with missions, 102
doctors, attitudes of, 138-9, 185-6
Dodson, Michael, 228, 229-30
Dodson, Patrick, 234, 235

Education Department *see* schools
employment, 163, 168-9
    farm work, 76, 169
    wages, 73-6
    War time, 72-3
    work permits, 73-4
eugenics, 33, 42-3, 45

Forrest River Mission, 136-7, 147
    behaviour problems in Wyndham, 151-2
foster families, white, 23-4, 101, 112-13
    abuse in, 198-200
Fraser, Rosalie, 10, 99, 19
    abused, 101, 113-14, 116-17, 120-1
    foster home, 115-16, 17-18
    removal, 114-15
Fremantle prisoners, 170-1
    segregation, 186-7
    see also prisons

Gare, Frank, 57-8, 95, 98-9, 130
genocide, 58, 249-51
    assimilation policy, 251-2, 257-8
Gnowangerup, 54, 153, 177, 197
Grayden, W, 125-6, 130, 131
guardianship *see* legal guardianship

'half castes' *see under* Aborigines; absorption policy; Neville, A O
Hasluck, Paul, 40-1, 70-1, 159, 174-5
Herron, Senator J, 236-7, 249
Hewitt, R, 179-80
Hill, Doreen, 13-19, 26-7
    marriage, 16-18
    parenting skills, 17
    removal of children, 19
Hill, Herbert Clem, 16-18, 26-8
    death, 27
    maintenance payments, 20, 24-5
    search for children, 24-5
Hill, Sandra, 10, 12
    foster family, 23, 25-6
    at Sister Kate's, 21-2
    removal, 19-20
    reunion with parents, 26
Hill-Keddie, Trish, 10, 12, 193
    continuing distress, 207-8, 210-11
    foster family, 23-4
    removal, 19-20
    reunion with parents, 26-8
Holocaust, 249-50
    survivors, 194-5, 198, 213
housing, 18, 70-1, 81, 171-2, 176
    government responses, 77, 78, 166-8
Howard, John, 254
    Aboriginal affairs policies, 238
    refusal to apologise, 236, 238, 244
    rejection of HREOC report, 235-6
    view of history, 252-3
Human Rights and Equal Opportunity Commission Report,
        196, 209, 213-14, 233, 235
    recommendations opposed, 245-6, 248-9
    recommendations supported, 254

justice system, 226-8
    arrest rate, 184-5, 218
    detention of juveniles, 229-30
    disadvantage not addressed, 222-5, 229-30
    discriminatory, 218-20, 221, 224

juvenile crime, 8, 172-4, 216-18
over representation, 191, 205, 220-1
see also police; prisons

Keating, Paul, 11-12, 235
Kidd, Jeanette, 171-3

legal guardianship, 14, 21, 37, 44, 55
responsibility for welfare, 119-21
Linnaeus, Carl, 32

malnutrition, 79, 80
in foster home, 116
marriages, control of, 44, 48, 49-53
maternal attachment, 128-9, 132-3, 196
mental health studies, 192
Middleton, S G, 86-7, 89
missionaries
racist views, 140-1
untrained, 147-8, 152
missions
abuse in care, 141, 153-4, 196-7, 199
accountability, 154
behavioural outcomes, 133-4, 147, 150-2
care lacking, 137-8, 140, 150-2
education inadequate, 140, 152-3
government funding, 135, 154
living conditions, 136-7
negligence, 135, 140
outcomes, 133-4, 162-3, 165-6, 187-8, 205
training inadequate, 151,163, 168-71, 173
Moore River, 39, 40
Moseley, H D, 40-1, 42

Native Administration Act (1936), 15, 56-7
guardianship extended, 21, 44
legalised removal of children, 56
Native American children, 58-9
effects of removal, 191, 202
Native Welfare Department *see* Department of Native Affairs
Nazi policies, 59, 61, 194

neglected children, 62, 67, 93-9
    abuse of system, 97, 98-9
Neville, A O, 30-2, 34-5, 60
    as Chief Protector, 14, 38-9, 55
    control of marriages, 48, 49-52
    'half caste' problem, 39, 48-50
    racist theories, 42-3, 47, 48, 50-2, 54
    removal of children, 30-3, 48, 55, 66
New Norcia Mission, 140-1, 147-8
    dormitories, 136, 150
    emotional deprivation, 122, 150-1
    government support, 148-9
    medical neglect, 138-9
    punishment, 145-7
nuclear tests, 124

Perth, 171
    Aborigines prohibited from city, 81
    East Perth, 81, 171-3
police
    racism, 82, 97, 184, 218, 221
    role of protector, 82
    treatment of juveniles, 218, 221-2, 228-9
poverty, 70-2, 79-80
    causes, 69-72, 75-6, 91-2
    desire to escape from, 68, 80-1, 83-4
    governments fail to address, 66, 68-9, 72, 79, 95, 130-1, 135, 165
    neglect assumed, 97
prisons
    background of prisoners, 206
    deaths, 206, 234-5
    deterrence limited, 206
    racial barriers, 178-9, 186-7
Prosser, Phillip, 10, 101-3, 120
    removal, 195
Public Interest Research Group study, 183-6
public opinion
    Apology, 237-8, 245-7
    assistance to Aboriginal people, 239-40, 242
    compassionate attitudes, 241
    racist attitudes, 180-7, 238, 241-2, 247

on reconciliation, 241

racism, 260-1
    attitudes, 40, 64, 90-1, 241, 242, 265-6
    disadvantage created, 89, 262-3
    experience of, 81, 82, 84, 175-8, 243-4, 266
    fear, 243
    history of, 31-3, 45-6
    hostility, 86-7, 89, 165
    institutionalised, 261-2
    prejudice, 85, 87, 174, 180-7, 241-2, 265
    segregationist, 81-5, 179-80, 248, 260-1
    white superiority, 61,
reconciliation, 11-12, 235, 252
    public opinion, 241
Referendum (1967), 239
    No vote statistics, 177-8
removal of children, 8-9, 15-16, 37-8
    age of removal, 17, 48-9, 128-9, 132-3
    emotional deprivation, 128-9, 132
    as government policy, 29-30, 35-6, 230-1
        see also absorption policy; assimilation policy
    moment remembered, 19-20, 114-15, 195
    neglect as justification, 62, 67, 79, 93-5
    numbers, 157
    opposition to, 124
    parents, treatment of, 97, 98, 142-3, 198, 208-10, 235
    in practice, 57-8, 93
    problems recognised, 93-4, 128-9, 132
    purpose, 12, 49, 62-3, 90, 92, 101, 159-60
    racist, 12, 255-6
    see also stolen generations, outcomes for
reserves, 39, 66, 165-6
    alcohol not permitted, 176
    conditions on, 70-1, 77-9, 166, 176
Roelands Mission, 87, 102-12, 149
    abuse of children, 102-4, 106-8, 110-12, 143-4, 149-50, 197
    child labour, 108-10
    outcomes, 149, 161-2, 189-90
Roth, E W, 35, 37
Royal Commission into the Conditions and Treatment of

Aborigines (1935), 40
Royal Commission on Aboriginal Affairs (1974), 188, 231-2, 234
Royal Commission on the Conditions of the Natives (1904), 35

Schapper, H, 167, 169, 173, 187-8
schools, 82-5, 87, 185
    racism in, 82-5, 178
    retention rates, 86-7, 185, 225
Select Committee into Native Welfare in the Laverton-
        Warburton Range (1956), 125-30
Sister Kate see Clutterbuck, Katherine
Sister Kate's Children's Home, 13, 43, 44
    child abuse, 22, 23, 28, 199
    cottage model, 21, 43
    cultural transformation aim, 49
    daily life, 21-2
    experience of Hill children, 17, 19-21
    family visits, 22-3, 49
    foster families, 23
Social Darwinism, 33, 46, 48
Special Committee on Native Affairs (1958), 130-4
stolen generations, outcomes for, 25-6, 191-2, 205
    abuse survivors, 197, 199, 200-1
    authority, problems with, 133, 147, 208
        see also under justice system
    children removed, 215-16
    family breakdown, 203, 207-15
    identity loss, 190-1, 201-3
    justice sought, 253-4
    mental health, 150, 192
    self esteem lacking, 134, 191, 203
    substance abuse, 172, 191
    traumatised, 193-4, 196-7, 201
    see also under missions; removal of children
Street, Jessie, 63, 162

Taft, Ronald, 180-1
Tardun Mission, 137, 142
Tuckey, Wilson, 246

United Nations Convention on Prevention and Punishment of
    the Crime of Genocide, 58, 250, 252
Universal Declaration on Human Rights, 58, 88, 126

Wagin, 175-6
Wandering Mission, 128, 155, 158-9
    isolation, 152-3
    missionaries untrained, 148
    neglect of children, 139-40
Warburton Mission, 124-5, 127-8, 131
Western Australia
    Aboriginal policies *see* absortion policy; assimilation policy
    Aborigines as cheap labour, 36-7, 91-2, 108-10, 153, 263-4
    causes of problems not addressed, 130-1, 135, 165, 222-5, 230-1
    continuing discrimination, 226-8, 230-3
    expenditure on Aborigines, 92-3, 131, 136, 154
    justice system *see* justice system; police; prisons
    white economic interests protected, 247, 263, 264